D1639416

Marie Antoinette

by the same author

THE FIRST BOURBON
THE MONKS OF WAR
PRINCE OF THE RENAISSANCE
THE BOURBON KINGS OF FRANCE
THE MOTHER QUEEN
THE HUNDRED YEARS WAR
MONKS AND WINE

Marie Antoinette on horseback, by Louis Auguste Brun

Desmond Seward

Marie Antoinette

Constable London

First published in Great Britain 1981
by Constable and Company Limited
10 Orange Street London WC2H 7EG
Copyright © 1981 by Desmond Seward
Phototypeset in Monophoto Garamond by
Servis Filmsetting Ltd, Manchester
Printed in Great Britain by
Ebenezer Baylis and Son Ltd
The Trinity Press, Worcester and London

FOR
Blanche Marie-Ange Thérèse Seward

Contents

Illustrations

Acknowledgements

I would particularly like to thank Mrs Prudence Fay for her helpful criticism. Also, I am grateful to the Count de Salis for information about the Swiss Guards in the service of the French monarchy. (His family had their own proprietary regiment, the Salis-Soglio, members of whom took part in defending the Tuileries in 1792.) I must also thank Monsieur Paul de Hevesy for details about the Habsburg dynasty during the eighteenth century; Mr Reresby Sitwell for pointing out to me that Louis XVI was the direct descendant of Charles I; and Mr William Drummond of the Covent Garden Gallery, who was most kind in arranging for the reproduction of the drawing of Marie Antoinette leaving the Conciergerie, now in the possession of the Pierpoint Morgan Library in New York.

As usual, I am indebted to the staffs of the British and London Libraries.

Foreword

. . . little did I dream that I should have lived to
see such disasters fallen upon her in a nation of
gallant men, in a nation of men of honour, and of
cavaliers. I thought ten thousand swords must
have leaped from their scabbards to avenge even a
look that threatened her with insult

Edmund Burke, *Reflections on the Revolution in
France* (1790)

*Calomniez! Calomniez! Il en restera toujours quelque
chose*

Beaumarchais

There have been so many lives of Marie Antoinette and so
little – if any – new information is to be discovered about her
that one may well ask if there is room for a new biography.
Yet her tragedy has a perennial fascination. Each time the
story is retold it sheds a little more light on this unfortunate
woman.

The dramatic quality of the Queen's life cannot be
exaggerated. Born an Austrian Archduchess and marrying
the heir to the richest monarchy in Europe, her early years
were passed in splendour and extravagant pleasure, years
which in retrospect have an air of unmistakable doom. By the
time of the Revolution she had become the object of a
terrifying, ever-increasing hatred. A detested symbol of the
ancien régime, she was swept to destruction as though caught
in some whirlpool; dragged from Versailles to Paris, failing
to escape to Varennes, insulted in the Tuileries by the mob,
fleeing from even that gloomy refuge, then immured in a
miserable prison from which her husband was taken to be

beheaded and where her small son was torn from her. Finally she was placed in a public gaol and subjected to every humiliation. Her thirty-seven years ended with an infamous, blatantly rigged trial, her gallant defence being followed by a brave death under the guillotine.

Another, subtler, drama was her ruin through slander. She was the victim of a vicious, shrewdly sustained process of character assassination from the moment she set foot in France, a sinister, carefully orchestrated campaign of calumny, which tried in particular to destroy her moral reputation. An intellectual climate fanatically hostile to traditional monarchy, and sheer human jealousy, exploited the xenophobic hatred of her as an Austrian and her own aloofness to make her the scapegoat for all French ills. The fact that royalists later acclaimed her as a martyr and revolutionaries as a whore of reaction obscures the reality – she was condemned long before 1789, not by *sansculottes* but by French courtiers, aided and abetted by fashionable writers. Her execution was not mere murder by an impetuous revolutionary tribunal in a moment of crisis, but the work of many years. She was no less a sacrifice to national prejudice than Captain Dreyfus a century later.

Both in prosperity and adversity Marie Antoinette was widely and deeply hated. Yet as soon as she was dead she became as revered as she had once been detested. She is still the object of an extraordinary minor cult. Oddly enough there remains much to say about her which has not been said before.

Even though no fresh, unprinted evidence is likely to be found, the memoirs and correspondence which her biographers have used certainly deserve reinspection. Some recent writers give the impression that these all yielded up their secrets long ago, or reject them because they are in part biased or inaccurate. So indiscriminating a dismissal overlooks material which can provide revealing insights.

Unquestionably her personality has been blurred by too much association with that of her husband in a tragic duo, while important influences have not received full attention.

The Queen's temperament was essentially Germanic, never French. She always remained a child of Austria and a daughter of Maria Theresa which, in her own generation at least, meant that she belonged to a family with sound bodies and minds. Though spoilt by lack of proper education, Marie Antoinette shared many of their gifts but her potentialities showed themselves only after the Revolution had begun and her greatest qualities only during the final agonized days of her short life. Contrasted with the normality of her own family, the physical and mental oddities of the later Bourbons must have made her realize that in Louis XVI she had married an amiable freak — from soon after their birth, however healthy they seemed to everyone else, she surely sensed that she was the mother of diseased children. Again, the intensity of her personal religion has been ignored in discussing her marriage and her strange, hopeless romance with Axel von Fersen.

Marie Antoinette may also be seen as the victim of men. Both Louis and Fersen failed her miserably and consistently, leaving her to cope with appalling situations in which she should never have been placed. Her brothers and her nephew let her perish when they might well have saved her. Eighteenth-century society could be hideously unfair to women — enemies invariably exploited the fact of her sex, and the humiliations of her imprisonment and trial are only the most obviously unpleasant instances.

If one tries to interpret events from her own point of view and to accept her as a serious — though hardly successful — politician, an unfamiliar Queen emerges. The real Marie Antoinette was in many ways very different from the traditional portrait.

[1]
Childhood

It may truly be said that the daughter of Maria Theresa
resembled her mother either too much or too little

Mignet

Mère qui tient un jeune objet
Dans une ignorance profonde,
Loin du monde,
Souvent se trompe en son projet

Marivaux, *L'École des Mères*

MARIA ANTONIA JOSEFA JOHANNA — later known as
Marie Antoinette — of Austria-Lorraine was born at the
imperial palace of the Hofburg in Vienna on 2 November
1755. It was *Allerheiligen*, the Feast of All Saints, but
nonetheless a date of ill omen, since the dreadful Lisbon
earthquake took place that very same day. She was the
sixteenth and last child of the Holy Roman Emperor Franz I
and of the Empress Maria Theresa, and therefore a Habsburg
Archduchess from the very first moment of her arrival in this
world.

The forcefulness of his magnificent consort has blurred
both the personality and origins of the Emperor Franz.
Admittedly his character was not strong. He was essentially a
man of pleasure, a keen hunter and womanizer, if also
charming, affectionate and unpretentious. An amateur of
science and an enthusiastic numismatist, he possessed a flair
for money unusual in one of his rank — managing the imperial
finances so well that he was nicknamed 'the court banker'.

But basically he was an ineffectual figure, saved from failure and obscurity only by his wife. Indeed some genealogists think that the Lorrainer blood was responsible for dimming the Habsburg brilliance in future generations, even though it does not seem to have affected his own children.

Franz's homeland was much more interesting than his personality. He was the last reigning Duke of Lorraine, a duchy on France's north-eastern frontier and a principality of the Empire. It dated from the time of Charlemagne's son Lothar and until the mid-eighteenth century was as separate a country from France as Belgium is today; in the early twentieth century Maurice Barrès could still refer to himself as a Lorrainer rather than a Frenchman. However France was determined to absorb the little state and did so in 1735 after the War of the Polish Succession, by means of a complicated treaty: Franz surrendered his duchy to Louis XV's father-in-law, the former King of Poland, Stanislas Leszczynski, who was to reign as 'King of Lorraine' at Luneville for the rest of his life on the understanding that the duchy would revert to France when he died; in return Franz received the Grand Duchy of Tuscany together with the hand of the Archduchess Maria Theresa, heiress to the Habsburg domains. Franz had no wish to give up his own country but both France and the Empire threatened him with the brutal ultimatum 'no renunciation, no Archduchess', and this timid man soon yielded. Nevertheless he always regretted leaving the land of his birth and, much to the irritation of the Habsburgs' nobles, filled Vienna with Lorrainer hangers-on who obtained enviable positions at court.

The Emperor Franz was very fond of Maria Antonia, perhaps because she was the youngest of his daughters and the baby of the family. Sadly, he died when she was only nine. She never forgot him and how he kissed her good-bye for the last time, saying 'I want to embrace this child once more,' just before leaving on a journey during which he suffered a sudden and fatal stroke. She often spoke of him in France years afterwards, telling her ladies-in-waiting that the house of Habsburg-Lorraine owed its popularity to the simple manners which her father had brought to Austria. Yet she did not take after him in any way at all.

Maria Antonia's feelings towards her mother were somewhat different. Maria Theresa was unquestionably the most remarkable of all Habsburgs, an Austrian Elizabeth Tudor. This great woman had succeeded her father, the Emperor Charles VI, on his death — as unexpected as that of her husband — when she was only twenty-three, with every prospect of seeing her inheritance stolen by the surrounding powers. Without adequate advisers, money or troops she nonetheless found the courage and skill to fend off her enemies, and even won the loyalty of the disaffected and impossibly turbulent Hungarian magnates who accepted her as their 'King'. If she lost Silesia to Frederick the Great of Prussia, she nevertheless managed to win the crown of the Holy Roman Empire for her beloved husband. She led her peoples through two long and miserable wars without losing their enthusiastic affection, while at home she began an administrative revolution which included reform of taxation, reorganization of the army and an attack on the power of the nobles and the privileges of the Church. She was genuinely anxious to alleviate the poverty and degradation of the peasants throughout the Habsburg lands, from humane and not merely economic motives. She was not always successful, but her endeavours were never less than heroic.

Although kind and affectionate, Maria Theresa must have been an uncomfortable mother. She was gay enough and enjoyed music, dancing and masked balls, yet at the same time she was almost excessively pious and puritanical; she outlawed illicit love affairs among her courtiers and actually set up a notorious 'chastity commission' which caused worry and embarrassment to the very greatest of her ministers. She was domestic to an almost bourgeois degree, living with her adored Emperor in intimate little apartments in which they shared a double bed, and interrupting a play to tell the theatre how she had just heard that she had acquired a new grandchild. But she was also a ferociously dedicated ruler who rose at five every morning to work at state papers

throughout the whole day. Indeed it is said that on the day
Maria Antonia was born the Empress toiled at her documents
until she felt the pains of labour, resuming her work as soon
as the child had been delivered. After her courage her most
striking qualities were her industry and her sense of duty.
They did not necessarily make for affection.

It was understandable, if regrettable, that her mother
should neglect Maria Antonia. Not only was the great
Empress preoccupied by cares of state but she already had so
many children. Early in her marriage she had produced quite
enough boys to ensure the survival of her dynasty and there
was no problem in finding thrones for the younger ones.
Some of her daughters had alarmingly poor health but the
others were strong and well set-up like their mother. There
was good reason for Maria Theresa to be blasé about children
by the time Maria Antonia was born. Mme Campan, a future
woman of her bedchamber and devoted friend for many
years, tells us that the Empress 'who inspired awe by her
greatness, taught the archduchess to fear and respect her
rather than love her,' and adds that she was much too busy
with politics 'to be bothered by the duties of a mother'. Maria
Theresa sometimes did not see her smaller offspring for a
week or even ten days, though admittedly this worried her.
Each evening the imperial physician, Gerhard von Swieten,
had to report to her about their health after paying them an
obligatory daily visit. And if anyone of sufficient importance
to be received by the imperial family visited Vienna, the
Empress would make a point of dining with all her children –
apparently in the hope that the visitor would think that they
were her chief concern. However, when Maria Antonia grew
older she was at last allowed to eat with her parents and her
elder brothers and sisters every evening.

Maria Theresa was occasionally terrifying. In 1767 her
daughter-in-law Josefa, wife of her eldest son, died of
smallpox. During the illness the Empress was brave enough
to kiss the girl and caught the disease herself. When she
recovered she told her daughter, another Josefa – about to
leave Vienna to marry the King of Naples – that she must

accompany her to the vault of the Capuchin church in the Neuer Markt, which was the imperial burial place, to pray by the dead Josefa's coffin. The poor Archduchess saw the order as a death warrant. Weeping, she picked up Maria Antonia of whom she was very fond and told her how soon she would never see her again because she had 'to go down to the tombs of her ancestors, and would shortly go there again and remain there'. The coffin had not been properly sealed and the Archduchess did indeed catch smallpox and die of it. According to Mme Campan, Maria Antonia could never forget the incident (though in part this may have been due to being vaccinated by Swieten in consequence, in those days a painful and alarming experience).

Maria Antonia's parents ruled an area which covered the modern countries of Austria, Hungary and Czechoslovakia, together with half of Romania, a third of Yugoslavia, most of northern Italy (including all Lombardy and Tuscany) and parts of Germany. Moreover her father was also 'Holy Roman Emperor of the German Nation'. The office was scarcely more than titular, but one should not underestimate its prestige; even in the twentieth century a Habsburg monarch, still the representative of the Holy Roman Emperors, was able to veto the election of a Pope. (As late as the 1960s, Catholic missals contained a prayer for the Holy Roman Emperor with, however, a note that the prayer was no longer said, 'the Holy Roman Empire being vacant'.) In theory Franz I was still the first sovereign in Christendom as well as in Germany.

Such a position required suitable settings. The two great Viennese palaces were the Hofburg and Schönbrunn – the latter just outside the capital and surrounded by a park of 500 acres. There was also a palace at Innsbruck and the shooting lodge of Laxenburg (between Vienna and the modern Hungarian border). Their decoration was in what has been called the 'Theresian' style. This was largely a cheerful Rococo which some interpret as reflecting the more informal spirit of the Empress contrasted with her Baroque pre-decessors' stiffness. Later it became Neo-Classical as well, a mixture which has a slight tinge of uneasiness, though its statues gave the imperial parks and gardens unquestioned grace, with all the elegant nostalgia for antiquity which was to be so fashionable in Louis XVI's France. It was a background both gay and intellectual, urbane and earnest.

Although the Empress kept a large enough court, ceremony was simplified to an extent which surprised foreigners, especially Frenchmen. The imperial nobility found itself in a very different position from that of France – there was no sense of kinship between monarch and nobles as at Versailles. Unlike the Bourbons, the Habsburgs regarded aristocratic privilege as positively harmful, an obstacle to the progress and well-being of society. Maria Theresa disliked her nobles, considering them too rich and greedy, too arrogantly independent, altogether a hindrance to good government. She bequeathed this dislike and distrust to her sons Josef and Leopold – in the former's case it became almost pathological – and Maria Antonia inherited a good deal of it herself. On the other hand, while the Empress kept very much aloof from her courtiers, she relied on favourites for both ministers and ladies-in-waiting. She even asked one minister to tell her about her faults, and many a poor girl of good birth owed a glittering career and a rich husband to her patronage. Maria Theresa was only happy when surrounded by trustworthy friends who would work for her and guard her against over-mighty subjects.

The Empress imposed her taste in music on the court and on her children. In 1754 Christoph Willibald Gluck, a Bohemian gamekeeper's son, became her court composer and conductor. An unorthodox figure – he composed in the garden, with two bottles of champagne on top of his clavichord – he soon ousted traditional Italian *opera seria*; first by providing tuneful airs for French comedies and turning them into comic operas, then by creating Neo-Classical *opera seria* with *Orfeo* and *Alceste*. Gluck himself taught Maria Antonia to play both the clavichord and the spinet, though without noticeable success. She also attempted the harp. Perhaps Gluck did not try hard enough, since Mme Campan

Marie Antoinette in 1767, aged 12, by the Master of the Archduchesses' Portraits

tells us that later 'music was the accomplishment which the Queen most enjoyed. She did not play any instrument well, but she learnt to read at sight like a first rate music master. She only became so expert in France, this part of her education having been as neglected at Vienna as the rest.'

During her childhood Maria Antonia met other great musicians, including Leopold Mozart and his little son who played before the imperial family at Schonbrünn in 1767. Wolfgang Amadeus Mozart was then about her own age and must have made some impression on the Archduchess, if only because he himself was so young. There is a charming legend that he and Maria Antonia played duets and that he proposed to her and was accepted – alas, there is not a word of truth in it.

Maria Antonia had a pretty voice. She sang French and Italian airs with her brothers and sisters at family concerts, when Josef would play the cello, Ferdinand the kettledrums and Maria Christina the clavichord. And from a very early age she danced in the stiff and formal court ballet of the period. A picture has survived of her, dressed with some splendour, in a ballet of this sort which took place at Schönbrunn on 24 January 1765 when she was little more than nine years old.

The only other art which she was taught – after a fashion – was drawing. She was said to have sketched an excellent likeness of her father. It may well have been the drawing which she presented to the French envoy when he came to Vienna to arrange her marriage contract, and of which she later said, 'I do not believe I even put a pencil on that sketch.' For no one realized the extent to which her governesses were neglecting her education.

The trouble with Maria Antonia's childhood was that it was too free. The Empress issued stern commands that her children were not to be pampered, especially in their food, but she was too busy with her papers to see that this was done. There is a gouache, painted by her sister Maria Christina and still at Schönbrunn, of Maria Antonia and her two brothers romping in their parents' breakfast room on

Marie Antoinette with her parents on St Nicholas's Day 1762, painted by her sister, the Archduchess Maria Christina

Christmas morning when she was only seven. It portrays a happy and thoroughly normal little girl. She was particularly lucky in her brothers and sisters.

Like every genius the future Josef II may have been a bit tiresome but at least he was fond of her. No less brilliant but more attractive was Peter Leopold, Grand Duke of Tuscany and also a future Emperor, who was to die tragically young. Nearer her own age were the Archdukes Ferdinand and Maximilian; the former was to become Viceroy of Milan while the latter would enter religion as Grand Master of the Teutonic Knights and reign at Mergentheim in celibate medieval splendour with his own little court. Two of her sisters were also to enter religion; the life of an eighteenth-century abbess of imperial blood was dignified and usually almost scandalously luxurious, with wide estates, large and beautiful convents and elegant summer palaces, together with a retinue of cloistered ladies-in-waiting. Maria Christina married Albert of Saxony-Teschen and was to be 'Governor General' of the Austrian Netherlands – modern Belgium. Maria Amalia, another sensible, strong-charactered girl, was to be Duchess of Parma; while Maria Carolina, no less forceful and Maria Antonia's best-loved sister, would be a most remarkable Queen of Naples. In appearance her features resembled Maria Antonia's and it is probable that their characters were similar. Her palace at Caserta was even larger than Versailles, but this after all was what she had been brought up to expect: in that age a girl of imperial family had only the careers of marriage or religion – kingdoms and palaces were her natural due if she was successful.

The circle began to break up when the Emperor Franz died in 1765. Josef became Emperor in his place, full of plans for reform and modernization, to rule side by side with his mother though not always in harmony. The delightful Leopold went off to Tuscany. As has been seen, poor Josefa died in 1767. The following year Maria Carolina left for Naples.

Maria Antonia's own fate was decided early enough, when she was thirteen. *Bella gerant alii, tu felix Austria nube* – 'others make war but thou, O happy Austria, makest marriages' – was a family motto: the rise of the Habsburgs and their acquisition of vast domains was due to a multitude of good marriages. Now however Maria Theresa hoped for an alliance which would not so much gain territory as secure peace with France, Austria's traditional enemy. The marriage of her youngest daughter to the Dauphin was intended to consolidate a revolution in foreign policy. Already Habsburgs and Bourbons had joined forces against Prussia in the Seven Years War and though they had been the losers they were determined to continue allies. The initiative came from France, the French foreign minister, the Duc de Choiseul, instructing the French ambassador at Vienna to ask for the hand of an Austrian Archduchess. The proposal was made in 1766 but the negotiations were so protracted that Louis XV's formal letter of confirmation did not arrive until 1768.

Maria Theresa at once set about preparing her daughter for her future role. A famous ballet master, Noverre, was engaged to teach her dancing and deportment, which he did with such success that she was later renowned for both. To polish Maria Antonia's French she also engaged two actors from a French company then in Vienna, Messieurs Aufresne and Sainville, in the hope that these exponents of the comedies of Marivaux would impart the best elocution. The French were horrified by her choice of such low instructors and insisted on sending a tutor of their own choosing. The incident underlines the contrast between the stuffiness of the Bourbon court and the comparative informality of that of the Habsburgs.

The new tutor was the Abbé Jacques de Vermond, a doctor of the Sorbonne and librarian of the Collège Mazarin. Opinions of the Abbé vary. Mme Campan, jealous and a snob, despised him as the son of a village surgeon and later wrote of him as being 'born into a low class of life, filled with all the ideas of modern philosophy . . . vain, talkative while sly and offhand at the same time, very odd and ugly'. In fact the young man – he was still only thirty-four – made an excellent impression on the imperial family and the Empress actually asked him to spend every evening with them. For his part he was full of admiration for the Habsburgs and their simple ways which were in such contrast to the unbending pomp of French royalty. He quickly won the respect and affection of his pupil who was to owe what education she had to him.

The Abbé has left us the first authentic description of the Archduchess: 'She has a most graceful figure; holds herself well; and if, as may be hoped, she grows a little taller, she will possess every good quality one could wish for in a great princess. Her heart and character are both excellent.' But Vermond was shocked by her lack of education. It seems that her governesses had tried to endear themselves by letting her do exactly what she wanted – they knew that they were in no danger of being discovered by the Empress, busy with her state papers. On one occasion, however, a governess had been dismissed after Maria Antonia told her mother that all her lessons and letters were first traced out in pencil for her by the lady, so all she had to do was ink them in. A new and excellent governess, Mme de Brandes, was appointed but too late. By the time she was thirteen, when Vermond arrived, Maria Antonia could not even write proper French or German, while her governesses' indulgence had frustrated attempts to teach her by the learned professors which her mother had engaged, so that she had absolutely no knowledge of history or many other subjects. The exception seems to have been Italian which she was taught by the court librettist, the playwright Pietro Metastasio. The Abbé reported to her mother: 'She is much more intelligent than people realize. Unfortunately up to the age of twelve she was not trained to concentrate in any way at all. Since she is rather lazy and very frivolous, she is therefore extremely hard to teach. For the first six weeks I tried to explain the basic elements of literature and saw that she could understand me perfectly if I gave clear explanations. She usually showed sound enough judgement but I could never persuade her to take sufficient pains to master a subject on her own initiative, though I suspected that she was perfectly capable of doing so.

In the end I was forced to admit that she would learn only if she found the lesson amusing.'

Maria Theresa herself gave her daughter tuition. Two months before Maria Antonia was to leave for France, her bed was moved into the Empress's bedroom. For the first time mother and daughter were close to one another and, judging from the tone of Maria Theresa's future letters, she obviously found a good deal in Maria Antonia's character to worry her. She tried to explain to the girl the duties of a Queen-consort and gave her a set of rules to follow, making her swear solemnly to read them once a month.

It might be thought that the Empress would naturally have instructed her in the mysteries of men and procreation, of pregnancy and childbearing. It is almost certain that she did not. At about this time poor Maria Carolina wrote of her own first experiences of marriage: 'The suffering is true martyrdom, made worse by being expected to look happy. I know what I speak of and I pity Antonia who has yet to suffer it . . . But for my faith which told me "think of God" I would have killed myself rather than endure what I have had to bear for over a week.' As will be seen, this omission was to cause the Queen of France even more misery than it did the Queen of Naples.

Maria Theresa did at least pay attention to the child's looks. At fifteen the Archduchess was by no means a beauty though she had the charm and freshness of youth and a pretty pink and white complexion. Besides the famous projecting Habsburg lower lip, she had a bulging forehead. The Empress imported a fashionable *coiffeur* from Paris to dress her daughter's hair – between blonde and light brown, with red lights – to conceal the unsightly outline of her brow. Her teeth were checked by a French dentist, sent to Vienna at her mother's request. In addition she was taught such worldly graces as how to gamble at the court gaming-table and how to preside over other games of chance.

On 21 April 1770 the Archduchess Maria Antonia left Vienna for ever. Her suite included fifty carriages, each drawn by six horses changed several times a day, and countless guards and outriders. Maria Theresa was in tears and prayed as though she foresaw disaster. But the procession was cheered by the Austrians, who had resurfaced the roads in honour of the occasion, and when the Archduchess spent her first night away from home at the great abbey of Melk she was joined by her brother, the Emperor Josef. Then she and her cortège travelled for a week through Austria and through Bavaria towards the French frontier. Eventually they reached the Rhine near Kehl.

Here, on an island in the middle of the river, a superb marquee had been erected. It consisted of a vast central *salon* with a room on either side – one for the Archduchess's Austrian suite and one for her new French suite, the latter being headed by the Comtesse de Noailles. (According to Mme Campan, who was not there, to symbolize that she was no longer Austrian her ladies handed her over naked to Mme de Noailles, an experience which reduced the poor girl to tears: in fact this ancient custom was mercifully omitted.) With due ceremony she was then entrusted to the stiff and unsympathetic Countess – later to be nicknamed *Mme l'Etiquette* – whom, in her nervousness, she embraced. After being presented with her new household, all middle-aged ladies, she began her journey to Versailles – no longer as Maria Antonia but as Marie Antoinette.

[2]
The child bride

Chacun court après le bonheur

Beaumarchais, *Le Barbier de Seville*

In maiden madness, virulently bold

Sheridan, *The School for Scandal*

MARIE ANTOINETTE's first day in France began with a triumphal entry into Strasbourg. When someone tried to deliver an address of welcome in German, the child – she was scarcely more – had enough tact to interrupt with the graceful plea, 'Don't speak to me in German, *messieurs*, as from now on I only understand French.' After public celebrations, which included a little surprisingly a Festival of Bacchus, she spent the night at the Archbishop's palace. She was introduced to two people of note. One, a woman of 105, wished the Archduchess a life as long as her own; it is a curious thought that had the wish come true Marie Antoinette would have been alive in the 1860s. The other was the Archbishop's nephew and coadjutor, a clerical exquisite who welcomed her with a florid speech. This was Louis de Rohan, the future Cardinal of the Diamond Necklace, whose folly and frivolity would one day do so much hurt to the reputation of the Queen of France.

Leaving Strasbourg she crossed her father's lost Duchy of

Lorraine, seeing his old capital at Nancy, and then went by way of Rheims – crowning place of the Kings of France – through the woods to Compiègne, where she arrived on 14 May. Here she was met by Louis XV and his grandson, her betrothed, who were waiting for her under the trees at a crossroad as though on some hunting party. The King was sixty but still the handsomest man in France, tall, high-coloured and athletic with a regal, enigmatic charm which women found irresistibly attractive. In the words of Mme Campan, who as a young girl had often seen and revered him, Louis's 'walk was easy and noble; he held his head in the most dignified way imaginable while his expression was imposing without being at all severe; he combined the utmost courtesy with a genuinely kingly manner and gracefully greeted the humblest female whom curiosity led into his path.' (One wonders if the 'humblest female' was Mme Campan herself.) Certainly Louis had already shown considerable curiosity about the latest addition to his family, closely interrogating an officer of his court, a M. Bouret, whom he knew to have seen her, about her breasts. When Marie Antoinette stepped down from her carriage to make him a deep curtsey, the King raised her up and kissed her enthusiastically on both cheeks. Soon it was evident that he was enchanted. No doubt Marie Antoinette was overwhelmed by the majesty and glamour of the man who was France. In a way he was her father-in-law – partly because of the premature death of the Dauphin's father, partly because he was so miraculously young for his years.

Every girl dreams about her future husband and Marie Antoinette can surely have been no exception. Louis-Auguste, formerly Duc de Berry and now Dauphin, was very different from his grandfather the King. Not quite sixteen but already nearly six feet tall, he was a fat, clumsy, slovenly youth, short-sighted, inarticulate and embarrassingly awkward in manner – he could not even dance. An ambassador thought he looked 'as though he had been brought up in the woods', and another ambassador saw in him 'a very limited intelligence, little comeliness and no sensitivity'. His supreme pleasures were eating and hunting, though he was also something of an amateur blacksmith and dabbled in lockmaking and bricklaying. Even Mme du Barry called him that 'fat, ill-bred boy'. When Marie Antoinette kissed him, he showed no emotion whatsoever.

Others introduced included the Dauphin's three aunts, Mesdames Adelaide, Victoire and Sophie. All were as ugly as they were eccentric, though no one knows why their father gave them such odd nicknames: Adelaide was '*Loque*' (Dishclout), Victoire '*Coche*' (Old Sow), and Sophie '*Graille*' (Scrap). The feline Horace Walpole once saw them with their fourth sister Louise – '*Chiffe*' (Bad Silk), who had since entered religion – and left an unpleasing but convincing portrait: 'The four Mesdames, who are clumsy, plump old wenches with a bad likeness to their father, stand in a bedchamber in a row, with black cloaks and knitting bags, looking good humoured, not knowing what to say, and wriggling as if they wanted to make water.' But today the three old maids were amiable enough to their new niece. Then there was the Orléans tribe, descended from Louis XIV's brother and with distant hopes of succeeding to the throne should the Dauphin and his brother prove childless – the Dukes of Orléans and Penthièvre and Orléans's son Chartres who, as Philippe Egalité, would one day vote for the execution of Louis XVI.

Marie Antoinette and her betrothed continued the journey in the King's carriage. They paused outside Paris at a Carmelite convent in Saint-Denis so that Louis's fourth daughter, the tiny, hump-backed Madame Louise who had taken the veil, could be presented. At last they arrived at the little château of La Muette, built by François I and of which no trace now survives. Here she met her two future brothers-in-law, the Comte de Provence and the Comte d'Artois. The former, Louis-Stanislas, was as fat and greedy as the Dauphin, though icily cold and selfish with a slyly amusing wit. However, Charles-Philippe of Artois, handsome, cheerful and warm-hearted, was the only normal one of the three boys, even if he was also the least intelligent. In addition she met their two sisters, Mesdames Clothilde and Elisabeth. The first was 'as round as a ball' and so greedy that she was known popularly as '*Gros Madame*'; later she was to be Queen of Sardinia. Elisabeth, still little more than a baby, was to be the last and possibly the noblest of all Marie Antoinette's friends.

The royal party dined at La Muette where Marie Antoinette was to spend the night before her wedding. There is a legend which may be apocryphal, or perhaps happened on another occasion. It is said that during dinner the little Archduchess asked Mme de Noailles who was the beautiful lady at the end of the table. On being told that it was Mme du Barry, she wanted to know her function. 'To make the King enjoy himself,' answered Mme de Noailles. 'In that case,' said Marie Antoinette gravely, 'I am going to be her rival'.

On 16 May 1770 Marie Antoinette drove from La Muette to her wedding at Versailles. However unpromising her bridegroom may have appeared, however much a child she may still have been and however timid, she must surely have been excited by the prospect of becoming the future Queen of what then appeared to be the greatest state in the world. France was the richest country in Europe and had the largest population, and European culture was essentially French culture – in Germany and in Russia rulers and ruling classes spoke French instead of their own native tongues. The very word 'French' signified civilization and elegance. Despite her recent defeat by England, even the shrewdest of contemporary observers did not realize that France was in decline, that her monarchy's strength was the hollowest of gilded illusions and that her social and economic system was grinding to a halt. As the child bride arrived at the vast palace of Versailles – much more beautiful and impressive to eighteenth-century eyes than to our own – she can only have had the happiest thoughts, though she was understandably nervous.

The service took place in the Chapel Royal and included a nuptial Mass which was celebrated by the Archbishop-Duke of Rheims, Mgr de La Roche Aymon, the same prelate whose privilege it was to anoint and crown the Kings of France.

Marie Antoinette was dressed in white brocade sewn with diamonds; not only had she brought many stones from Vienna, but Louis XV had given her the *parure* of her bridegroom's late mother. In odd contrast to such glittering adornment, her wedding dress did not fit properly, both her stays and petticoats showing through a gap. She was so overcome that when she signed the register she spelt her name wrongly and spilt some ink – a large blot can still be seen on the page. Louis-Auguste, in a golden suit also sewn with diamonds, was even more nervous than his wife, trembling and blushing.

After the service the new Dauphine went to her temporary apartments to receive her household's oaths of allegiance. Over a hundred persons swore, including a wigmaker, a bath attendant and a fencing master. Then she proceeded to the Hall of Mirrors to play cards with the King and her husband; this was not so informal as it sounds, being primarily a spectacle – no less than 6,000 specially invited guests passed through the hall while she was playing, and many others who had not been invited also attended. Outside there was a fireworks display, but it was spoilt by a thunderstorm.

Finally there was a banquet in the Versailles opera house (only recently completed by the architect Jacques Ange Gabriel). Here some twenty-two members of the royal family dined, still in the presence of the 6,000 guests, while guardsmen from the *Maison du Roy* (the household troops) dressed as Turks played Turkish music; some of these guardsmen were Swiss. The Dauphin devoured his food with more than usual gusto and his grandfather noticed. 'You mustn't have too heavy a stomach tonight,' whispered the old King. 'Why not?' asked Louis-Auguste, 'I always sleep much better after plenty to eat.'

The happy couple were put to bed with traditional ceremony. Young Mme de Chartres assisted Marie Antoinette while Louis XV himself handed the nightshirt to his grandson. The Archbishop-Duke chanted the *asperges* as he sprinkled the bed with holy water and then prayed for a fertile union. At last the great four-poster's curtains were drawn. It is probable that the Dauphin went to sleep immediately without so much as touching his wife. For such a pious youth procreation was not everything. His grandfather had commented, 'Marriages are never happy but occasionally they are pleasant – let us hope that this one will be so.' To Marie Antoinette even that modest hope may now have seemed excessive.

Celebrations continued for a fortnight, culminating with a grand *feu d'artifice* in the capital, which the Dauphine was to attend. Paris was still very much a medieval city, with countless narrow streets full of wooden houses. The boulevards had not yet been built nor had the Louvre been completed – both the Louvre and the Tuileries were more or less derelict, empty save for colonies of ragged squatters. Yet a modern visitor to eighteenth-century Paris would find much that was familiar. There were such great buildings as the Invalides and the École Militaire and also the vast Place Louis Quinze (now Place de la Concorde). Thousands – some said hundreds of thousands – swarmed into the Place Louis Quinze, excited by wine running from the fountains. Marie Antoinette's carriage was late and delayed still further by the huge throng. Suddenly her coachman shouted that a dreadful accident had happened in the Place Louis Quinze – an overturned wagon had caused a bottleneck and at least 150 Parisians were trampled to death. She drove home tearfully and cried for days. She and the Dauphin sacrificed a year's private spending money to help the victims' families.

Slowly the little Dauphine settled into the stately routine of Versailles. She rose between nine and ten, breakfasted, then visited the three old aunts where she might also find King Louis. At eleven her hair was dressed and at twelve she held her *lever*, attended by any gentlemen or ladies who cared to do so: first she rouged her face and washed her hands, after which the men left and she dressed ceremonially, before attending Mass with the royal family.

Mass was followed by the daily ordeal of dining in public with her husband, which must have been intolerable for a girl accustomed to the comparative informality of the Viennese court. Every member of the Bourbons had to submit to this tiresome practice, a spectacle which delighted sightseers from the country, the palace ushers being instructed to allow anyone properly dressed to come and watch. 'At the dinner hour there was none to be met upon the stairs but honest folk who, when they had seen the Dauphine take her soup, went to see the Princes eat their *bouilli* and then ran till they were out of breath to behold Mesdames at their dessert.' At these dinners Marie Antoinette and her young husband were served by five women, the lady of honour who handed them their wine kneeling on a low stool. Most people would have found it impossible to swallow even a mouthful but the Dauphine, gifted with a youthful appetite, solved the problem simply by eating very fast.

Having finished dinner the Dauphine visited the Dauphin. If he was busy she returned to her own apartments where she read, wrote letters, or sewed – one piece of needlework was a waistcoat destined for the King 'which makes almost no progress, but which I hope with God's grace to finish in a few years' time'. At three she again visited the old aunts, at four the Abbé de Vermond came to give her lessons, and at five she received an hour's tuition from a music master (either the harpsichord or singing). The evening was spent with the aunts and her husband, supper being at nine; usually they were visited briefly by Louis XV, but so late that Marie Antoinette frequently dozed on a sofa until he arrived. Normally she and her husband retired at eleven. This routine seems to have been scrupulously observed, as the Dauphine had apparently little time to herself; in a letter to Marie Theresa she apologizes to her mother for its being dirty again 'but I had to write it at my dressing-table two days running'.

Such a routine must have been hard to tolerate for so high-spirited a girl as Marie Antoinette. She found the constant nagging of Mme de Noailles especially irritating – the stiff Countess even objected to her playing with her maids' children. Looking back with the wisdom she had acquired as a headmistress under Napoleon, Mme Campan commented that 'the Comtesse de Noailles was thoroughly disagreeable

in appearance and held herself bolt upright with a most
severe face. She was an expert on etiquette, but merely
succeeded in boring the young princess without making her
realize how important it was.' Vermond, who had breathed
the more sensible air of Vienna, was constantly joking about
Mme l'Etiquette and her lessons.

The three eccentric old maids with whom she had to spend
so much time were not the most exciting company for a girl.
The eldest, Madame Adelaide, was haughty and abrupt in
manner, harsh-voiced, totally lacking in charm. Before the
Dauphin's marriage she had expressed her disgust at the
choice of an Austrian and, though she relented sufficiently to
give Marie Antoinette the key to the secret passage which led
to her apartment, she never really overcame her dislike of an
Austrian Dauphine – she found her youthful high spirits
particularly irritating. It was Madame Adelaide, not some
sansculotte, who first called her '*l'Autrichienne*'. The second,
Madame Victoire, was in contrast sheepishly amiable. Her
two obsessions were good food and piety; sometimes they
conflicted, as on fast days, and she was tormented by scruples
about eating waterfowl in Lent. She seldom left her sofa –
where she played the bagpipes – but was mildly fond of her
new niece. The third aunt was the oddest of the lot. Even
loyal Mme Campan says of Madame Sophie, 'I have never
seen anyone else quite so revolting in appearance; she walked
as fast as possible and, from trying to recognize people
without looking at them, developed a sidelong leer like that
of a hare.' In manner she was ludicrously stiff and reserved,
taking no notice of anyone and rarely saying a single word;
she only relaxed out of fear during thunderstorms, when a
flash of lightning would make her clutch the nearest person's
hand and a second flash would make her throw her arms
around them.

It was at her aunt's apartment that the Dauphine first
became acquainted with Mlle Genet, their official reader.
Only three years older than Marie Antoinette, she was the
daughter of the Chief Clerk at the then equivalent of the Quai
d'Orsay. When she was still very young her father recognized

the quality of her intellect and procured her the best education available – her tutors included the moralist Marmontel, the Venetian playwright Goldoni and the great Roman *castrato* Albanese. She possessed a perfect command of Italian and English, singing charmingly in both languages. But where she most excelled was in reading aloud, which she developed to a fine art and for which she became something of a celebrity at only fiftcen. The little prodigy speedily endeared herself to her difficult mistresses and the Dauphine took no less of a fancy to her. (They must have found her name peculiarly comic; the genet was a rare, mongoose-like little animal then existing in France's southern wildernesses, whose fur could be worn only by the King.) The young reader would accompany Marie Antoinette on the harp or the pianoforte when she sang her favourite songs – such as those by Gluck, which reminded the Dauphine of Vienna. Like her mother the Empress, once Marie Antoinette had chosen servants she was devoted to their welfare. Soon she obtained little Genet's appointment as a woman of her bedchamber and got the King to give her a small pension. Nor was this all. Mlle Genet speedily became Mme Campan, her husband being the son of the secretary to the Dauphine's closet.

Our knowledge of Marie Antoinette's early years in France comes largely from Mme Campan's memoirs, which were not published until her death in 1823. It has long been recognized that she was to some extent writing to ingratiate herself with the restored Bourbons and is often untruthful as well as inaccurate. But it is wrong to dismiss her testimony out of hand. (One historian shrugs her off as 'that old gossip collector'.) Any study of Marie Antoinette, however scholarly, contains countless anecdotes and details known only from Campan's memoirs, and a cautious – very cautious – re-examination of the memoirs can be of great value. If especially unreliable about political matters or those people whom she dislikes, she is otherwise excellent at putting her mistress's point of view. A close association over a period of many years enabled her to understand the Queen much better than most other contemporary observers.

Mme Campan is plainly unsafe on the subject of Mme du Barry. The ravishingly beautiful Jeanne Bécu, a former shopgirl and high-class tart, had been Louis XV's official mistress since 1769. She made the King a happy man, not only by the prowess in bed of which he claimed cheerfully, 'She's the only woman in France who can make me forget I'm nearly sixty,' but also by giving him a simple, intimate feminine companionship which clearly suited him very well – at breakfast she would say, in her lisping, vulgar accent, 'France, you're making a muck of the coffee.' After he met her he had no other mistresses. His affection made her powerful. She persuaded 'France' to dismiss Choiseul because the great minister sneered at her: as Horace Walpole put it, 'Choiseul has lost his power ridiculously, by braving a *fille de joie* to humour two women – his sister and his wife.' In fact the dismissal, which took place a few months after Marie Antoinette's arrival in France, was not entirely due to the 'Roxalana of familiar gaiety' (Mme Campan's description) – Choiseul had nearly embroiled France in another war with England. But the du Barry was certainly able to impose her will on the Dauphine, though only after an epic struggle.

Marie Antoinette seems to have learnt from the aunts how Mme du Barry made the King 'enjoy himself'. She expressed her horror of the 'stupid and impertinent creature' in a letter to her mother quite soon after her marriage, and refused to address a single word to her. The spectacle caused considerable amusement at court while ladies who were friends of the royal mistress began to fight like cats with the Dauphine's supporters, and a great deal of unpleasantness resulted. Infuriated, Mme du Barry complained to 'France', who in turn grew angry. He told Mme de Noailles to tell Marie Antoinette to behave herself. By way of Vermond and the Comte de Mercy-Argenteau, the imperial ambassador, the French King's displeasure became known in Vienna. Somewhat unexpectedly Maria Theresa wrote to her daughter ordering her to humour Louis XV, otherwise 'I anticipate nothing but pain, sadness and petty intrigue, which will be very unpleasant for you'. At last, in 1772 the Dauphine said coldly to the du Barry, '*Il y a beaucoup de monde aujourd'hui à Versailles*,' (There are lots of people at Versailles today) during a New Year's Day reception. The King was delighted with her and sent her a beautiful present. It was all very different from Schönbrunn and the chastity commission. However Marie Antoinette refused to say anything else to the wretched woman.

There were perhaps deeper undertones to the battle with Mme du Barry, who was popular with the anti-Choiseul party. These people are said by Mme Campan to have been the secret enemies of the little Dauphine before she even arrived in France. They disliked and distrusted her as an Austrian; for centuries the Habsburgs had been the traditional enemies of France. It was the seed-bed of a conspiracy of hatred which would eventually destroy her. But at this early date she was protected by Louis XV's obvious liking for her and by the inescapable fact that she was the future Queen of France. Nonetheless, 'surrounded by enemies at Versailles' as she was, she must surely have sensed their covert hostility.

Marie Antoinette's isolation in a strange and foreign land was very real. Her only friends were Madame Victoire, Mme Campan, Vermond and the old King. She wrote to her mother that 'the King shows me a thousand kindnesses and I love him dearly', while Louis constantly praised her elegance and vivacity. Even so she must have guessed that Mme du Barry was constantly trying to poison his mind against her, and in any case she saw little of him apart from his fleeting visits to the aunts. And if full of useful advice, her mother's letters were not entirely a help; Maria Theresa never ceased to chide her. Two footmen and a maid were in M. de Mercy-Argenteau's pay, while the Abbé de Vermond told the excellent ambassador everything that Marie Antoinette told him outside the confessional. In addition one of the aunts' ladies-in-waiting brought him news from their quarter. 'There is not a single hour in any one day of which I do not have information on the Archduchess,' Mercy-Argenteau claimed. No one but the Empress saw his reports, not even the Emperor Josef. Poor Marie Antoinette was bewildered by her mother's seemingly uncanny knowledge of her every action. The Empress was brutally frank to her ambassador about her own low opinion of her child – 'I am well aware of my daughter's youth and love of pleasure, and of her lack of industry, not to mention her ignorance.' The extraordinary behaviour of the Dauphin was worst of all. It is likely that Mme Campan is speaking all too truthfully when she says of this early period of Marie Antoinette's marriage, 'The most humiliating indifference and coldness, often turning into sheer rudeness, were the sole feelings the young prince showed. Her charms could apparently make no impression on him; he slept in the Dauphine's bed only out of duty and often went to sleep without saying a word.'

One can only admire this young girl's resourcefulness in coping with her difficult situation. She tried to recreate something of that *gemütlich* world at Schönbrunn which she so much missed, to replace her beloved brothers and sisters. In 1772 Provence married Maria Giuseppina of Savoy, the King of Sardinia's daughter, and the following year Artois married her sister Maria Theresa. Neither girl was exactly attractive in personality, let alone appearance. The elder was small and ugly, with deep red skin and a weirdly heavy bosom, so dirty that Louis XV wrote to her parents begging them to make her wash her neck; surly, irritable and unfriendly. Her principal interest was trapping small birds to be made into soup. The younger was even smaller – barely four foot high – cross-eyed, with a grotesquely long nose, though at least good natured. The Dauphine did what she could with such unpromising material, insisting that she and her husband and the other two young couples saw as much of each other as possible. Save for dinners in public they ate all their meals together, always using the Provences' flat in the left wing at Versailles – perhaps because Provence was already so fond of good food. Occasionally the aunts were invited and later, when she grew up, Madame Elisabeth (the Dauphin's sister) but no one else.

Helped by Mme Campan, Marie Antoinette also formed a

tiny drama group. It consisted of the three couples – minus the boorish Dauphin – and Mme Campan's husband and father-in-law. Provence and Artois were quite good actors but their wives were deplorable. The theatre was a room in the Versailles attics with a collapsible stage hidden in a cupboard, and the sole audience was the Dauphin since Marie Antoinette was frightened that the aunts would disapprove. In the end a servant one day entered the room by accident and the Dauphine was so alarmed that she stopped her plays. Yet they seem to have achieved their object – not just to copy the cheerful little world left behind in Vienna but to civilize the Dauphin. In Mme Campan's opinion it was the theatricals which began to overcome his gaucheness and timidity.

Louis-Auguste started to enjoy his wife's company, but for an unknown reason would not consummate the marriage. People began to comment on the Dauphine's barrenness. Then rumours began to circulate that the fault was her husband's. In 1771 no less a personage than George III copied out a report by an English agent that, 'The King in speaking about a month ago in Mme du Barry's apartment said: "The Dauphin is well made and perfectly well formed yet has hitherto shewn no desire for women, nay rather seems to loathe them."' The same year the Empress told her daughter not to be too impatient with Louis-Auguste, as increasing his uneasiness would only make matters worse; by the end of the year however she was asking Swieten for his professional opinion on the young man's extraordinary coldness. In 1774 it was popularly reported that the marriage had still not been consummated and the Spanish ambassador at Paris heard that Louis-Auguste suffered from some form of phimosis – an irretractable foreskin – which made it painful for him to accomplish the sexual act, though it is quite likely that Mercy-Argenteau may have put about such a rumour to avert any suggestion of sterility on the Dauphine's part. Some sort of sexual relations between the couple began probably as early as 1774, though they were clearly unsatisfactory. But if Marie Antoinette remained unfulfilled, she at least made her husband fall in love with her.

The little Dauphine was growing up. Protected though she was by the artificial atmosphere of Versailles, she must to some extent have noticed the old King's unpopularity. He was at loggerheads with the Parlements. These in no sense resembled the English Parliament, but were both law courts and powerful legal corporations which were largely here-ditary in composition and whose members formed a judicial aristocracy. Bastions of privilege and reaction, they neverthe-less claimed to be custodians of the 'Law of France', and to be 'Fathers of the People'. They hoped to unite into a single body under the Parlement of Paris and to turn themselves into something like Parliament in England. Even great nobles who looked down on them as lawyers began to hope they would regain the powers they had lost under Henri IV and Louis XIV, and they were starting to attract considerable popular support. They were in fact aristocratic revo-lutionaries – Louis XV called the Parlement of Paris 'an assembly of republicans'. They were also the greatest obstacle to reforming the *ancien régime*. Time and again they tried to obstruct the King's government. By 1770 they were refusing to transact any legal business at all and deliberately bringing the courts to a standstill. It is in this context that Louis XV's famous comment '*Après moi le déluge*' must be seen. Idle and irresponsible as the old King was, when they tried to prosecute his first minister the Duc d'Aiguillon for misgovernment he stopped them by a *lit de justice* – a session of the Parlement of Paris over which he presided in person – and at the beginning of 1771 dissolved all the Parlements of France. They were replaced by new law courts set up by the Chancellor Maupeou, the 'Maupeou Parlements' whose co-operation allowed the introduction of revolutionary new taxes which even the most privileged could not escape. The Dauphine must have heard many grumbles. They cannot have made her look forward to her husband's accession to the throne.

In June 1773, after she had approached the King herself, Marie Antoinette made her *joyeuse entrée* into Paris – the ritual entry into the capital by Kings, Queens and Dauphines. A long train of carriages drove from Versailles to the gates of Paris, where she was presented with the keys of the city. There were fountains running with wine, set speeches, triumphal arches, artillery salutes, and vast crowds of cheering Parisians. When she looked out from the balcony of the Tuileries she was frightened at seeing such a multitude and exclaimed '*Mon Dieu*, there are so many of them!' The Duc de Brissac responded, 'You see below you 200,000 people who are in love with you.' Shortly after, she wrote to the Empress how deeply she had been touched by her enthusiastic reception by the poor – 'I cannot even begin to give you an idea of the wild joy and affection they showed us.' She also notes – like the true daughter of a benevolent despot – that these poor people were 'crushed by taxation'.

She now began to spend a good deal of time in Paris, incognito, cloaked, and masked, visiting the Opéra, theatres, and even gaming-houses. A shrewd observer, the Prince de Ligne, tells us that people arranged masked balls purely to give her the pleasure of going incognito and that 'she always thought that no one recognized her though in fact everyone did'. He also admits that her 'ceaseless chatter about masquerades' could be tedious.

In 1774, at one of these masked balls, she met a man who would play a most important part in her life. On 30 January a young Swede on the grand tour, Count Hans Axel von Fersen, went to a masquerade at the Opéra where in the early hours of the morning he struck up a conversation with a youthful lady in a grey velvet mask, who eventually introduced herself. It was the Dauphine, to whom he had already been presented at Versailles. He met her once or twice again that year, during the Carnival, but only briefly. Fersen was very handsome, tall and slim, always beautifully dressed and with graceful, rather serious, manners, chiefly memorable for strange blue eyes and a charming Swedish accent. Marie Antoinette seems to have remembered the glamorous Count, only a year younger than herself, though perhaps simply from pleasure at impressing a foreigner – already one of her weaknesses.

Beyond question she impressed another distinguished foreigner, who never actually met her but who never forgot her beauty. In 1790, in *Reflections on the Revolution in France*, Edmund Burke was to write, 'It is now sixteen or seventeen years since I saw the Queen of France, then the Dauphiness, at Versailles; and surely never lighted on this orb, which she hardly seemed to touch, a more delightful vision. I saw her just above the horizon, decorating and cheering the elevated sphere she just began to move in – glittering like the morning star, full of life, and splendour, and joy.'

Marie Antoinette's amusements were not invariably vapid nor even frivolous. At the Opéra – a huge, round edifice built in 1770 and able to hold 3,000 persons – the music of Rameau still held sway, though rivalled by that of such fashionable Italian composers as Jommelli and Piccini. Few Frenchmen had ever heard of Gluck who in Vienna was making such progress as harmonizing arias and in dramatic action. The Dauphine's old music master wished to make his name known to the cultural capital of the world so the Empress wrote to Marie Antoinette asking her to help him. Always good-natured, and usually anxious to please her mother, she promised to attend the first performance of his *Iphigénie*. Although it had been given a French libretto, it was especially daring to produce this work in Paris since Rameau had written an opera with the same story. The French musical establishment spoke of a 'barbarian invasion'. Gluck's overbearing temperament nearly caused a disaster: not only did he bully and shout at the singers in rehearsal, but he insisted on postponing the opening performance, to the irritation of the fashionable world who had already booked its seats. He was saved by the Dauphine who obviously enjoyed all the excitement. So thoroughly did she lobby that the first night, on 19 April 1774, was attended not only by the three young royal couples but by Louis XV himself with Mme du Barry. In consequence all Paris came too – including a Swiss visitor, Jean-Jacques Rousseau. The orchestra, the cast and the chorus were so bad that Gluck was in despair. Nevertheless Marie Antoinette determinedly clapped each aria, supported by her husband and her in-laws, and the audience followed them – in any case, by the end the vast majority were conquered by the sheer beauty of the opera. Although many influential critics remained hostile, Gluck had conquered. However, the real triumph belonged to Marie Antoinette.

During Lent the King and Mme du Barry had been frightened by a preacher who had ended his sermon with the words, 'Forty days more and Nineveh shall be destroyed.' On 27 April 1774, only a week after seeing *Iphigénie*, Louis woke up feeling feverish, but hunted as usual. That night he became so ill that the doctors made him go back to Versailles. He developed a severe fever and was bled drastically. On 29 April he broke out in a terrible rash. He refused to believe that it was smallpox, as he thought that he had had it when he was a child and was therefore immune. But it was the most virulent form of all, in which the pustules overlap and form a single scab. Eventually the King asked for a mirror and realized the truth. 'This is smallpox,' he gasped; 'at my age one doesn't recover!' He sent away Mme du Barry, who had been nursing him devotedly, though he wept when he learnt she had gone. His body turned black, as though covered with a sort of leprosy, and gave out a sickening smell. On 7 May, now a living, rotting corpse rather than a man, Louis was shriven and received Communion. He was so strong that he survived the eleventh, crucial day of illness and there were rumours that he was recovering, but he had been virtually unconscious for some time. He died at three o'clock on the afternoon of 10 May. So horrible were his putrefying remains that one of the workmen who placed them in their lead coffin is said to have died from uncontrollable vomiting.

When Louis XV died, a lighted candle placed in a window of his room was extinguished, as a signal. Mme Campan, who was present, says that suddenly 'a terrible noise, just like thunder' was heard in the ante-chamber where the Dauphin and Marie Antoinette were waiting. It was the court running to acclaim its new sovereign and his consort. Mme Campan adds that the royal couple fell on their knees, crying, 'God guide and protect us! We are too young to govern.' This detail has been questioned as a pious invention, but there is no reason to do so. Such behaviour at so emotional a moment was in keeping with Marie Antoinette's character. Soon afterwards she wrote to her mother that she and her husband were 'appalled at having to reign so young'. But she added, with a hint of pride, 'I can only be amazed by the will of Providence that I, the youngest of your children, should have become Queen of the finest kingdom in Europe.' Meanwhile the drums rolled and the heralds shouted, '*Le roi est mort: vive le roi!*'

[3]

Frustration and frivolity

. . . le goût pour le plaisir, qui alors faisait de Versailles
un séjour de délices

Prince de Ligne, *Lettres à la Marquise de Coigny*

Meanwhile the fair young Queen, in her halls of state,
walks like a goddess of beauty, the cynosure of all eyes;
as yet mingles not with affairs; heeds not the future;
least of all dreads it . . . fair young daughter of Time,
what things has Time in store for thee!

Carlyle, *The French Revolution*

AT RHEIMS on 11 June 1775 Louis XVI was crowned King
of France and Navarre. It was Trinity Sunday and a day of
stifling heat. The great cathedral was packed, while an
enormous crowd thronged the streets; among the spectators
were the young Abbé de Talleyrand and Georges-Jacques
Danton, who was only fifteen. Louis's silver robes were
removed, and through slits in his crimson shirt he was
anointed with oil from the Sacred Ampulla, that 'precious
treasure sent down from Heaven to our great St Rémy for the
consecration of Clovis and his successors'. He swore many
excellent oaths – including a promise 'to exterminate
heretics' – and then, in a golden chasuble and blue velvet
tunic and dalmatic, holding the sceptre and the sword of
Charlemagne, he had the crown of France placed on his head.
He complained that the crown was hurting him; superstitious

observers thought it an evil omen, remembering how Henri
III, the most disastrous of the Valois, had made a similar
complaint. But it did not seem to worry Louis, who was led
to his throne on a high platform where he received the
homage of the Princes of the Blood. Finally, still in his
crown, the King banqueted on a dais with the Princes.

Marie Antoinette wrote to her mother that she would
never forget the wonderful day 'even if I live for two
hundred years'. The Duc de Croy says that during the
coronation she shed floods of tears and had to wipe her eyes
with a handkerchief. He is corroborated by Mercy-
Argenteau who reported to the Empress that the Queen cried
so much that she had to leave the gallery, and that when she
returned the entire church cheered and applauded. Louis was
delighted and smiled at his wife for the rest of the day 'in utter
adoration'.

Next day the King 'touched' for the King's Evil – scrofula
– which could only be cured by the hands of an anointed
monarch. Indeed he would have to live his life henceforward
with almost as much ritual as at his coronation. When he
travelled from one palace to another he was accompanied by
an entire army; four trumpeters came first, followed by the
Hundred Swiss in uniforms like those of the Papal Guard,
and then the royal coach surrounded by the Bodyguard in
blue and red, while on one side was a long line of the French
Guard and on the other a long line of the Swiss Guard. At
table he was served by nearly four hundred servants at the
Grand Couvert on Sundays, and by scarcely less at other times
when he dined in public. His rising or *lever* was almost
liturgical in its reverential ceremony.

At not quite twenty-one, King Louis was grossly over-
weight, with a pot-belly and a pronounced waddle. His face
was slack and podgy, its prognathous jaw hidden beneath
double chins, even if the nose over his thick lips was the
eagle's beak of Louis XIV. He had a heavy, apathetic
expression and was so short-sighted that without a lorgnette
he could not recognize his valet at six feet. His very laughter
was lethargic, though when excited his voice occasionally

rose to a high squeak. A miserable childhood – an orphan since the age of fourteen, he had suffered under a narrow-minded pedant of a governor – had afflicted him with an ineradicable lack of self-confidence. His brothers were far more suited for the throne, and he knew it. Tom Paine hit the mark in observing, 'Perhaps no man ever bred up in the style of an absolute King, ever possessed a heart so little disposed to the exercise of that species of power as the present King of France.'

Yet Louis XVI was thoroughly well intentioned, with a profound sense of duty. He had already tried to improve himself. Such boyish amusements as shooting the Versailles cats and beating dogs senseless had been replaced by a love of hunting which amounted to a passion, though he was still most cheerful in the smithy and forge which he had installed next to his library. Although bored by the arts he was very well read, especially in history and not only French history – among contemporary authors he was familiar with Hume and Gibbon, and he followed important debates in the English Parliament.

Unfortunately, in those days his wife was not interested in history. She also disapproved of his lockmaking and smithying. She told a friend, 'You must agree that I wouldn't look very beautiful standing in a forge and that Vulcan's role doesn't suit me at all.' At this stage of their marriage the couple's incompatibility was particularly noticeable. The Empress was clearly very worried about it. Learning that Marie Antoinette in a letter to Count von Rosenberg – an old Viennese friend – had referred to her husband as *'le pauvre homme'*, Maria Theresa actually suspected her daughter of 'intrigue worthy of a Pompadour or a du Barry'. What upset the Empress still more was Mercy-Argenteau's report that Marie Antoinette never went to the King's bedroom and had ceased to do so by pretending that she had a cold. (By tradition French Kings and Queens occupied separate bedrooms.)

Louis's father had told him – on his deathbed in 1765 – that at least two strong reigns were needed to save the monarchy,

Marie Antoinette playing the harp in her bedroom at Versailles,
by Gauthier D'Agoty

and certainly the new King hardly thought of himself as a strong ruler. Nor did his consort. Shortly after Louis XV's death she wrote to her brother the Emperor Josef that, 'The King's death has left us with a prospect which is all the more terrifying since M. le Dauphin is completely unversed in matters of state, which the King never discussed with him.' She adds that while she writes Louis is weeping on her shoulder 'and only just now compared himself to a man who has fallen out of a belfry'. She asks for prayers.

Maria Theresa was no less pessimistic, commenting to Mercy-Argenteau, 'I fancy her days of happiness are over.' Other foreign observers were scarcely more sanguine. Frederick the Great of Prussia likened Louis to 'a sheep among wolves', prophesying that to escape them he was going to need 'truly wonderful ministers'.

However, the French were not so gloomy. At first Louis XVI was wildly popular. By the time he died the old King had become much disliked and everyone had been looking forward to the new reign. Solemnly declaring 'I want to be loved', the young monarch announced that he would forgo his *joyeux événement*, a heavy tax traditionally levied at the accession of every new king. Soon porcelain medallions were being manufactured with the legend *Louis le Populaire*. To keep him company Marie Antoinette gave up her *ceinture de la reine* – the Queen's girdle tax which had always been imposed with the 'joyous event' – commenting 'anyway, nobody wears girdles nowadays'.

As regards 'truly wonderful ministers', Louis's father had left him a list of reasonably reliable men but by now most of them were growing old. Having sacked Louis XV's ministers, who were loathed by the entire country, the young King consulted the list. The first two names on it were of men both in their seventies. However poor Louis felt safer with old men. He would probably have preferred Machault, but his aunt Adelaide hated Machault because he was a Jansenist. In the event he chose Maurepas as his First Minister, although Maurepas had been banished to his estates since 1749 (for writing a spiteful poem about Mme de Pompadour).

This aged but plausible cynic was essentially a courtier who was not going to risk exile again. Already seventy-three, he would retain power until his death at eighty. He and his rouged crone of a wife did not know how to grow old gracefully; on one occasion, although famed since his youth for impotence, the venerable statesman took part in one of Marie Antoinette's charades, clad in pink silk as Cupid. His attitude to public affairs was equally frivolous and irresponsible. On the other hand he had an extremely good brain and was one of the last genuinely able men available to the *ancien régime*. He also had an excellent adviser in the wily Abbé de Véri. But Maurepas was too tired and too pleasure-loving to serve Louis properly.

The Queen tried to persuade Louis to make Choiseul Foreign Minister. In consequence historians accuse her of 'meddling in matters of State'. Yet one should not blame her – it shows her good sense rather than otherwise. Not only was the Duc de Choiseul the Austrian alliance's architect and its most loyal supporter, the man who had made her Queen, but he was one of the ablest statesmen produced by *ancien régime* France. Unluckily he had incurred the enmity of the King's father as a rake and freethinker and, above all, as the man who had bullied Louis XV into banishing the Jesuits and had then frightened Rome into suppressing the whole order. Nor did such a record endear him to the King's aunts. Marie Antoinette did her best for Choiseul, coaxing and sulking, and finally Louis agreed to recall him to court. The Duke was summoned to La Muette (where the King was staying until Versailles was free of smallpox). Choiseul arrived triumphantly and the Queen tricked her husband into speaking to him. Alas, Louis simply observed that the Duke had grown fat and bald, which was all the conversation Choiseul got from His Majesty. Two days later the unhappy man left court for his estates in Touraine.

For the King had already decided on his Foreign Minister. It was to be the vulpine-countenanced Comte de Vergennes, the French ambassador to Sweden, amiable and excessively reassuring in manner like so many of his profession. He had a

common wife and overdressed and was not quite a gentleman
– at any rate not by the standards of the Prince de Ligne –
while not only had he been sacked by Choiseul in the latter's
days of power, but he was lukewarm about the Austrian
alliance. Even so he was genuinely able, the *ancien régime*'s last
truly successful minister – despite the ultimately disastrous
gamble he would take on America.

Marie Antoinette was furious and the King was anxious to
soothe her. He knew that, like many people of fashion, she
had acquired a taste for nature in consequence of the mood
set by Rousseau, and that she was fond of the open air;
Beaumarchais gives a pretty picture in his secret memoirs of
Louis coming home through the park at La Muette and
'finding the Queen and other great ladies sitting on a bench
eating strawberries and cream; she had refused a chair or even
a stool and everyone was behaving in the most informal way
imaginable'. The King also knew that Marie Antoinette
wanted a country house of her own and when, almost at the
very moment of Vergennes's appointment, she asked him for
the Petit Trianon he was only too pleased to let her have it.
This charming little rustic pavilion, standing by a pleasant
lake in a corner of the grounds of Versailles, had been built
for Mme de Pompadour but she had died before its
completion, so Louis XV had given it to Mme du Barry. No
toy ever gave the Queen more pleasure.

To some extent the King may also have been trying to
please his wife in his treatment of the Petit Trianon's former
occupant. The du Barry was forbidden to appear at court
and, escorted by a policeman, was sent to a convent. Marie
Antoinette has been accused of 'hounding' the fallen cour-
tesan, of pettiness and spitefulness, but this is most unjust.
Mme du Barry was confined on the orders of the King
himself; the principal reason why she was allowed to see no
one was because there were fears that she might reveal state
secrets told to her by Louis XV. In the event her confinement, in apartments of the utmost luxury, lasted only a year;
within three years she was actually allowed to return to court
– at the Queen's intercession.

From Marie Antoinette's point of view Louis's most objectionable appointment was going to be that of the new Controller-General, though she did not realize it for some time. This was Baron Turgot de l'Aulne, a brilliant, charmless administrator whose job was to put the country's finances in order. He told the King, 'I shall be feared and hated by most of the court and by everyone who sells pensions or wants them.' The Queen did not yet appreciate how much she was going to be irritated by him.

Turgot was determined to stop the royal household's worst extravagances. To this end he obtained the appointment of his ally M. de Malesherbes as Minister of the Royal Household in June 1775, instead of Marie Antoinette's own candidate. Malesherbes was likeable enough, a distinguished magistrate, patron of literature and amateur botanist, a bluff, untidy figure, rather like a French Dr Johnson, in snuff-stained clothes, smoking a perpetual pipe and carrying a thick stick (mannerisms which had a tragic private history). But he was not the Queen's sort, nor did he even want the post – he had to be bullied into accepting. Marie Antoinette had no particular animosity towards him but his appointment made her dislike Turgot still more.

The King's choice of Turgot delighted the intellectuals, who were astonished that he had picked a known freethinker. Louis also won tremendous popularity by a less inspired gesture – recalling the Parlements. Surprisingly, Turgot took little interest in the return of these turbulent courts which were the chief obstacles to introducing into France the sort of enlightened despotism which existed in Habsburg lands. It is possible that Turgot's reforms might have saved the French monarchy, but it is indisputable that the Parlementaires were to bring it crashing down.

Meanwhile the Queen was changing Versailles. Having escaped first from her mother and now from the old King and the gloomy aunts, this headstrong girl, still in her teens, was determined to enjoy herself as much as possible. Her pitifully inadequate young husband had no idea whatsoever of how to control her. Marie Antoinette laughed out loud at the old-

fashioned mourning dresses of certain great ladies, referring
to them as 'stiff-necked old centenarians who live in the last
century'; hearing some had declared angrily that they would
leave 'the little girl's court' for ever, she said it was a mystery
to her how anyone over thirty dared appear there anyway.
Mme l'Etiquette was speedily dismissed, her dismissal being
the prelude to many relaxations in court ceremony. The
Queen insisted on footmen being allowed to serve her;
hitherto a Queen of France could only take food and drink
from ladies-in-waiting. She simplified the ritual of her *lever*,
depriving several duchesses of some much-prized prece-
dence. Even Mme Campan criticizes her mistress for this,
pointing out that she was hurting the duchesses' vanity.
Older and more conservative courtiers began to dislike the
young Queen. Rumours of their irritation caused a jingle to
be sung in the corridors at Versailles, to the effect that if
Marie Antoinette went on upsetting people like this she
would be sent back over the frontier:

> *Petite reine de vingt ans,*
> *Vous qui traitez si mal les gens,*
> *Vous repasserez la barrière . . .*

She was popularly known as *la petite moqueuse*. The imperial
ambassador sent gloomy reports to Vienna about the
antagonism she was arousing; predictably, a stern letter
arrived from the Empress warning her daughter that she
must not offend valuable friends just to please herself and a
few cronies. The Queen took no notice – after all, her mother
had taught her that aristocrats had no particular right to their
privileges.

Maria Theresa bombarded her with letters. Plainly she
considered that her daughter was going to the devil. 'I
foresee nothing but grief and misery for you,' she groaned.
The Empress was quite right in suspecting that Marie
Antoinette was throwing herself into frivolous amusements.
It does not seem to have occurred to Maria Theresa that this

thirst for pleasure could well have been the direct consequence of Louis XVI's physical inadequacy.

The Queen was used to normal men who begot children,
like her fondly-remembered father who had sired sixteen and
her brother Leopold who was in the process of siring another
sixteen. As has been seen, her mother had failed to instruct
her adequately on sexual matters and she was pathetically
ill-equipped to cope with the situation. Moreover she
realized very well that it was the duty of a Queen of France to
bear a Dauphin, that already there were malicious murmurs
about her barrenness. It was only natural that such a healthy
and energetic girl should try to find an outlet for her
frustration and do so with the most manic enthusiasm. After
receiving another dreadful letter from her mother, she
blurted out to Mercy-Argenteau, 'What does she want? I am
so frightened of being bored!'

There were race meetings, hunting parties, masked balls,
plays, operas, gambling, clothes and jewels. Mercy-
Argenteau reports that on 11 May 1775 she was driven to a
race-course in the Bois de Boulogne by her brother-in-law
Artois in a fast open carriage 'called a "devil"'. She
continued to frequent the course, the Plaine des Sablons, with
her new circle of young friends and favourites – a special
stand like a rustic gazebo was built for her. (The King had it
demolished since he thought it might give scandal.) She
cheered and shouted like a full-blooded Austrian, to the
horror of a world which had not yet forgotten Louis XIV.
Mrs Thrale saw her hunting in 1775, riding side-saddle on a
grey horse and wearing a shovel hat with plumes, and noticed
how dangerous and vicious-looking were the hunters she and
her ladies rode. On occasion she rode astride, with a leopard-
skin saddle-cloth, dressed like a man in green pantaloons and
an English riding-coat and round hat – something again
which would not have been done under Louis XIV. During
the winter of 1775–76 the snow lay for six weeks and,
remembering the sledging parties of her Austrian childhood,
the Queen had several sledges built; the painted, gilded
vehicles, the bells and feathers of the horses and the furs of

the occupants made an enchanting spectacle and sledging became the rage among younger courtiers.

She shared the popular taste for English fashions. She wore English-style riding habits, danced English country dances – one of her favourites was '*Over the Hills and Far Away*' – and enjoyed Fanny Burney's popular novel *Evelina*. She even tried to speak the language. Once, to Lady Spencer's horror, she confused the word 'inexpressibles' and said of the Duke of Dorset's flashy buckskin breeches, 'I do not like dem yellow irresistibles' – collapsing in laughter when she realized her mistake. Then, as now, there were traditionalist Frenchmen – and Frenchwomen – who deeply distrusted an excessive love of anything English.

As for plays and operas, Marie Antoinette was unflaggingly loyal to Gluck. She invited him to Paris every year until 1778 and supported him in the battle with his rivals Piccinni and Sacchini, attending his new operas – *Orfeo* in 1775 and *Alceste* in 1776, and a fresh production of *Iphigénie* in 1777. From deference to her sister Queen Maria Carolina she had to give a mild welcome to the Neapolitan Piccini and his *La Buona Figliola*, but on the whole the Opéra rarely staged any works other than those of Gluck after Marie Antoinette became Queen, at any rate during her early years. Her patronage ensured Gluck's lasting success.

Louis shared her tastes for hunting and the play and billiards, but not for gaming. Every evening when she was not dancing at a masked ball or at the theatre or the Opéra, she played cards for very high stakes indeed. Faro was the popular game, much to the disapproval of the King who was horrified by the enormous sums involved. Her gambling parties often went on all night – on one occasion for thirty-six hours – and after a marathon of this sort her husband was angry enough to tell her and her friends, 'You really are a useless lot!' By January 1777 she owed 487,272 livres for debts contracted in the previous year alone, mainly from gambling, which she could not pay. Louis settled them from his private resources. Informed by the zealous Mercy-Argenteau, the Empress remonstrated in tones of horror –

'Beyond question, gaming is the very worst of all amusements, attracting evil companions and giving rise to spiteful
rumours.'

She overspent on clothes. In 1774, even before Louis XV
died, the Duchesse de Chartres presented a certain Mlle Rose
Bertin to her. Soon this grasping, snub-nosed Norman
businesswoman was visiting Her Majesty at Versailles every
morning, bringing a troop of assistants together with
patterns and materials which made up into such dresses as
désir masqué, soupirs étouffés or *plaisirs indiscrets*. Mlle Bertin ran
a most profitable racket, ruthlessly exploiting her young
patron. On average the Queen bought 170 creations a year
and, not surprisingly, exceeded her dress allowance by an
annual 40,000 livres. She also patronized the famous hair-
dresser Léonard Hautier, who came out from Paris each day to
pile her hair into tall strange shapes, to such effect that when
someone unkindly sent a sketch of her to Vienna Maria
Theresa asked to be told whether it was the Queen of France
or an actress.

Her worst extravagance was diamonds, for which she had
a passion. Mme Campan, writing much later and with the
awful Affair of the Diamond Necklace in mind, claims that
Marie Antoinette's first purchases were very modest and
from her own purse since 'she didn't wish to burden the
Royal treasury with the expense of a mere whim'. Indeed in
1775 Mrs Thrale noticed, 'There were no diamonds at all at
Court but the Queen's ear-rings, and she had no other jewels
on her head – a pair of pearl bracelets with a picture on each
were all that looked like ornaments of expense; her gown was
a gauze adorned with flowers.' Alas, the solitary earrings
were the start of a monumental spending spree. They had
been sold to her the previous year for 369,000 livres – almost
as soon as she ascended her throne and could do what she
liked – by a sharp German jeweller, a Jew called August
Böhmer. Partly by offering lavish credit, Böhmer then
managed to sell her a diamond spray for 200,000 livres and a
diamond bracelet for 250,000, followed by some 'chandelier'
earrings for 30,000. She bought more bracelets as well. The

Empress was appalled when she learnt of these purchases from Mercy-Argenteau and sent yet another all-but-hysterical remonstrance: 'A Queen can only degrade herself by such impossible behaviour and degrades herself even more by this sort of heedless extravagance, especially in difficult times. I know only too well what expensive tastes you have . . . I hope I shall not live to see the disaster which is all too likely to occur.' Marie Antoinette can hardly have mollified her mother by replying, 'I would not have thought anyone could have bothered you about such bagatelles.' Maria Theresa was quite right: one day Böhmer and his wares would bring disaster upon her daughter.

Now that the King was busy with affairs of State and the rituals of his position, the little circle of the three young royal couples broke up. Monsieur, as Provence was now known, led his own life. He loved pageantry and display and spent vast sums on it, dressed in diamond-studded suits and keeping an enormous stable although his deformed hips made it impossible for him to ride. Unpleasantly haughty in manner, icily cold and selfish, he was an unattractive even repellent figure whose fat, if hawk-featured, face habitually wore a sly, malicious grin. He was also slightly ridiculous – Mme Campan informs us 'he had more dignity of demeanour than the King, but his size and obesity gave him an ungainly walk'. His sexuality was ill defined; it was rumoured that his impotence had driven his dirty and half-mad wife to drink. However he was undeniably the cleverest member of the family and, as an enthusiastic patron of letters, filled his palace of the Luxembourg with writers. He could not hide a consuming envy of his elder brother, writing a number of anonymous pamphlets – one sneered at Louis as 'the leading dummy in the kingdom' and another abused Turgot whom he called a 'despot'. Despite his impotence he boasted loudly that he could do what his brother could not – supply France with an heir to the throne. Marie Antoinette had to meet him occasionally and sometimes went to his parties – once he gave a fête for her at his château of Brunoy which she told Mme Campan was the most magnificent she ever saw, a combi-

nation of masque and tournament – and he was frequently at
the balls at the Opéra.

The one member of the royal family of whom she saw
more than ever was Artois, so much so that enemies
circulated rumours of incest. He accompanied her everywhere and was the leading spirit in all her revels. Charles-
Philippe was wild and reckless and had plunged into
scandalous dissipation, accumulating vast debts. When
drunk, which was only too frequent, he was violently rude
and fought at least one duel. A pathological sensualist like his
grandfather, besides patronizing all the most expensive
prostitutes in Paris he seduced countless court ladies and saw
little of his wife after he had presented her with two sons. The
Comte d'Hézecques says of him, at a slightly later date, he
'possessed that fashionable ease and light amiability which
please women', while he was surprisingly popular with the
Parisians who admired his good looks – he had the nose and
eyes of his grandfather – his amiability and dashing turnout,
and liked his habit of driving himself about their city. With
all his wildness, and despite being rather stupid, he was
nonetheless genuinely fond of his sister-in-law whom he
treated with the utmost respect (though on occasion he was
seen to pinch her). At this period he was the Queen's leading
chevalier servant, escorting her to every smart play and ball. In
1779 he wagered his sister-in-law 100,000 livres that he could
build and furnish a new palace in nine weeks, and he won his
bet. This was the Bagatelle in the Bois de Boulogne. In style it
is the purest Neo-classical and with its furniture and
decoration is a perfect example of the period's taste, since
Artois was the only member of the royal family to interest
himself in such things – he may well have influenced Marie
Antoinette's own ideas on décor.

There were others who might also be described as the
Queen's *chevaliers servants*. They included the Duc de Lauzun,
the Prince de Ligne, the Baron de Besenval, the Duc de
Guines, the Duc de Coigny, the Marquis de Ségur, the Comte
de Vaudreuil, the Comte d'Adhémar, and the Vicomte
Dillon. Some of these men were slightly shady.

Among the latter was Louis-Armand de Gontaut-Biron, Duc de Lauzun, a free-spending rake from Gascony. He was undeniably clever and witty, always doing the unexpected. An Anglophile, he had an English mistress, he dressed like an English hunting man and imported English jockeys from Newmarket. Marie Antoinette was very taken with him and allowed him to escort her to the race meetings at the Plaine des Sablons. However, voraciously sexual, he could not contain himself and tried to make love to her; according to his own account he actually embraced her. What is certain is that he was shown the door and banished from the Petit Trianon.

The Prince de Ligne was a very different figure. This grandee from the Austrian Netherlands was in his forties, irresistibly civilized and amusing, as lively as he was witty, an easy cosmopolitan who was at home in every court, interested in neither money nor advancement, the very personification of an eighteenth-century *grand seigneur*. He had commanded his private family regiment, the *Ligne-Infanterie*, with distinction during the Seven Years War and was a respected adornment of the Hofburg. He first came to Versailles in June 1776 at Artois's invitation, spending several months there every year for the next decade. Because of his honesty and detachment, the Prince's opinions on Marie Antoinette and her circle are of special interest. He remembers, 'I never saw anything in her company which was other than distinguished by elegance, good feeling and taste. She could detect an intriguer a league away. She loathed every sort of pretence.' He had many conversations with her and particularly admired 'the graceful way in which she extricated herself from any little embarrassments, arising from a kind of naivety which suited her very well, emphasized the kindliness and sensibility of a very sweet nature and made her face even more charming'. He explains away any imputations of flirting. 'Her affected flirtatiousness was only from friendliness and reserved for very few people, while there was also that natural *coquetterie* of a woman and a Queen intended to please everyone.' Speaking not only for himself but for the other men in Marie Antoinette's little circle, he adds, 'We adored her, without ever dreaming of falling in love with her.' Ligne knew Vienna and the Viennese, still more he knew Maria Theresa and the Queen's brothers and sisters, and he was therefore better equipped to understand Marie Antoinette than almost anybody else at Versailles.

Even older than Ligne and still more amusing, though less honourable and less intelligent, was the Baron Pierre-Victor de Besenval from Solothurn, a pink-cheeked, prematurely white-haired lieutenant-colonel of the Swiss Guards who was in his fifties when Marie Antoinette became Queen. The Duc de Lévis-Mirepoix, a notably sour observer, informs us that Besenval 'had the cunning found among so many of his countrymen, who under a wooden-faced, clumsy appearance frequently show themselves much shrewder than any Frenchman'. In reality this handsome soldier – who in any case was half Polish – was far from wooden-faced or clumsy, being both elegant and dignified. Like many distinguished military men, off the battle-field he was a hard-drinking, woman-chasing man of pleasure, though he also had a beautiful house in the rue de Grenelle (today's Swiss Embassy) with magnificent pictures. He entertained the Queen with a vast repertoire of funny stories and sang both Swiss airs and the latest French songs. He was very popular with the ladies of the court, no doubt because he made them laugh so much. Ligne, who knew him well, describes him (in a letter to the Russian Empress) as *'un de nos très aimables roués'*. Unlike Ligne, Besenval was silly enough to fall in love with Marie Antoinette and fell on his knees before her, declaring his passion. The Queen replied coldly, 'Rise, sir. The King shall not be informed of an offence which could disgrace you for ever.' For a long time she hardly spoke to him, though he was not banished completely from the Petit Trianon. Mme Campan says that Besenval, 'like an experienced courtier', knew how to live down her mistress's displeasure; it is more to the point that, as a Swiss and a cosmopolitan, he probably had a much shrewder understanding of Marie Antoinette's Austrian temperament than most Frenchmen.

It was only to be expected that so many of the Queen's closest male companions should be northerners – Ligne, Besenval and later Fersen. Another was the 'brutally handsome' – and seemingly insufferably haughty – Count Bálint Miklós Esterházy of Frakno (a distant kinsman of Haydn's Prince Esterházy), who was fifteen years older than herself. She knew all about the curious mentality of Hungarian magnates from her mother's court, and immediately divined the loyalty, generosity and grandeur of spirit concealed by an arrogant exterior. Like many of her men friends he was a professional soldier, so she quickly obtained him the colonelcy of a regiment of hussars, making sure it had pleasant quarters. 'Why have you sent Esterházy's regiment to Montmédy, a nasty garrison!' she asked the War Minister angrily, insisting that it be moved at once to the much sought after garrison town of Rocroy. In addition she paid the Hungarian's debts. During the French Revolution few foreigners were to be kinder to its exiled victims than Count Bálint Miklós Esterházy.

The Queen's closest friendships were with her own sex. She had three special favourites. Marie-Thérèse-Louise de Savoie-Carignan, Princess de Lamballe was the daughter-in-law of the Duc de Bourbon-Penthièvre, a Prince of the Blood, and was herself a princess of the royal house of Savoy. Four years older than Marie Antoinette, she had been widowed at nineteen when her appalling young husband died of syphilis after having told her exactly how he had caught it. Perhaps in consequence she suffered from hysteria and fainting fits; it was said that even a bunch of wilting violets could send her into a swoon. Opinions vary about her appearance: characteristically Mme Campan describes her in her winter furs as 'looking like Spring peeping from beneath sable and ermine'. Others disagree, and portraits show an excessively long neck, clumsy hands and an undeniably vapid if amiable expression. Mme de Genlis says of the Princess that 'she never possessed a single opinion of her own'.

The Princesse de Lamballe had been present at Marie Antoinette's first meeting with the royal family at Compiègne in 1770, but the friendship began only after Louis XVI's accession. Mme de Lamballe seemed so simple and innocent that even Mercy-Argenteau approved of her, reporting to the Empress in 1774 that 'besides being sweet and charming she is thoroughly honest and has no taste for intrigue or for anything improper'. But in September 1775, despite Malesherbes's horrified protests, the Queen insisted on reviving the moribund office of Superintendent of the Queen's Household for her, at a salary of 150,000 livres a year. The Princess then began to give herself almost regal airs, while showing herself ludicrously incompetent. By the following spring Mercy-Argenteau was writing to Vienna that everyone was in a bad temper and the household badly run, that Mme de Lamballe 'who is usually to blame, is slowly falling out of favour with the Queen and the time is approaching when . . . Her Majesty will be both sorry and embarrassed at having revived a perfectly useless household post'. In the event the Princess never lost Marie Antoinette's friendship, though she soon had to compete with a new favourite.

Yolande de Polastron, Comtesse de Polignac, was six years older than the Queen. Her husband was an army colonel of good, though not as yet great, family, with fashionable tastes but insufficient means. However the principal man in her life was the Comte de Vaudreuil, her lover, for whom she would do anything. Marie Antoinette first saw her at a court ball and, so the Duc de Lévis-Mirepoix tells us, was delighted by her 'angelic face' and 'heavenly figure'. Mme Campan gives a gushing description of the new friend: 'She was of medium height with a very fair complexion, dark brown hair and eyebrows, dazzling white teeth and an enchanting smile and altogether radiantly graceful. She disliked formal clothes and was almost always simply dressed.' The Queen asked Yolande why they had not met before; the Countess answered she was too poor to come to court often. Her husband was speedily made First Equerry, he and Yolande being given a magnificent flat at Versailles 'at the top of the marble staircase'. Mme de Lamballe was so upset that she burst into tears and Marie Antoinette had to soothe her by taking her for a walk in the gardens with her arm around her waist.

The third girl friend, not so close, if even prettier despite being older, was the Princesse de Guéménée. She was of greater stock than Yolande, being a Rohan who had married another Rohan. Very smart and dashing, when she went to the races she was always surrounded by an admiring crowd of *jeunesse dorée*. She was also a firm friend of Lauzun and in fact very much a member of the fast set – her drawing-room was once described as being little better than a gambling hell.

The Queen's fondness for these female favourites was one of her few real weaknesses, more serious than any extravagance on clothes or jewels. She cost the State much more by lavishing places and pensions on them and their friends, which caused understandable jealousy at court. What in fact were acts of pure kindness were turned against her by secret enemies who presented them in the vilest terms. Unquestionably they were ill-balanced and ill-judged pieces of patronage but the Queen was certainly not a Lesbian as now began to be rumoured, however passionate and over-sentimental the friendships may have been. Even if sometimes hysterically demonstrative, they were never more than retarded adolescent crushes resulting from the frustration of an unsatisfying marriage.

The Petit Trianon was also a cause for scandal. At first people were pleased that Louis had given it to the Queen, but they soon grew angry when stories circulated about the amount of money she was spending on her toy palace. Its rooms were refurnished with the utmost luxury in what is sometimes wrongly called the *style Marie Antoinette* – in reality *Louis Seize* – which meant the light, elegant, long-legged bureaux, commodes, and cabinets made by such *ébénistes* as Reisener, Molitor and Jacob, all Neo-classical in inspiration, as were their delicate tables and straight-lined chairs. Curtains and wall coverings were fussier; flowered silks and velvets festooned with draperies and tassels. The Queen herself paid considerable attention to detail, having the books which she never read bound in blue leather. Nor were the gardens neglected. She ordered the creation of a *jardin anglaise*, a 'Graeco-English' garden with footbridges and obelisks, pagodas, gazebos and temples, which would eventually cost 200,000 livres.

However, she did not begin the construction of the Hamlet next to the Petit Trianon from which it was separated by the lake until 1782. It was a miniature farm with eight cottages, cows, sheep, goats and chickens, and also fruit trees, raspberry bushes and strawberry plants. Indeed it was run commercially by a professional bailiff called Vally Bussard, earning an average of about 6,000 livres annually. Some admirers of Marie Antoinette claim that it was a model farm based on the new, scientific agriculture, rather than a toy, but this is an exaggeration. On the other hand, tales of the Queen playing at milkmaids dressed as an Arcadian shepherdess and milking beribboned cows and goats are equally wide of the mark – even if she did once order a Swiss billy goat which had to be 'clean and white and unsmelly'. Certainly Marie Antoinette shared the fashionable taste for nature disseminated by Rousseau, but the Hamlet was essentially a piece of landscape gardening, a theatrical backcloth intended to create the illusion that the Petit Trianon was in the depths of the countryside.

Although only a mile from the palace of Versailles, to Ligne the Petit Trianon seemed 'a hundred leagues from court'. He adds nostalgically that there 'one could breathe the air of happiness and freedom'. Of necessity very few guests were invited, since the little pavilion contained only seven rooms. It was a very intimate and a very private place, and manners were relaxed accordingly. No one dressed formally, and when the Queen entered ladies did not trouble to stop their embroidery while gentlemen continued with their billiards, their backgammon or their cards, which was just as she wished. There were such frolics as blindman's buff, and country dancing on the lawn. Sometimes, though rarely, large parties were given, such as that on 3 September 1777 to mark the completion of the 'Temple of Love' in the *jardin anglais*. A miniature fair was erected, complete with booths, sideshows and open-air theatre, and the guests danced to music played by bandsmen of the *Maison du Roy* dressed as Chinamen, while the Queen and her ladies served wine or lemonade. Those who disapproved of Marie Antoinette called the Petit Trianon 'Little Vienna' – perhaps not entirely without justification, but certainly with malice.

If the luxury and exclusiveness of the Petit Trianon upset many, it was nothing to the offence caused by the advancement of the Polignac set. Yolande herself was not especially greedy, but she could deny nothing to her lover Vaudreuil, and she seemed almost as anxious to please her husband's voracious clan. Eager for friendship, the Queen was only too ready to oblige, 'to correct the injustices of fortune' as Mme Campan amiably puts it. M. de Polignac was made a Duke, Postmaster General – a most lucrative office – and Master of the Horse, while all his debts were paid, to the tune of 400,000 livres. Yolande's father was given a fat pension and her daughter an equally rich dowry. Her brother-in-law became ambassador to the Swiss. Her husband's sister-in-law, Diane de Polignac, was made a lady-in-waiting despite a most unsavoury reputation. Such favours infuriated families of genuinely high standing like the Noailles, not to mention Princes of the Blood such as the Orléans. They had reason to be jealous; it has been estimated that over a period of years the Polignac set annually milked the royal treasury of not less than half a million livres. The horrified Mercy-Argenteau wrote about it to the Empress, groaning that he had never heard of 'royal favour conferring such enormous benefits on such a family in so short a time'. Admittedly Marie Antoinette was very much at fault, yet there is something to be said in her defence. Beyond question Yolande was genuinely sweet-natured and likeable. Mme Campan considers her character above reproach and argues convincingly that she never wanted anything for herself, that she was as incapable of seeing through her venal relatives as was the Queen herself. And all Marie Antoinette sought was 'the sweets of friendship'.

The Queen's preference for the Petit Trianon and her favourites had more harmful consequences than merely causing offence. Under the *ancien régime*, Versailles, so far as government and the ruling classes were concerned, was the centre of France. But now some noblemen began to avoid it. In an often quoted passage the Duc de Lévis-Mirepoix explains what was happening: 'In those days of pleasure and frivolity, intoxicated by her power, the Queen had no inclination to submit to routine and she found court ceremony tedious in the extreme.' He says that she plainly thought it ridiculous to imagine the common people's loyalty depended on the amount of time spent by the royal family among boring courtiers. The Duke continues, 'Apart from a few favourites to whom she had taken a fancy or who knew how to intrigue to ingratiate themselves, everyone was excluded from the royal presence. Rank, service, reputation, birth, were no longer enough to gain admittance . . . Only on Sundays could persons furnished with proper introductions manage to see Their Majesties for even a few minutes . . . and deciding that it was a waste of time to make a long journey simply to be received ungraciously, they preferred to stay at home.' He adds that Versailles started to decline into 'a minor provincial town which one visited reluctantly and left as quickly as possible'.

The Duke exaggerates. Perhaps he himself had been – or at least thought he had been – 'received ungraciously'. Until 1789 Versailles ran no danger whatsoever of becoming 'a minor provincial town' and until the very end was always thronged with courtiers, even if they were not quite so awed by the royal majesty as they would have been in Louis XIV's day. But M. de Lévis-Mirepoix is perfectly correct in thinking that many people were deeply offended by the Queen's attitude. It was not just her aloofness. She had a mocking Viennese wit which could hurt, and she spared no one. Moreover Lévis-Mirepoix puts his finger on the true danger of Marie Antoinette's behaviour – to a large extent the common people's view of her was indeed derived from the upper nobility. It was the latter whose wounded pride was the real origin of the hatred of the Queen displayed by all classes during the Revolution; who were the first to condemn her as frivolous and useless, as extravagant and depraved, as a foreigner and an enemy of France. Marie Antoinette was quite unaware of any such danger, nor can one altogether blame her. When the Empress warned her daughter that she must accept the boredom of 'a representative position' among 'so touchy a nation' as the French, the Queen might well have replied that her mother had always had a very poor opinion of her own nobles.

Undeniably Marie Antoinette was foolish and spendthrift, but she was also a very innocent young woman. Her extravagance was not so very great (she spent a mere fraction of what the Empress Joséphine was to spend). Writing in 1911 Hilaire Belloc, no admirer, admits that 'her gambling was not often excessive; her expenditure upon jewellery and dress would be thought most moderate today in the case of any lady of our wealthier families' – though here he is referring to her more mature years. And despite her sexual frustration, this most full-blooded of girls did not take a lover. She was a practising Catholic, if not noticeably devout until much later; she confessed regularly to Vermond and went to Communion. Stories of Sèvres cups moulded from her breasts are nonsense. Mme Campan testifies to what nowadays seems an almost comic degree of modesty; the Queen 'bathed in a long flannel gown, buttoned up to the neck, and when her bathing women helped her out of the bath always made one of them hold a cloth in front of her so her ladies-in-waiting could not see her'. Her chosen companions may have been fast, but she showed herself responsible enough where young girls of her household – 'from the Maison de Saint-Cyr, all well born' – were concerned, forbidding them to see 'unsuitable' plays. Nor was she a greedy person. In a court noted throughout Europe for its delicious cuisine she herself was very far from being a *'fine fourchette'*; almost invariably she dined on a chicken, roast or boiled, while for breakfast she had only coffee and 'a sort of bread to which she had been used during her childhood in

Vienna'. Normally she drank nothing but water, though very occasionally she took a little watered wine for her health.

In fact Marie Antoinette had many good qualities and hardly any bad ones. The trouble was that not only had her education been neglected but that since the age of fourteen she had lived an isolated and severely repressed existence before achieving almost inconceivable eminence and power, and that Louis XVI was not the man to discipline any woman, let alone such a strong one as his wife. Moreover, not only were his courtiers anxious to please her, but his ministers were always amiably ready to indulge any extravagance, however much they might secretly disapprove.

The Queen is often blamed as a principal architect of the fall of Turgot, the reforming minister who *might* have saved the monarchy. As Controller-General (and therefore Minister of Finance) he was admirably determined to reduce government expenditure, which of course included court expenditure. Understandably he and Malesherbes, the Minister of the Royal Household, deplored pensions and places for friends together with diamonds and gambling debts, though they remained deferential enough. Malesherbes's appointment had irritated Marie Antoinette in any case. She blamed Turgot. The latter angered her still more in March 1776 when he insisted on recalling her crony the Comte de Guines from London where he was ambassador, on justifiable grounds of incompetence. Guines was elegant and civilized, the patron to whom Mozart dedicated his flute and harp concerto – indeed he wrote it so that the Count could perform it with his children – and so careful in his dressing that to look thinner he wore such tight breeches that he could not sit down. He was excellent company, very witty and amusing. Unfortunately as a diplomatist he was a disaster, at the same time both idle and intriguing, and very nearly upset the 'family compact' between France and Bourbon Spain. During his time in London he even indulged in smuggling on a large scale and was later to be tried for it.

The Queen knew nothing about foreign policy or diplomacy but she was unfailingly loyal to a cheerful companion.

Turgot had to go. In April the King asked Marie Antoinette if she had been cheered at the Opéra. This was because the capital was in uproar on account of the Parlement's opposition to the Draconian new edicts proposed by the Controller-General. She answered smartly that if Louis had been there with his Turgot, he 'would have been well and truly hissed'. Turgot went the following month.

Many historians consider that his dismissal finally doomed the French monarchy and many blamed the Queen. It is true that a very clever, indeed a brilliantly gifted, wife might possibly have stopped Louis XVI from sacking Turgot – or might have tried, though not succeeded – but it was too much to expect from an inexperienced girl of twenty-one. However weak Louis may have been, he would probably have shrugged off Marie Antoinette's grumbling if Turgot had not upset practically everybody else. His abandonment of controls on the grain trade had sent wheat prices soaring and caused bread riots (which were popularly known as 'The Grain War') all over the country and even in Paris, while his proposed attacks on privilege and tax immunity had infuriated the entire nobility and the clergy. Even the bourgeoisie and the intellectuals were turning against him. He had finally antagonized the King himself with an almost unbelievably tactless letter which insisted on calling a national assembly and included the reassuring warning, 'Never forget, Sire, that weakness put Charles I's head on the block.' Had there been such an anachronism as a foreign correspondent in Paris during the spring of 1776 he would surely have concluded that while the Queen's dislike of the Controller-General had had small influence on her husband's decision to dismiss him, she was nevertheless showing herself admirably in sympathy with popular opinion. The fact that Guines was made a Duke in June is a testimony to Marie Antoinette's capacity for friendship rather than a monument to her 'destruction' of Turgot.

Alas, Guines's dukedom was not seen in such an approving light. By now, for an increasing number of Frenchmen and Frenchwomen, the Queen could do nothing right. Her greatest weakness was that she was so very foreign – so Austrian. All too many French nobles had had fathers, brothers, husbands or near relatives killed by Austrians in quite recent wars, while many others had fought against Austrian troops. Fighting at the side of the Austrians during the disastrous Seven Years War (1756–63) had scarcely been a happier experience; after a mutual defeat even friendly allies have little love for one another, and the Franco-Austrian alliance had been stormy at best. The word *Autrichien* was no less emotive a word than *Boche* during the 1920s and 1930s. Significantly the French upper nobility began to speak of *l'Autrichienne* when they talked of the Queen, and they stressed the second half – *chienne* means bitch.

Certainly few women have been more Austrian than Marie Antoinette. She would have made the perfect heroine for a Mozart opera or a Strauss operetta. Cosmopolitans like Ligne or Besenval found her charming, but the French aristocracy saw little to admire. Viennese gaiety was not at all the same thing as the gaiety of Versailles, whose inhabitants found the Queen's cheerfulness much too Germanic and boisterous. She lacked the subtle, cerebral elegance of a French *grande dame*. Those outside her tiny circle knew nothing of that *gemütlich* warmth, kindliness and simplicity which so endeared her to her friends, and were immune to her *stimmung*, her dynamic compound of optimism, self-confidence, boundless energy and zest for life – they plainly considered it thoroughly unfeminine and improper. Her flamboyant amusements were sniffed at as verging on the bourgeois.

Marie Antoinette played into her enemies' hands. At heart as well as in temperament she always remained a loyal Austrian. Indeed, her revered mother had told her to 'stay a good German', whatever happened. Moreover she was incapable of comprehending or sympathizing with the French nobility. Hilaire Belloc observes perceptively that 'she did not understand its stiffness, its exactitude, its brilliancy or its hardness; and she heartily disliked all four'. Belloc was writing at a time when the French aristocracy had not yet become today's discreet body, and when it was still

Proust's Faubourg Saint-Germain and still clearly identifiable
with the world of Versailles.

The enmity openly displayed by the French princes for her
brother Maximilian when he came to visit her in February
1775 would have warned someone older and more experienced. The eighteen-year-old Archduke was an ugly,
uncouth boy with a harelip and misshapen jaw, slow to the
point of clownishness, but this was no reason for the French
Princes of the Blood to insult him. According to protocol it
was their duty to call on him; the Duc d'Orléans, the Duc de
Chartres, the Prince de Condé and the Prince de Conti all
refused, a gesture plainly intended as a snub.

The Queen appears to have ignored the insult. She was
unfeignedly delighted, if a little nervous, when she learnt in
1777 that another of her brothers, the Emperor Josef II, also
intended to visit her.

[4]
Children at last

Vos folies, méritent elles de la pitié?

Beaumarchais, *Le Mariage de Figaro*

Slander's mark was ever yet the fair

Shakespeare, *Sonnet LXX*

THE EMPRESS Maria Theresa trembled as much as ever for her daughter's marriage. It is plain, from Mercy-Argenteau's dispatches and from her own letters, that she had guessed that something was very seriously wrong. Whether or not she attributed Marie Antoinette's frantic love of pleasure to sexual frustration, she was clearly horrified by its consequences. Now Mercy-Argenteau was reporting that Versailles had been all but deserted during the winter of 1776–77 because of the Queen's amusements and wild behaviour. The Empress decided to send her son Josef to Paris to investigate.

Certainly there is reason to think that Marie Antoinette was still very far from being in love with her husband. Just what she had to put up with has been dwelt on in detail by many biographers, but it is too important not to repeat. To begin with, she shared none of the King's interests. He was always happy in his library while, according to Besenval, the Queen scarcely opened a book during these early years. His hobbies irritated her, especially the fact that his hands were often filthy from working in his smithy – on more than one occasion she screamed at him for being so dirty. Louis was also slovenly; when the Swedish King Gustavus III, a homosexual exquisite, was received by the ruler of the most elegant nation in Europe, he found the French monarch in a dressing-gown and odd shoes with uncombed hair. Mme de La Tour du Pin – a lady-in-waiting and the author of some particularly observant memoirs – remembers 'there was nothing stately or regal about him. His sword was a continual embarrassment to him and he never knew what to do with his hat'. Nor had Marie Antoinette any wish to join in his gluttony. One of Louis's breakfasts consisted of a chicken, four chops, some thick ham and six baked eggs washed down by a bottle and a half of champagne; while his dinners, especially after hunting, were so gargantuan that Mercy-Argenteau believed 'they deprive him of reason'. After these orgies of gorging and swilling he frequently had to be carried to bed, practically unconscious and emitting *'un bruit très suspect'*. In his cups he could swear with surprising foulness, and he had a weakness for irritating practical jokes. The only thing which saved this awkward, ineffectual ox of a man from being a laughing-stock was the simple fact that he was King of France. The Queen was far too young and immature to appreciate his decency and goodness – indeed his good intentions may well have got on her nerves.

Above all, the man was still inadequate in bed. Lauzun tells of a significant incident at about this date. Once, after she had lost her temper with the Duke, Marie Antoinette suddenly flung her arms around him and then fled in an agony of embarrassment; it is clear that the poor girl was beginning to lose her self-control. Quite apart from physical frustration, the Queen was humiliated by not being able to produce an heir – and sometimes humiliated in public. In the autumn of 1775, at a race meeting, Mrs Thrale heard Parisian fishwives shouting revolting obscenities at Marie Antoinette and asking why she didn't have a Dauphin. The same year the Queen wrote unhappily to the Empress about the birth of Artois's first son – 'There's no need to tell you, dear Mama,

Louis XVI, by Duplessis

how much it hurts me to see an heir to the throne who isn't mine.'

Josef II must have seemed hardly the person to help her. He was a strange creature, brilliant but icily cold, a classic example of the benevolent despot, determined to be a real father to his country – the Habsburg domains – and a 'people's Emperor'. Full of schemes to improve the lot of his humbler subjects, he tried driving a plough himself to see what it felt like, wore patched clothes, ate nothing more luxurious than boiled bacon, walked the streets of Vienna in disguise to learn public opinion, and had himself shut up in prison to understand a prisoner's reactions. He distrusted aristocrats and, though a good Catholic, priests. In the event his measures probably saved the Empire as a whole from revolution, even if they drove some parts of it into revolt. His basic flaw was sheer coldness, which crushed his wives and repelled most people. The Prince de Ligne, who knew him well, comments that Josef 'never yielded to love or friendship, perhaps he feared involvement; there was invariably too much self-interest in his relations with others; he trusted no one, since he had grown used to seeing other sovereigns deceived in their mistresses, their confessors, their ministers or their friends'. Ligne adds that the Emperor 'sacrificed all pleasure in order to make others work harder; what he detested most in the world was idleness'.

Perhaps not surprisingly Mercy-Argenteau reported to Vienna that 'despite genuine joy at the prospect of seeing her august brother again, the Queen is obviously most uneasy about the impending visit and what he may think of her court and, in particular, of the Queen's own way of life'. It looks as though Marie Antoinette was feeling a little guilty. It is also clear that she regarded her eldest brother as one of the two or three men in the world whom she could consider her superior, though he too, as she knew, had to defer to their mother. Moreover she must have been aware how little she had in common with him, how far too austere and intolerant he was to pardon even the simplest amusements. On the other hand she had a deep affection for a member of the beloved family in Vienna, one who had sung with her in his fine bass voice and accompanied her on the clavichord – music being almost his only indulgence. She awaited his coming with mixed feelings.

The Holy Roman Emperor, using the name Count Falkenstein as an incognito, arrived in Paris in April 1777 and installed himself at an ordinary hotel. The following day he took a cab to Versailles and booked a room in a cheap lodging-house, where he was to sleep wrapped in a cloak on a camp bed. Then, wearing a 'puce' suit of bourgeois cut, he called at Versailles, a tall, thin man of thirty-six with an aquiline nose and his family's protuberant jaw and lower lip, and bulging eyes. There was a touching reunion between brother and sister, who at once retired to a private room where they spent two hours together alone. Marie Antoinette was clearly overjoyed, despite her earlier misgivings. Apparently she at once asked Josef if he was going to criticize her, but he answered that he needed time to think.

In the days that followed the Emperor Josef II plainly thought a good deal. He gives his impressions of the Bourbons in letters to his brother Peter Leopold, the Grand Duke of Tuscany. Louis XVI is 'a little weak though no fool' yet oddly listless in both mind and body. Monsieur is 'an inscrutable creature; he is better looking than the King, though mortally cold, and his belly stops him from walking properly'. As for Artois he is 'a complete fop'. Madame is ugly, coarse and an intriguer, Mme d'Artois 'hopelessly mad'. These, it must be remembered, had been the only companions available to Marie Antoinette during her first years in France. She told Josef without mincing her words that she had no deep affection for either brother-in-law, though Artois was useful socially.

The Emperor did not waste much time at Versailles. He insisted on inspecting all the practical buildings in Paris – including the prisons – and then toured the French provinces for several weeks. Although he got on well enough with Louis, his moodiness and sarcasm, and his unconcealed contempt for aristocrats, made him unpopular with the

French nobility. He confirmed many people's dislike of Austrians in general and of his sister in particular.

Yet in one vital matter Marie Antoinette had good reason to be deeply grateful for the visit of the Emperor Josef. He solved the physical problem of her marriage, simply by discovering that Louis 'never completes the [sexual] act . . . saying he does it from duty and without any enjoyment at all'. Incredibly, like his wife, the King had never received any instructions in sexual matters and remained ludicrously ignorant; the Emperor writes to Grand Duke Leopold that the King and Queen of France 'make a hopelessly clumsy pair' in bed. It has been suggested that Josef invented his account purely to entertain Leopold, but in view of what happened almost immediately after his departure from France it is more than likely that he was telling the truth.

On the debit side, Josef upset Marie Antoinette a good deal. He complained of 'a proneness to impatience and to melancholy which hinders any serious conversation', that she cries too much – 'floods of tears which only exhaust her' – and that she shows a tendency to both hysteria and the vapours. Even if he ascribed the latter weaknesses to her unsatisfactory marital life, he was harsh enough with her. One evening at Versailles he told his sister she must not accompany her husband on any royal progress or tour 'because she would be absolutely no help to him whatsoever'. He also reproved her for not treating Louis with sufficient dignity, and reproached her for her haughty and aloof manner. Where he really upset her was in his horror at her frivolous way of life. Nor did he merely rebuke her for her gambling parties.

When he finally left Versailles he pressed into her hand a written 'Instruction' of some thirty pages, a truly extraordinary document. Like the Emperor himself, it should most certainly not be taken as infallible, even if much of it shows considerable knowledge of the Queen's nature. Her imperial brother warns her that if she continues to be so very irresponsible she will end as 'an unhappy woman and an even more unhappy Queen'. He blames her for not responding to her husband's affection – 'aren't you cold, disinterested when he caresses you or tries to speak to you? Don't you look bored, even disgusted? If it's true, then how can you possibly expect such a cold-blooded man to make love to you and be genuinely fond of you?' He tells her to make herself useful and to make him need her. He asks her if she has ever bothered to think of the impression which her flash friends have upon the French public, and indeed on anyone worthwhile in France. He expresses horror at what she has told him about her adventures at the balls at the Opéra which 'possesses a most evil reputation', at her 'rubbing shoulders with rakes and loose women', at Louis being 'left alone at night at Versailles while you degrade yourself by consorting with the scum of Paris'. His advice that she should spend at least two hours every day reading serious books may make one smile a little, but not this prophecy – 'The revolution will be a cruel one and you may well be the cause of it.'

No doubt the Emperor's 'Instruction' was arrogant and sanctimonious in its tone, but Marie Antoinette had sufficient sense to follow some of the advice. In July Mercy-Argenteau writes that the Queen is behaving much more sensibly, spending far more time with the King – 'Almost every day they pass an hour or so alone together after lunch in one of their bedrooms.' Still more important, Josef had clearly had an instructive talk with his brother-in-law, details of which he omitted from the 'Instruction' – no doubt from delicacy. On 16 June the Queen had to write to her mother that Mme d'Artois was again expecting a baby but that, even if it humiliated her, she would try not to show any resentment. In the same letter she also says, 'I am not altogether without hope; my brother will tell my dear Mama about my situation.' Then on 29 July she writes ecstatically about 'the happiness so essential for my entire life. My marriage was consummated more than a week ago; the experiment has been repeated, and again yesterday and more successfully than before.' The Queen adds that even if she is not yet pregnant she can at least hope to be so one day. Josef commented smugly that both Louis and Marie Antoinette had written to thank him for the advice which had made it possible – 'I certainly discussed the matter in considerable detail during my conversations with him, and came to the conclusion that the only obstacles were his laziness, clumsiness and apathy,' says the Emperor.

Louis XVI was happy too. Naively he told his spinster aunts that the physical pleasure was even greater than he had anticipated and he was very sorry he had had to wait such a long time before enjoying it. (One doubts if this revelation did anything to make the old maids like their niece any better.) The King continued to enjoy himself, and towards the end of 1777 Marie Antoinette confided in Mme Campan that at last she really was Queen of France and hoped she would soon have children; she added that until now she had hidden her disappointment, though secretly she had cried a good deal. By then Louis was spending three or four nights a week in her bedroom.

At the end of April 1778 Marie Antoinette proudly told her husband that she was expecting a baby. She expressed herself with Teutonic humour: 'I have come to complain, Sire, about one of your subjects who has been rude enough to kick me in the belly.' Louis immediately flung his arms around the Queen. He did everything he could to please her, ordering a ballet whose theme was maternity and a *fête champêtre*: it was then that Maurepas appeared in pink silk as Cupid. The Abbé Vermond's brother was appointed *accoucheur*. On the evening of 18 December bells announced the beginning of Marie Antoinette's labour. Over fifty uninvited courtiers filled her bedroom – 'so motley a gathering, one would have thought oneself in a place of public amusement,' complains the outraged Mme Campan. This 'cruel etiquette' was abolished shortly afterwards, so badly did the spectators behave, pushing and jostling to see better; the screens round the bed would have been knocked over if the King had not taken the precaution of having them secured with ropes. It was such a painful birth that the loyal Mme de Lamballe swooned and was carried out insensible. The room was stiflingly hot. As soon as the child was born the Queen gasped, 'Help me, I'm dying,' and, bleeding from the mouth, lost consciousness. The *accoucheur* shouted 'Give her air and bring warm water – she must be bled from the foot.' Louis, strong as an ox, smashed the windows himself, while officials ejected the uninvited courtiers by the scruff of the neck. Marie Antoinette soon recovered and a twenty-one-gun salute rang out to announce the birth of the Princess Marie Thérèse – Madame Royale, whom her parents later liked to call *Mousseline la sérieuse* because of her comic baby gravity. All France rejoiced, and when Marie Antoinette went to Notre-Dame for her churching she was cheered with genuine enthusiasm. Monsieur alone was displeased, asking sourly at the christening, 'Who's the father?'

This happy event was followed by two sad ones. A short time after Madame Royale's birth Marie Antoinette again became pregnant but suffered a miscarriage. She was in tears for days and it was some months before she recovered her health completely. Then in December 1780 news came from Vienna that the Empress Maria Theresa had died of inflammation of the lungs. Only recently she had written to bully her daughter about not having a boy – 'We simply must have a son' – and to grumble about the Queen's keeping late hours when the King kept early ones, and thus reducing her chances of conceiving an heir to the throne. She had also warned Marie Antoinette not to discontinue receptions – 'the troubles which would ensue would be far worse than the petty inconveniences of receptions'. Yet for all the nagging the Queen was inconsolable, shutting herself up in her closet, seeing no one but the royal family and Mmes de Lamballe and Polignac. She spoke ceaselessly about her mother's virtues – she particularly admired the fact that the Empress had made her own shroud.

It was not an easy time for the King. Against his better judgement he had been persuaded by Vergennes to recognize the American Declaration of Independence, signing a treaty of commerce and friendship with them, together with a secret military alliance in February 1778. Even Vergennes was nervous about his gamble and American levelling – as Tom Paine tells us, 'The fact was that Count Vergennes was an aristocratical despot at home, and dreaded the example of the American Revolution in France.' England immediately declared war on France.

At home the country had now entered a long economic depression, both agricultural and industrial. There was unemployment and poverty throughout France, all classes finding themselves short of money. The war with England at least served as a distraction.

Many French noblemen fought by the side of the Americans, either as volunteers or with the 8,000 royal troops sent by Louis. They included some of the Queen's circle, notably Lauzun. Unlike recent wars with the British this one went well, and soon there were hopes of a glorious victory. The American Ambassador Benjamin Franklin, with his rustic manners and scientific interests, became the idol of both the court and Paris – they called him *l'ambassadeur électrique*. No doubt Marie Antoinette heard all too much about him from his unlikely but devoted admirer, Diane de Polignac.

The Queen continued to live with her usual lighthearted disregard for boring conventions. When she contracted measles (sometimes a serious disease for an adult) she installed herself at the Petit Trianon with four gentlemen to wait on her – Besenval, Coigny, Guines and Esterházy.

Axel von Fersen returned to Paris. Although his stay was comparatively short, this time he clearly made a considerable impression on Marie Antoinette. The Swedish ambassador reported that Fersen seemed on excessively close terms with her, telling King Gustavus that during the days before he left the Queen 'could not take her eyes off him, and when she looked at him they filled with tears'. The ambassador was convinced Marie Antoinette was in love, though he admits she 'shows much more self-control and prudence than formerly'. However Fersen departed for a second time, for America, where he became aide-de-camp to the French commander-in-chief Rochambeau.

At the beginning of 1781 the Queen found herself pregnant once more. On 22 October 1781 she gave birth. This time it was comparatively easy. The room was so quiet –

Marie Antoinette *à la rose*, by Mme Vigée-Lebrun

the jostling mob of the previous occasion having been banished – that she thought the baby was a girl. Then King Louis, weeping, said to her, 'Monsieur le Dauphin wishes to be presented.' A hundred and one cannon rang out, and Parisians kissed total strangers in the streets. The capital's tradesmen – chimney-sweeps, sedan-chairmen, butchers, cooks, blacksmiths, masons, locksmiths, tailors, shoemakers and even undertakers – marched to Versailles to the sound of music and carrying emblems of their crafts, that of the tactless undertakers being a small coffin. Market women to the number of fifty came in black silk dresses and, according to Mme Campan, 'almost all were wearing diamonds'. Throughout France there was rejoicing in town squares and on village greens, with bands and dancing and free wine. At court the King made everyone smile by referring at every possible opportunity to 'my son, the Dauphin'.

One person who did not smile was Monsieur, seemingly deprived of any hope of ever succeeding to the throne. He wrote to Gustavus III of Sweden how it was 'a blow to my heart', and did his best to spread a rumour that the child's real father was Artois. The latter, if scarcely overjoyed, was more philosophical. When his own son, the little Duc d'Angoulême (destined to be the last Dauphin) saw the baby and said 'What a tiny cousin,' Artois answered, 'One day, my son, you will find him quite big enough.'

The Orléans clan were even crosser. They had disliked Marie Antoinette from the beginning. Moreover Chartres compounded their fury by making a fool of himself over a sea-battle with the English off Ushant: when he returned with dispatches, rumours circulated that he had engaged seven enemy vessels single-handed and at the Opéra he was cheered to the echo; but it then emerged that his ship had hardly fired a shot and he became a laughing-stock. A chance reference by the Queen to the action ruined, so he believed, his chances of becoming Lord High Admiral of France.

Marie Antoinette was nothing if not tactless, and the Dauphin's birth made her still more enemies. During the following year, 1782, Mme de Guéménée's husband suddenly went hopelessly bankrupt and the King ordered her to leave court and resign her post as governess to the royal children. (M. de Guéménée's cousin, the Cardinal de Rohan, commented with some pride that only a Rohan could succeed in going bankrupt for so vast a sum.) The Queen took the opportunity to insist on the appointment of Yolande de Polignac in her place. Yet even Marie Antoinette had misgivings, asking Mme Campan's advice: what the Queen dreaded, so this faithful lady tells us, was 'the jealousy of other courtiers'. The advocacy of Besenval, a good friend to the Polignacs, seems to have made up her mind and Yolande was appointed, receiving still more handsome appointments and a splendid salary. Just as Marie Antoinette had feared, all too many people were indeed furiously jealous. But at least they could no longer sneer at her for being a barren woman.

[5]

'A nice little smear of dirt'

Come and mourn for your Queen, insulted and
sacrificed by plotters and by injustice

Marie Antoinette

... an obscure plot, contrived by swindlers and
hatched in the haunts of darkest depravity

Mme Campan

DURING THE 1780s the campaign of calumny against the
Queen grew to a crescendo, culminating, as will be seen, in
the Affair of the Diamond Necklace, which finally destroyed
her reputation with the French people. However the Necklace scandal was to be disastrous only because of all the
preliminary slurs on her name. It is necessary to understand
just who were her enemies and the extent of their ruthless-
ness, together with quite how extraordinarily fertile was the
atmosphere for their plots.

The first among these enemies was the nobility. Not the
French nobles as a whole – that infinite host of *noblesse de
l'épée*, *noblesse de la robe* and *noblesse de la cloche*, from
Parlementaires and provincial landowners down to little
hedge-squires with incomes of barely £30 a year – but *Les
Grands* and their hangers-on. The 'Great Ones' were the
world of power and pleasure, those enormously rich families
who dominated Parisian society and who in their decline
were later to be known as the 'Faubourg Saint-Germain'.

Their members came partly from the ancient feudal houses, partly from parvenu dynasties who had risen under Louis XIV. (Contrary to popular opinion, social climbing was very easy in the *ancien régime* – any rich man could, and did, buy a title while obliging heralds would forge pedigrees of impressive antiquity.) They were united by wealth and inter-marriage. The old aunts, who had turned bitterly against their niece and retired to their château of Bellevue, provided a gathering place for all the stuffy grandees among *Les Grands* whose noses had been put out of joint by Marie Antoinette's disregard for them; *Mme l'Etiquette* may have been something of a joke but her clan, the Noailles, was rich and influential, as was that of men like M. de Lévis-Mirepoix. There were other royal salons frequented by the 'Great Ones' where hatred of the Queen was in fashion – notably those of Monsieur and Chartres.

At the Luxembourg Monsieur schemed indefatigably to discredit his brother's inept government, and naturally exploited his sister-in-law's unpopularity. It is an exaggeration to claim that he was a secret pretender to the crown, however much he may have coveted it; what Louis-Stanislas wanted at this period was for France to be transformed into a 'benevolent' despotism, with himself as the absolute power behind the throne. It is also an exaggeration to suggest he was Marie Antoinette's most dangerous enemy. But there is no doubt that Monsieur's circle was the source of pamphlets which heaped vile and filthy abuse on the Queen.

Marie Antoinette's most energetic foe was certainly Chartres, who became Duc d'Orléans in 1785. He too was furiously ambitious, privately seeing himself as head of a rival dynasty rather than a junior Prince of the Blood. Orléans, as he was now called, had a certain originality. He was a Freemason, he had been up in a hot-air balloon and he had an unusual knowledge of England, where he was a member of Brooks's and dined with Charles James Fox. Although smaller and older, in appearance he resembled Monsieur – if better built and not so fat and with a moon-face spotted with the pox and crimson from hard drinking. There were rumours of orgies; on one occasion he was said to have run stark naked through the Paris streets for a bet.

However the Prince de Ligne says such stories are ridiculous and gives rather an engaging portrait of the Duke: 'He was always good company, even among bad; exquisitely polite though with perhaps a certain haughtiness when speaking to men, if invariably respectful and attentive towards women; naturally cheerful, his jokes were in unfailing good taste, though he had more personality than conversation . . . He was well set up and beautifully dressed, with a nice expression.' The Prince, a lover of pleasure himself, is unlikely to have been shocked by Philippe d'Orléans's drinking, whoring and gambling. Yet even Ligne was shaken by the Duke's superstition and claims that his head was turned by being told by a fortune-teller in the rue Froidmanteau – the 'great Etrella' – that one day he would be master of both Versailles and the kingdom. The Prince also admits that Orléans was 'mean in small things, though generous enough in big', which is a charitable way of putting it.

In fact the Duke combined avarice with debauchery, although he owned about a twentieth of France, at least 10,000 square miles, and had an income of £400,000 in English money of the period. When his gaming losses grew out of hand he more than recouped them by building three arcades of shops around the Palais Royal, which were soon filled with cafés, casinos and brothels. Here he held court among bankrupt noblemen and speculators and other hangers-on – briefless advocates, broken officers, unsuccessful authors, out-of-work journalists and prostitutes. In a sense he was King of Paris, with the Palais Royal for his Versailles. Scores of pamphlets against the Queen, and still more lying rumours, originated in this flashy haven of discontent.

The writers who surrounded Monsieur and the Duke were perfect tools for their purpose. Among intellectuals of the Enlightenment it was the fashion to sneer at kings and queens, to express a hope that the last priest would be strangled with the entrails of the last monarch; with comparative moderation the English historian Gibbon claimed that 'the generality of princes, if they were stripped of their purple, and cast naked into the world, would immediately sink to the lowest rank of society, without a hope of emerging from obscurity'. Most writers of the day, especially the French equivalent of Grub Street, shared this attitude. Even the most successful pens would produce pamphlets, provided the money was right; Beaumarchais is known to have written several, and may have been among Marie Antoinette's slanderers. It was he who urged 'Calumny! Calumny! Something will always stick!'

There were a multitude of little printing presses in Paris – not to mention London – and few problems of circulation. The most secret, and far from least venomous, enemies of the Queen were among those courtiers who bowed or curtsied to her at Versailles but fumed inwardly at not being in the tiny chosen circle of the Trianon. Avidly they devoured the flood of pamphlets, passing them from hand to hand so that they reached every corner of the palace; the King even found them on his desk among the State papers, while one was wrapped up in Marie Antoinette's table napkin; bundles of them were actually thrown through the famous *oeil de boeuf* window (so called from being shaped like a bull's eye) which gave its name to the most beloved drawing-room in Versailles. If they included songs, these would be sung at night in the palace gardens when the Queen was in earshot.

The libels attacked her on every possible ground. She spent too much on clothes, on gambling and on parties, she could not even dance properly. Most wounding of all were sexual smears. It has been said that the *polissonneries* aimed at Marie Antoinette during her first years as Queen were comparatively mild; in reality, within two months of her husband's succession to the throne they accused her of sleeping with Orléans (who later pretended he had had to rebuff her advances), with Lauzun 'on moonlit walks', with Mme de Lamballe's brother-in-law, and with many others, including Coigny, Dillon, and of course Artois.

As early as July 1774 when she had only just made friends with Mme de Lamballe Marie Antoinette was popularly rumoured to sleep with her, and soon she was also being accused of unnatural relations with Yolande de Polignac. It is very much to the point that eighteenth-century France's name for Lesbianism was the *vice allemand*, something which was only to be expected from an Austrian Queen. Disgusting verses were circulated, telling of Sapphic orgies. The poor young woman had to learn to live with such libels, writing sadly to her mother that 'two tastes have been widely attributed to me, one for women and one for lovers'. It is quite possible that the mysterious high fever which made her take to her bed for three weeks in 1776 and caused her hair to fall out, was due to hysterical revulsion at these smears.

Above all, Marie Antoinette was accused of cuckolding the King. The campaign intensified noticeably after the birth of the Dauphin, which indicates a source near Monsieur or Orléans, or even Artois – though the latter was much too good-natured to encourage this sort of thing personally. A good example is the following:

Veux-tu connaître
Un cocu, un bâtard, une catin?
Voyez le Roi, la Reine,
Et Monsieur le Dauphin.

Only one of the authors has been identified, a certain M. Champcenetz de Riquebourg – only eighteen but already noted both as a duellist and a satirist – who was caught throwing an entire volume of such songs, all in his own handwriting, through the *oeil de boeuf* window. It is probable that he was working for friends of Artois, who hoped for the latter's succession and in consequence were trying to make out that the Dauphin was a bastard. The King had no wish to discredit his brother, who was quite innocent, so Champcenetz escaped scot-free, although Louis declared that slandering the Queen deserved the death penalty.

It is impossible to guess with any certainty who were the

other authors. Beaumarchais has already been mentioned. One might also suggest the novelist Choderlos de Laclos (author of *Les Liaisons Dangereuses*), the 'journalist' and pornographer Restif de la Bretonne (creator of *La Paysanne Pervertie*) and the future Revolutionary giant, Mirabeau. Good money would be paid for libels on the Queen, enough to attract the most distinguished writers. The cynicism of such men is illustrated by a passage in Beaumarchais's preface to his *Le Barbier de Séville*, in which he speaks of a 'quibbling century where everything is turned into a joke; where the least difference of opinion sows lasting hatred, where every gain ends in a battle; where repaying an insult only earns another insult'. In the play Beaumarchais puts a paean in praise of calumny into the mouth of Don Basile: 'Calumny, Sir! You don't know what you are disdaining. I have seen even the best people all but overwhelmed by it. Please realize that there is no outright lie, no nasty tale, no ridiculous story which one cannot make the gossips of a capital circulate enthusiastically . . . until it becomes, by divine grace, a general clamour, a public crescendo, a universal chorus of hatred and outlawry.' As Figaro observes later, 'Where calumny is concerned, one needs a position, a name, a family, a rank of real substance, to make a sensation in society.'

A veritable industry sprang up. The sheer forcefulness and flamboyance of Marie Antoinette's personality made her a figure of consuming interest to the French – and therefore all the more liable to be attacked. She was the outstanding figure at court, indeed in all France. Admittedly, as the sovereign Louis of course occupied the first position in the realm. But few French kings possessed a duller personality while few French queens combined such allure with so colourful a character as his wife. There was little competition from the rest of the royal family, all of whom – especially its female members – were insignificant in comparison. Had Marie Antoinette been a native Frenchwoman and a mere mistress she might not have aroused such hatred. Unfortunately she was not only an Austrian but Queen as well. In a time of economic recession, of general poverty and hardship, she and her little circle were singled out for everyone's opprobrium. Not just in Paris but in Bordeaux or in Lyons or in any other provincial town, every man attributed his wife or his daughter's extravagance in dresses to Marie Antoinette's evil example. But it was *Les Grands* who disliked her, detested her, most of all.

The Prince de Ligne tells us how impossible it was for the Queen to please such people. Her very beauty of feature, of complexion, of carriage, counted against her. Stateliness was seen as arrogance, amiability ascribed to frivolity. She laughed a great deal and was therefore considered mocking. If she dined at a woman friend's house people accused her of not living up to her position – *Les Grands* thought her little parties at the Trianon bourgeois, yet called her extravagant because she bought Saint-Cloud for her children's health. Her most innocent pleasures were regarded as vices. Small gambling losses were described as 'wasting State treasure'. Even walking through a gallery at Versailles accompanied by only a single footman was condemned as scandalous. Marie Antoinette admitted ruefully to Ligne that every one of her amusements was being spoilt by the poisonous gossip of her '*charmants vilains sujets*'.

One day the slanders would be transformed into criminal charges which would cost the Queen her life. In retrospect it can be seen that she was already being tried, without any chance of defending herself. One has to agree with Stefan Zweig – her somewhat romantic biographer of the 1930s – when he claims that Marie Antoinette was doomed before the Revolution even began. 'The axe of hatred which severed the Queen's neck had been put into the executioner's hands by the delicate and bejewelled fingers of the aristocracy.' For aristocracy one must of course read *Les Grands*, though France's intellectuals were scarcely any less guilty.

The irony is that by the 1780s Marie Antoinette was settling down. As Ligne observes, 'She laughed, sang and danced until she was twenty-five.' Clearly her children gave her a sense of responsibility, although it was only later that she became so obsessed with them; her character was of the sort which matures very slowly – she was what would nowadays be called a late developer. She continued to enjoy herself, but not so frenetically; she no longer lived for pleasure. The Trianon and the Hamlet – which was only begun in 1782 – became increasingly refuges rather than places of amusement. She gambled less and started to dress with deliberate simplicity. In 1783 Mme Vigée-Lebrun painted her *en Gaulle* – i.e. wearing a Créole dress of the cheapest gauze. The portrait was exhibited at that year's Salon of the Academy of Painting. (Needless to say, the same public which accused the Queen of dressing extravagantly at once claimed that she was ruining the silk-weavers at Lyons.)

Marie Antoinette made quite a friend of the painter. Always sympathetic towards her own sex, especially towards those with unpleasant husbands, she encouraged her and found her commissions. M. Vigée-Lebrun was a picture dealer and theoretically a tradesman, which effectively barred his wife from the Academy, from which in any case her sex excluded her. The Queen persuaded the King to intervene and Mme Vigée-Lebrun was admitted as the first woman member. The friendship endured and she painted Marie Antoinette and her children several times.

King Louis himself was maturing, acquiring more self-confidence. Thomas Blaikie, Artois's Scots gardener, who saw him about 1780 describes the King as 'dressed almost like a country farmer, a good rough stout man of about twenty-five'. Despite his gross figure and his waddle he had now developed considerable dignity and even charm. The Comte d'Hézecques, a former royal page, informs us how 'I spent nearly six years at court and I never once saw the King act rudely, not in the slightest way, to any one of all his servants'. Louis was by now extremely popular with the French, able to tap that extraordinary reverence which they still felt for the monarchy. Children brought him much closer to Marie Antoinette, who increasingly returned his affection. Mme de La Tour du Pin was struck by the way in which she greeted him at Sunday morning audiences, 'with a charming air of pleasure and deference'.

Louis XVI was hopeful about his government's prospects. Turgot had warned him that France would be ruined from the moment she fired her first shot in support of the American Revolution, and the King had an uneasy suspicion that he was right. However his suspicions had been assuaged by the triumph of defeating the old enemy across the Channel in 1783, and also by M. Jacques Necker, a Swiss banker and economist of brilliant reputation, who was Director of Finances from 1776–1781 and who floated imposing long-term loans. Necker reassured all France by investing his own fortune in government stock and by producing a book on the glowingly healthy state of the national finances, the *Compte rendu au Roi*. In reality his loans were raised at ruinous interest while the *Compte rendu* was a thoroughly dishonest cooking of the books which ignored the enormous State debt incurred during the American war. But for a time everyone felt safe, except for sharp old Maurepas who told the King to sack Necker.

Necker, fat, pot-bellied, yellow-faced, over-dressed, with awkward, oily manners and uncouth hats, was ludicrously vain and had social ambitions. He was the only one of Louis XVI's ministers before 1789 who was not a nobleman, so he bought a title. His wife Suzanne – Edward Gibbon's boyhood sweetheart – held a somewhat *louche* salon where she acquired a strange if not uninfluential selection of friends for her husband. Necker insisted on presenting his promiscuous blue-stocking daughter Germaine at court, an occasion of some comedy. When her parents' carriage arrived at Versailles the future Mme de Staël leapt down with such eagerness that she tore her dress; in consequence her train fell off as she curtsied at her presentation, to the courtiers' malicious amusement. Marie Antoinette saved the situation by taking the poor girl into her apartments to be sewn up; during the operation the Queen chatted to Germaine to restore her self-confidence.

Even the King's brothers were settling down. Monsieur, perhaps surprisingly in view of his ill-defined sexuality, had acquired a beautiful, high-spirited young mistress, the

Comtesse de Balbi. Her husband, grandson of a Genoese Doge, was jealous to the point of insanity and in 1780 thrashed his wife with his cane when he caught her with a lover; he was speedily confined in a madhouse – with Monsieur's connivance, some suspected. Louis-Stanislas installed her in apartments at Versailles and allowed her to preside over his literary gatherings at the Luxembourg. Artois remained wild enough but at least less ostentatiously so, having developed a passion for boar-hunting and also a calming mistress, Louise de Polastron.

The Queen's one new indiscretion was at least mature, even if one must admit that, while innocent enough, her predilection for Axel von Fersen was as excessive as it was unwise. The Count returned from America in June 1783. Illness had aged him, obliterating much of his good looks and giving him a gaunt, haggard appearance. Marie Antoinette was playing the harp when he arrived – she stopped as soon as he was announced, though she had not finished the piece. She tried to ensure that he would now remain in France by persuading the King to buy Fersen the colonelcy of the *Royal Suedois* (a regiment of Swedish mercenaries in the French service). But after only a short stay the Count went on leave, to accompany Gustavus III of Sweden on what was perhaps a somewhat overwrought tour of the Empire and Italy. He returned the following summer with King Gustavus who – disguised as Count Haga – wanted to sample all the pleasures of Versailles. A phrase of Fersen's in a letter to his sister of 1783 shows that he had already fallen in love with the Queen: 'I cannot belong to the one woman to whom I should like to belong, the only woman who really loves me, so I will belong to no one else.' However after six weeks of '*fêtes, plaisirs et divertissements*' (during which Axel noticed ungallantly that Marie Antoinette looked almost beautiful, 'as though by some miracle'), he escorted his King back to Sweden. From there he corresponded with her – discreetly calling her 'Joséphine' – and at her request bought a large Swedish dog for her. In 1785 he returned to France once more, to command his regiment, though being stationed at Valenciennes on the

Belgian border he could only visit Versailles infrequently.

Some historians believe that Fersen and the Queen actually slept with each other, others that he was no more than a 'well-liked courtier'. Undoubtedly she wrote him passionate letters with such expressions as 'I kiss you tenderly' and told him she loved him. Yet the strange, wistful affair was almost certainly never more than platonic.

Fersen's forebears had been Baltic Germans, not Swedes, and his temperament was of a recognizably Teutonic type in its romantic gloom and introspection. An intensely private and secret creature, his elegant exterior concealed some extremely unattractive qualities; these included overweening arrogance, ruthless, loveless womanizing – he was interested only in sensual gratification in such affairs – and morbid self-pity. He once wrote complacently, 'I am fated never to be happy.' There were also rumours that *'le beau Fersen'* had a homosexual relationship with his King; certainly Gustavus III, a complete and passionate homosexual, had been devoted to the Count since his youth and never flagged in his friendship. There is a legend – admittedly on poor authority – that during their tour together in 1784 Gustavus took Fersen to the top of Vesuvius and then threatened to throw himself down into the crater if the Count did not give up the Queen of France. Even if Fersen was not a practising homosexual, there was undoubtedly more than a streak of narcissism in his nature.

One may well ask why this complicated neurotic, so morose and solitary, appealed to anyone as healthy and as extrovert as Marie Antoinette. She may have been attracted by the very fact that his temperament was so difficult, one which she as a German alone could understand at Versailles. Perhaps in her eyes his exaggeratedly aloof bearing and extraordinary reserve enhanced his good looks. Moreover, his romantic and infinitely respectful devotion, so different from the straightforward desires of a Lauzun or a Besenval, flattered a markedly sentimental streak in the Queen. For his part Fersen's pride was gratified by the love of so great a personage, while he may well have had what is sometimes

Count Axel von Fersen aged 28, from a contemporary miniature

called a *princesse lointaine* complex. Physical relations would have destroyed the magic for both of them. Only two northerners could have had such a strange and unreal romance – it is possible that they revelled in its very unreality.

In March 1785 Marie Antoinette bore her husband a second son, Louis-Charles, Duc de Normandie (the future 'Louis XVII'). It was a savage blow to Monsieur and to Orléans. The pamphleteers of the Luxembourg and Palais Royal grew desperate. No doubt they were encouraged by the Parisians' reception of the Queen when she made her ceremonial entry into Paris after the birth. There was not a single cheer, only icy silence. When she returned to Versailles she wept bitterly, crying 'What have I done to them?'

Even so Marie Antoinette felt safe enough, having borne the children it was her duty to bear. Nowadays her amusements were more staid than formerly. On Sundays there were gay little balls on the lawns in front of the Petit Trianon. She particularly enjoyed making her friends' children and their nurses join in the English country dances.

Nevertheless she continued to indulge her love of theatricals. She and her little circle formed their own 'company of seigneurs' who, in the Trianon's tiny white and gold theatre, played in such light operas as Sedaine's *Rose et Colas* and in many other cheerful plays and musical comedies of the moment. Apart from herself the only member of the royal family to take part was Artois, who once gave an epic performance walking the tightrope. Some of the players were hilariously inept; M. d'Adhémar, although elderly, insisted on juvenile roles in which his tremulous singing convulsed the Queen. She herself enjoyed acting, ably supported by Yolande de Polignac and Madame Elisabeth. A German diplomatist, Baron Melchior Grimm, was most impressed by her dashing Jenny in *Le Roi et le Fermier*. She also played Colette charmingly in Rousseau's *Devin du Village* and was considered even better as Babet in Dezèdes's operetta *Matinée et la veillée villageoise* – long-forgotten works but plainly much appreciated. At first limited to perhaps no more than forty people, the audience was later widened; officers of the

Bodyguard, and equerries of the King and his brothers, were allowed to come, together with certain favoured ladies – there was frantic competition for invitations. Louis was present at every performance, arriving long before they began. However Monsieur and his wife disapproved and never attended, considering such antics beneath royal dignity. The last production of all was Beaumarchais's *Le Barbier de Séville*, in the fateful August of 1785. Marie Antoinette played Rosine and Artois Figaro, while a musical accompaniment was specially commissioned from Paesiello. It was a strange choice, in view of the play's authorship.

Beaumarchais was an adventurer as well as a playwright. He was a shady if amusing jack-of-all-trades, once watchmaker to Mme de Pompadour and teacher of the guitar to the royal aunts, a spy and pamphleteer, who had been a secret agent and gun-runner for the Americans, besides being involved in all sorts of court and diplomatic scandals. He had published a peculiarly irritating paper which argued the claims of the Spanish Bourbons to the French throne because of King Louis's supposed impotence, and he had actually called the Queen's mother, the august Empress, a swindler ('*friponne*') in print. Moreover he had written another play which slyly attacked the entire established order. *Le Mariage de Figaro* was accepted by the Comédie Française in 1781 and sent to the authorities for approval. The King, who had it read to him by Mme Campan, was horrified, shouting 'Detestable! It must never be performed . . . that man mocks everything which ought to be respected.' Beaumarchais not only portrayed a nobleman as a fool but implied he was a fool because he was a nobleman, making the valet address such remarks to his master as 'You nobles merely take the trouble to be born.' Such insolence seems mild enough but then it was regarded as breathtaking – years later Napoleon said it showed that the Revolution was already happening. Louis banned the play. Unabashed, the author enlisted support from among the great, who should have known better. Eventually Marie Antoinette persuaded the King to allow its performance, although he had once said to do so would be 'as much a disaster as pulling down the Bastille'. *Figaro* was produced at the Versailles theatre in the spring of 1784 and was a *succès de scandale* with the glittering audience.

The Queen, if only momentarily, felt even more secure then because of a new Controller-General. Necker had gone in 1781, succeeded briefly by nonentities. Marie Antoinette herself was responsible for the appointment in 1783 of Charles-Alexandre de Calonne, Comte d'Hannonville, after glowing testimonials from Artois and Yolande de Polignac and even from Vergennes. To begin with she was deeply impressed by this paragon. But soon after the appointment the Queen began to regret it, possibly because she sensed instinctively that in some way Calonne – a complex, secret creature who hid behind a mask of frivolity – was deceiving her husband. She blamed Yolande for recommending him and grew noticeably less friendly towards her. Yet Marie Antoinette could easily have stopped the appointment and undoubtedly she at first welcomed it; only afterwards did she convince herself that she had always disapproved of him. In fact her original judgement had been correct – the new Controller-General really was the best man available.

Still under fifty and looking younger than his age when he received the post, Calonne was very presentable indeed, an accomplished courtier who was just the sort of person a frivolous favourite would recommend, handsome, perfectly dressed and unfailingly charming, famous for his mistresses and his pictures (he had ten Titians); even the haughty Duc de Lévis-Mirepoix said he was the only member of the *noblesse de la robe* who knew how to behave like a gentleman. Calonne's attitude towards his country's economic problems was most entertaining; he joked, 'The finances of France are in a deplorable state and I would never have accepted responsibility for them if my own were not in an equally shaky condition.' He had always lived above his means, stating that 'a man who wants to borrow must appear rich; to seem rich one has to impress by lavish expenditure'. At the start he enchanted Marie Antoinette; when she made a demand for a large sum in ready cash, he replied, 'If it is

possible, Madame, it is already done; if it is impossible it shall
be done.' Like Necker he appeared to think that all the
nation's financial problems could be solved by borrowing.

In reality, for all his raffishness and jokes, Calonne was
another Turgot, but in disguise. He enjoyed work as much as
he enjoyed pleasure. He had the same background and the
same attitudes as Turgot, having been an *Intendant* in charge
of entire provinces for almost twenty years, with a specialist
knowledge of the textile industry. In 1766 he had tried to
force the Breton nobility to shoulder some taxes, outraging
the Parlementaires. He knew perfectly well that, because of
Necker's cynical financing of the war with England without
more direct taxation, the State was in danger of bankruptcy.
A private pessimist, he also considered that France was so
ramshackle as to be almost ungovernable. Nevertheless he
believed that he might just save his country by gentle steps
and by concealing his true aims. In 1784 he set up a sinking
fund to service the national debt, in 1785 he reformed the
gold coinage and in 1786 he obtained an Anglo-French
commercial treaty – admittedly on not over-advantageous
terms. He hoped to start a French industrial revolution on
the English model, encouraging rich noblemen to invest in
mines and factories, and he launched an ambitious programme of public works to bolster French credit. All the
time he was conscious that the deficit was increasing, though
he dared not reveal the true state of affairs to the King – he
still thought he could save the situation. Talleyrand com-
pares him to 'the clever steward of some ruined spendthrift'.
Calonne distrusted the Queen who eventually came to
distrust him too. If he had been open with her, this
excessively cynical man might have achieved more.

The King bumbled on, oblivious of impending disaster
like most of his subjects. His weakness and his insensitivity to
popular opinion had been all too evident in 1781 when he
allowed the Parlements to enact new qualifications for
commissioned rank in the army; henceforward no one
without four generations of nobility could be promoted
captain or above, while no one who was not a nobleman

could be even a lieutenant. It is possible to interpret the edict as no more than an attempt to secure by law the situation prevailing in contemporary England, where army officers were usually gentlemen of three generations. However Mme Campan, who came from the class which suffered from the edict, says it aroused widespread indignation. She explains why: 'The provinces were full of non-noble families, who for generations had lived as people of substance on their little estates and paid the taxes. If they had several sons, they put one into the King's army, one into the Church, one into the Order of Malta as a serving brother and one into the legal profession, while the eldest inherited the family manor . . . I knew someone belonging to this worthy class, who had spent years in the diplomatic service and actually been a minister plenipotentiary, the son-in-law and nephew of colonels and majors and on his mother's side nephew of a lieutenant-general who was a knight of St Louis, unable to get his sons made ensigns in an ordinary regiment of foot.' Loyal lady-in-waiting though she was, Campan believed the edict to be one of the causes of the Revolution. Undoubtedly an increasing number of the monarchy's natural supporters were growing dissatisfied.

Ironically, Louis had agreed to the edict in the hope of winning popularity. Both he and the Queen were obsessed with their subjects' attitude towards them. Marie Antoinette's letters to her mother are full of the Parisian crowd's reactions; she and Louis were constantly asking each other if they had been cheered in the streets or at the Opéra. Fersen noticed the Queen's preoccupation with this topic, how depressed she became when she thought she detected any coldness. But, however hard he might try, the King would never be able to please the Parlementaires or satisfy their political ambitions. They showed this all too clearly in their reactions to the Affair of the Diamond Necklace.

A young adventuress (and occasional prostitute), the 'Comtesse' de la Motte-Valois, made the acquaintance of 'Count Cagliostro' – Giuseppe Balsamo – a self-styled alchemist, magician and prophet. Cagliostro told her that one of his clients, Cardinal de Rohan, had dreams of becoming a second Richelieu and felt that only the Queen's disfavour stood in his way. Louis de Rohan, Grand Almoner of France and Archbishop of Strasbourg (where he had welcomed Marie Antoinette so fulsomely on her arrival in 1770) was a prelate from the world of *Les Liaisons Dangereuses*, an ornament of the boudoir rather than the altar, a womanizing fop whose behaviour as French Ambassador in Vienna had been so scandalous that Maria Theresa demanded his recall. Not only was he a member of Mme du Barry's *louche* circle, but he had infuriated the Queen by gatecrashing a party at the Trianon. Little Mme de la Motte-Valois, penniless but obviously very clever, saw golden possibilities in the fatuous Cardinal's dreams.

By the spring of 1784 she had not only made his acquaintance but had convinced him that she was a close friend of Marie Antoinette. She then produced letters to her, apparently in the Queen's handwriting, which persuaded Rohan to write secretly to Marie Antoinette to justify himself, and to use the 'Countess' as a courier. She soon brought a gratifying response from Her Majesty – 'I am very pleased that I no longer have to consider you guilty. However I cannot as yet grant the audience for which you ask.' In August Mme de la Motte-Valois arranged for a discreet meeting between the Queen and the Cardinal, at night in the park at Versailles. Marie Antoinette wore a white dress and gave the Cardinal a rose. Had not Cagliostro prophesied that 'a woman in white' would transform his life? In fact 'Marie Antoinette' was Nicole, a young *fille publique* from the Palais Royal with some resemblance to Her Majesty, whose face was shaded by a broad-brimmed hat. Now that the enraptured Cardinal was well and truly hooked, it only remained to make money out of the situation.

Within a short time Mme de la Motte-Valois and her seedy husband were borrowing large sums from Rohan 'for the Queen'. In a few months he was selling his plate to assist her Majesty, whose debts and shortness of ready cash were common knowledge.

Marie Antoinette's love of diamonds was also common knowledge. For some years M. August Böhmer, mindful of early profits, had been collecting the finest diamonds he could procure to make up a necklace of several rows, which he hoped to persuade her to buy. The price was the then incredible sum of 1,600,000 livres. But the Queen, more sensible these days, was quite content to have her old diamonds reset. Böhmer obtained an audience. He cried that he was ruined if she would not purchase the necklace, and threatened suicide. Marie Antoinette was very angry, telling the man that she had already been offered it as a present by the King but had declined, and that Böhmer must never again behave in this way. The Motte-Valois and her husband heard the story and resolved on a final coup.

The Cardinal was informed that the Queen wished him to buy the necklace for her in such a way that the King would not know. Rohan drew up a 'contract' which received 'the royal signature', authorizing the purchase. Accordingly he arranged with the jeweller to pay by instalments and handed the necklace to Mme de la Motte-Valois whose husband sold it in London. For a few months the couple lived like royalty themselves. Alas, Rohan was slow in raising the first instalment and so August Böhmer complained to Marie Antoinette about the delay. The theft was discovered. The Queen was certain that Rohan had stolen the necklace and she convinced the King of that as well.

Louis XVI proceeded to handle the affair in the clumsiest way possible. Instead of hushing it up by buying the jeweller's silence, he had the Cardinal arrested in full view of the entire court, in the Hall of Mirrors at Versailles as he was proceeding, vested for Mass, to the Chapel Royal. The disgrace was compounded by the fact that the Minister for the Royal Household, the Baron de Breteuil, who made the arrest, was known to be a bitter personal enemy of Rohan. Still worse was the choice of tribunal. As Napoleon put it, 'The Queen was innocent and, to make certain that her innocence should be recognized publicly, she chose the Parlement of Paris for her judge. The result was that everyone thought her guilty.' Meanwhile the wretched Cardinal was incarcerated in the Bastille.

Such treatment outraged every great noble in France, lay or clerical, who – unlike Louis and Marie Antoinette alone – realized that however foolish Rohan might be, he was hardly capable of theft. Through the usual pamphlets they portrayed him as the innocent victim of a stupid and malicious tyranny. The Queen's secret enemies hastened to exploit the scandal, circulating rumours of her extravagance and of her baneful influence on the country's finances. Intellectuals rejoiced at the spectacle of a Cardinal being tried for theft in such unsavoury company and at the tarnishing of Marie Antoinette's reputation, if only by association with such a tawdry business. There were rumours, widely believed, that Rohan was deliberately making himself a scapegoat in order to hide the real story and shield the Queen.

On 31 May 1786, to the horror of Louis and Marie Antoinette, the Parlement acquitted Cardinal de Rohan. It worded its verdict with an intentional ambiguity which seemed to cast doubt on the Queen's innocence. Mme Campan found her in tears at the news. 'Come and mourn for your Queen, insulted and sacrificed by plotters and by injustice,' she asked her lady-in-waiting, adding, 'I am sorry for you as a Frenchwoman. If *I* cannot find honest judges in something on which my reputation depends, how would *you* be treated in a trial where your future and character were at stake?' Plainly she saw the verdict as yet another rejection by the French. Louis came in and told Mme Campan how sorry he felt for his wife, and that he too was sure that Rohan was guilty – 'it was all a scheme to put money into his pocket, but in trying to do so he found himself cheated instead of being the cheat'. He at once deprived the Cardinal of all his offices and exiled him to an abbey. This only antagonized the public still more – at the news of Rohan's acquittal they had shouted '*Vive le Parlement! Vive le Cardinal!*' and danced in the streets.

Even Mme de la Motte-Valois's condemnation and sentence damaged Marie Antoinette. Never particularly merciful, the Parlement ordained that the poor little adventuress be first branded in public and then spend the rest of her life in the appalling prison of the Salpétrière. She struggled so violently on the scaffold that, half naked, she was branded on a breast instead of a shoulder with a red-hot iron whereupon, howling, she bit the executioner through his coat. The horrible tale aroused widespread indignation. After a year she managed to escape from the Salpétrière and fled to London. Here she issued the vilest 'memoirs' in edition after edition. She claimed to be innocent of the theft of the necklace, to have confessed only from loyalty to the Queen, and to have had Lesbian relations with her. She also alleged that Marie Antoinette had become Rohan's mistress when she arrived in Strasbourg in 1770. Thousands of copies circulated all over France, and indeed throughout Europe. The French government tried vainly to buy off Mme de la Motte-Valois. Half unhinged, she merely took the money and then went on to publish even more disgusting fantasies.

The harm done to the Queen's reputation by the Affair of the Diamond Necklace was incalculable. Her reputation was in tatters among high and low, from great nobles and prelates down to *sansculottes* and fishwives. Even her friends began to suspect, most unjustly, that this unusually good-natured and magnanimous woman could be a venomous and spiteful enemy. The Affair had discredited not only Marie Antoinette but her husband's government as well – Napoleon regarded it as one of the causes of the Revolution. A councillor of the Paris Parlement was speaking no more than the truth when he commented smugly that it was, 'a nice little smear of dirt on both crown and crozier'. One must agree with Mme Campan when she says that for the Queen the Affair marked 'the end of happy times'.

Madame Déficit

C'est déjà fait, madame, un faux avis donné sur vous

Beaumarchais, *Le Mariage de Figaro*

Slander
Whose sting is sharper than the sword's

Shakespeare, *A Winter's Tale*

EVERYBODY remembers Talleyrand's saying that no one knew what pleasure meant who had not lived before 1789. Beyond question life was both stately and elegant for those of the richer aristocracy. Yet the last decade of pre-Revolution French pleasure also had an underlying sourness, a *fin de siècle* quality of corruption and dissatisfaction. A modern historian, the Duc de Castries, discerns '*un snobisme du vice et de la décadence*'. There was a morbid cult of death, which anticipated the guillotine, and a thirst for pornography – the Marquis de Sade was experimenting with 'pleasure' and writing about it, and Restif de la Bretonne's nasty little *La Paysanne Pervertie* was a best-seller – while gambling had become a mania. The decline in morals was accompanied by a symptomatic relaxation of manners. Many people of fashion ceased to powder their hair, the younger nobles tried to dress like English grooms or hunting men, and smart intellectuals aped homespun Americans. There was a cheerless and widespread conviction that not only was the machinery of government failing but that the very foundations on which society rested were hollow and without meaning. The heady intellectual winds which were blowing – Rousseau and trans-Atlantic liberty, the Enlightenment apparently on the verge of triumphing – induced an unsettling mood which contained as much despair as optimism. In addition there was the financial insecurity of the economic recession. A considerable part of the nobility faced ruin.

By the mid-1780s Marie Antoinette was very different from the frivolous 'Queen of the Rococo' who had once made daring visits to the wicked balls at the Opéra. She was now a large, plump, Junoesque woman, though so lively and graceful that it was not apparent. If hardly beautiful in the strict sense, she nonetheless succeeded in giving the impression of being a very great beauty indeed. Her most obvious assets were her ash-blonde hair and the transparent skin and pink-and-white complexion which she had retained from her childhood – the too prominent forehead was artfully disguised, while the drooping Habsburg lip became a permanent half-pout which gave a not unattractive illusion of disdain. She held herself superbly and was famous for her remarkably graceful gliding walk – 'it marked her out as the sovereign in the midst of her court', says Mme Vigée-Lebrun. Nowadays the Queen often dressed in dark, dignified reds and greens, which set off her hair and colouring. Her effect overall was fascinating, one of mingled *joie de vivre* and stateliness according to those who saw her at Versailles. Châteaubriand tells us 'she seemed enchanted with life', while Hézecques remembers her unmistakable majesty – 'One would have offered her a throne without thinking, in the way one would offer any other woman a chair.' Ironically, she had become *digne*, truly worthy of her rank and position, that quality so much admired by the French nobility which detested her.

Her distress at the Cardinal's acquittal was to some extent soothed by the birth of a fourth child in July 1786, Sophie Béatrice. However there was little else to console her. Her husband's government was now approaching the financial

Marie Antoinette, by Mme Vigée-Lebrun

crisis which it had tried to postpone for so long. The Controller-General's credit had been seriously damaged in 1785 by a pamphlet written by the envious Necker, and in 1786 the Parlement, which had enjoyed flexing its muscles during the Cardinal's trial, refused to register Calonne's reform of the gold coinage on the specious grounds that it would impose 'hidden taxation'. The Controller-General's situation was desperate – the Treasury was in debt for millions upon millions of livres and at least half the revenue for 1787 had already been spent. If he really was the only man who could save France, he must act now. Seemingly undismayed, Calonne presented Louis XVI with a 'Précis of a Plan for Improving the Finances'. It contained the reforms once urged by Turgot and insisted above all on abolishing the exemption from direct taxation enjoyed by the nobility and clergy, emphasizing how unfair it was that 'the richest class is taxed least' – there was to be a land tax from which no one would be exempt. The Controller-General knew very well that the Parlements would never accept his plan, but he had a solution: the King must summon an Assembly of Notables who would surely realize the gravity of the situation and that their fortunes were bound up with those of the monarchy, and who would therefore co-operate, even if unwillingly.

The Assembly met at Versailles in February 1787 and Calonne managed to convince Louis. Unfortunately the 144 Notables – princes, *grands seigneurs*, prelates, high officials – simply could not see that it was in their interest to co-operate. They refused to pay. The Archbishop of Narbonne declaimed wittily, 'M. de Calonne wants to bleed France and he is asking the Notables' advice on whether to bleed her in the foot, the arm or the jugular vein.' The Duc d'Orléans grumbled with no less elegance, lamenting that the proposed reforms would cost him 300,000 livres annually, and then left ostentatiously to go hunting – killing a stag within sight of the Bastille. The Controller-General treated the Assembly to an impassioned, indeed brilliant, address but he weakened rather than strengthened his appeal by disclosing that the deficit was 113 million livres instead of 80 million as previously stated. Debates became bogged down in arguments and recrimination. The only thing that the Notables could agree on was not to pay taxes.

Calonne, overworking night and day in his carriage or in his bed as well as at his desk, began to crack. He lost his judgement and tried to frighten the Assembly by publishing a pamphlet explaining the benefits of his tax and how it was only justice that the nobles and clergy should pay it. Instead of gaining popular support, the unfortunate Controller-General was turned on by the entire country. The King was no help at all; when he heard the new figure for the deficit, he smashed a chair in his rage and bellowed that he should have had Calonne hanged; later he wept, moaning that Vergennes – the Foreign Minister, who had just died – was no longer alive to help him out of the mess. The Controller-General appealed to Marie Antoinette as a last resort, trying to win her support by offering to bring personal reports on the Assembly to her every day. She was not interested, having long since decided that he must go. Louis assured him that he would not be treated like Turgot – 'Don't be afraid, I was a boy then. Now I'm a man.' A few days later the King sacked the last minister who might have saved the *ancien régime*. Calonne was burnt in effigy in front of the Palais de Justice – the first of many occasions – but escaped to a comfortable and elegant exile in London.

The Assembly of Notables and its public discussion of the deficit damaged Marie Antoinette's reputation even more than the Affair of the Diamond Necklace. It revealed to everyone that 1,250 million livres (well over £50 million in English money of the period) had had to be borrowed during the last decade and that a large proportion of this had been spent by the royal family, whose households had several thousand members many of whom received enormous sums for doing nothing. But although Monsieur or Artois were indefensibly extravagant, France blamed only one person. In February, shortly after the Assembly had met, the Queen was hissed at the Opéra. A few days later she had to leave her box at the theatre when a speech against a tyrannical Queen (in

Racine's *Athalie*) was pointedly applauded. A host of new libels circulated about her, claiming that she spent wildly on vicious amusements. It was rumoured that she had suggested starving peasants ought to eat cake if they could not afford bread; she never said any such thing – the remark dates from a century before, when it was supposed to have been made by Louis XIV's Queen. (Marie Leszczynska, the consort of Louis XV, has been credited with saying something similar about pâté.) Slander has seldom been so deadly or so long lasting. More and more Frenchmen began to believe the tales about her. At Versailles young courtiers refused to make up sets for dances if it was at Marie Antoinette's request. All classes were united in their loathing for *Madame Déficit*.

The Queen remained surprisingly calm. She was prepared to admit that Mme de Polignac had been rapacious, and believed she was taking the blame for her favourite who, as far as she could see, was the sole cause of the public's 'odious and unfair outburst'. Characteristically she refused to abandon Yolande and tried to remain on friendly terms with her. There were good reasons for Marie Antoinette's strange detachment. In the summer of 1787 her baby Sophie died from tuberculosis, while it was probably becoming increasingly obvious that the Dauphin was also tubercular. Fortunately Fersen was in Paris for most of that depressing year – they used to ride out alone, to meet discreetly in the Versailles woods.

However gloomy she may have felt, the Queen cannot possibly have sensed that France was on the verge of Revolution. It is true that the 1780s were a period of recession after one of booming prosperity, that there was dreadful poverty – many of the urban proletariat and poorer peasants were starving. Yet the French had known such misery before, not all that long ago; in his diary the Abbé de Véri notices how everyone seems dissatisfied, although most people are more prosperous than when he was a boy. (The British economist Arthur Young's eye-witness accounts of the sufferings of French peasants in 1787–89 may still harrow us, but the Irish, the Highland Scots and many other

Europeans were enduring much worse.) However the end of boom times meant that the nobles and bourgeoisie were increasingly discontented. They knew that both government and society were not what they wanted – the system no longer worked. In 1751 the Marquis d'Argenson had written how even then there was a 'wind' of freedom and anti-royal feeling, how France was in an 'inflammable' condition. Intellectuals rejected Catholicism and the *loi fondamental* (by which King and subjects accepted each other's rights and privileges as unchallengeable), which together were the basis of the *ancien régime*. The writings of Rousseau and others created a willingness to look for alternatives. Educated Frenchmen saw a new, thrilling society being built in North America – the Declaration of Independence, for which some of them had actually fought, caused many Frenchmen to regard the *ancien régime* as morally inferior to what was emerging in the New World. Tom Paine testifies that 'a vast reinforcement to the cause of Liberty spread itself over France, by the return of the French officers and soldiers' after the American War. Even the old enemy across the Channel seemed to have a fairer society and a more efficient form of government.

In fact, the French nobility wanted a political system like that of Britain, governed not by the monarch but by the upper classes. France, as everyone knew, was the richest country in Europe, yet through trade and industrial manufacture the British appeared to be far more prosperous. In a France ruled by the aristocracy it would be possible to exploit both the country's natural wealth and, as they saw it, the brilliance of its nobility. From great princes like Monsieur and Orléans and *Les Grands* to disinherited roués like Mirabeau, from dissatisfied prelates like Talleyrand to landless younger sons of country gentry like René de Châteaubriand, the entire *noblesse* felt that there was a role for them in this *révolte nobilaire* and in the new constitution which must result from it. In Paris and in every provincial city, political discussion groups sprang up – in clubs, in the salons of duchesses, in masonic lodges.

What the *noblesse* failed to recognize was the astonishingly bitter hatred and envy of them and of their privileges which prevailed among the bourgeoisie great and small, even among people like Mme Campan's worthy relations. The upper bourgeois – what in Victorian England were called 'business and professional gentlemen' – had lucrative privileges of their own, such as extensive concessions in trade and industry, and were often much richer than many poor noblemen. But, as has been seen, they deeply resented being barred from careers in the army, the magistracy and the higher ranks of government administration, let alone from politics. They especially resented the nobility's exemption from direct taxation.

In the meantime however the nobles of France were the spearhead of revolution. The instruments with which they intended to force Louis to transform himself into a constitutional monarch were the Parlements – if the Assembly refused to co-operate with him, he would eventually have to submit to the magistrates of the red robe.

It is not too much to say that Marie Antoinette, however unskilful, organized the defence of the royal power against this neo-feudal reaction. As soon as the French monarchy found itself under really serious attack, the daughter of Maria Theresa showed her true metal. In any case she had no sympathy with the new ideas – she had never concealed her dislike of the American Revolution. It was she who brought down Calonne, encouraging Miromesnil – Louis's Minister of Justice – to go to the King and insinuate that the Controller-General was setting him against his Notables and 'making an appeal to public opinion which could have very dangerous consequences'. At the end of 1787 Fersen wrote to his friend Gustavus III that Louis XVI was still weak, still suspicious – 'He trusts only the Queen and it is quite clear that she does everything. Ministers visit her frequently to ensure she is informed of any matter of importance.' He adds that the Parisians believe silly rumours that the King has taken to the bottle and that Marie Antoinette is encouraging him to drink in order to make him sign whatever she wants.

In April 1787 the Queen persuaded Louis to appoint Loménie de Brienne, Archbishop of Sens, Controller-General in Calonne's place. Her husband disliked the man and held out for ten days. When he gave way Marie Antoinette swept out of the King's Council – a cabinet meeting was hardly the place for a Queen consort, but she was not Maria Theresa's daughter for nothing – with the triumphant remark, 'Depend on it, Sirs, now we have a real Prime Minister.'

Marie Antoinette told Mme Campan how, when crossing the *oeil de boeuf* room after the meeting, 'I heard a Chapel musician say, very loudly so as to make me hear every word, "A proper Queen ought to stay in her apartments and get on with her needlework."' Yet at the time Loménie de Brienne appeared an excellent choice. Indeed the sainted Turgot had said he would be more than consoled if Loménie could one day step into his shoes as Controller-General. Although he was a priest, and an archbishop at that, the smart intellectual world was delighted and considered that Turgot had come again. In a letter to George Washington M. de Lafayette praised the new Controller-General's ability and honesty. 'When I came to France, in the Spring of 1787, the Archbishop of Toulouse was then Minister,' Tom Paine remembered, 'and at that time highly esteemed.' The surest testimony to Loménie's reputation is that government bonds rose as soon as he was appointed. Marie Antoinette may well have been domineering, but it is scarcely fair to blame her for bad judgement in this case.

Etienne Loménie de Brienne was the last of France's statesman prelates, the heir of Richelieu and Mazarin. A member of the Académie Française and a true intellectual of the period, a Deist if not an atheist, he had no real Christian beliefs, having entered the Church solely to recoup the fortunes of his distinguished though hardly ancient family. A bitter foe to monasticism, he was acclaimed as the 'anti-monk', while his private life was not allowed to suffer from his profession and he collected women with as much enthusiasm as Calonne – contracting secondary syphilis.

Louis XVI was profoundly shocked by Loménie and had only recently refused to make him Archbishop of Paris on the grounds that, 'We must have an Archbishop of Paris who does at least believe in God.' Yet, however scandalous, the sixty-year-old prelate was an experienced and gifted administrator, very much of Turgot's school. When Archbishop of Toulouse he had built a most important canal joining the River Garonne to the Canal du Midi, and to the admiration of all intellectuals and progressives had opened his superb personal library to the townsfolk. He now donated his revenues from his rich abbey at Saint-Ouen to the poor, and his Controller-General's salary to the Treasury. These actions were not merely cosmetic. In easier times he would have been an excellent minister.

The Queen was not altogether happy about her new role in politics. Once, as she was parcelling up some files handed to her by ministers to give to Louis, she remarked, 'Any wife who meddles with matters above her understanding or out of her line of duty is nothing more than an intriguer . . . French Queens are only happy so long as they don't meddle.' But the King's weakness and indecision would have made any wife meddle. Until Loménie's appointment Louis had kept affairs of State away from her. He continued to try to do so, which did not help her.

Politics apart, Marie Antoinette was able to make Louis do almost anything she wanted. His early inadequacy in his physical relations with her had probably left him with a sense of inferiority towards her from which he could never recover. Besenval, with surprising sentiment for such a man of the world, tells us that not only would the King never oppose the Queen but 'when she was speaking I have a thousand times seen his eyes and face light up with a love and enthusiasm which even the most beloved of mistresses could hardly hope to inspire'. Louis's enslavement was displayed at the beginning of 1788, just after Fersen had had to return to Sweden. During his absence the King was handed a parcel of letters while hunting. They apparently contained vivid and plausible allegations of a torrid affair between his wife and the handsome northerner. Louis was so dreadfully upset that for once he stopped hunting and came back weeping to Versailles. Marie Antoinette knew exactly how to manage him. She demanded that Fersen be no longer received at court, thus manoeuvring the simple King into insisting that she must go on seeing Fersen.

Louis's dislike of Loménie forced the Queen to persevere with her 'meddling'. She gave the new Controller-General her full support when he admitted tacitly that his predecessors' plans had been basically on the right lines and when he tried to persuade the Notables to compromise – suggesting that the proposed land tax be reduced by half. But, like Calonne, Loménie simply could not see that the deficit was not being treated as a problem to be solved but as a pretext for an aristocratic revolution. The Assembly had no intention whatever of compromising, let alone co-operating, and the King had to dissolve it at the end of May, barely a month after Calonne's dismissal. Loménie decided that perhaps the Parlement might be more amenable after all.

In the meantime the court must set a good example by making drastic economies. The Controller-General had Marie Antoinette's enthusiastic backing. No less than 173 of her courtiers lost their places, Rose Bertin was sent packing, gaming tables made way for billiards and there was an end to masked balls. Many of her favourites had their allowances cut – Yolande de Polignac's husband had to surrender his office of Postmaster-General. The King's measures were even harsher. He sacked the Grand Falconer, disbanded 600 guards and cavalry and sold his wolfhounds, while several royal châteaux were put up for auction or demolished to avoid the cost of maintenance. Many household posts were abolished. Besenval moaned to the Queen that it was like being in Turkey, dependent on the Sultan's every whim – 'in a country where one cannot be sure what belongs to one from one day to the next'. Alas, public opinion was not impressed by these sacrifices.

The Parlement of Paris met in July 1787. The Queen was optimistic, though Besenval warned her that she was flattering herself if she thought it would be won over. Yet at first the magistrates of the red robe were surprisingly reasonable, registering the dismantling of internal customs barriers, the abolition of the *corvée* and the scheme for provincial assemblies. But then it refused to register the raising of the stamp tax, let alone the land tax – pointing out menacingly that Britain's Stamp Act of twenty years earlier had led to the American Revolution. The Parlementaires demanded the publication of national accounts and sent the King a remonstrance which declared that 'the Nation, represented by the Estates General alone has the right of granting subsidies to the King, the need for which must be proved to its satisfaction'.

Loménie, supported by Marie Antoinette, persuaded Louis to use his ultimate sanction – a *lit de justice*. This was a plenary session of the Parlement presided over by the King whose presence secured, under the laws, the automatic registration of any edicts he wanted. The magistrates were summoned to Versailles on 6 August where, perched high on the purple velvet cushions of the *lit*, Louis made them register both the land tax and the increased stamp tax. He was so unaware of their resentment and fury that he fell asleep on the cushions. But next day the Parlement reassembled at the Palais de Justice in Paris to declare angrily that forced registrations were illegal, and on 13 August it declared that any attempt to levy the taxes would be 'contrary to the Rights of the Nation'. The King thereupon exiled the entire Parlement to Troyes.

Uproar broke out in Paris, with demonstrations and riots which anticipated those of the Revolution. The police were stoned and shops looted. The mobs, led by the magistrates' clerks, were largely working-class in composition, including many artisans and apprentices. The usual stream of pamphlets were rushed out by Orléans's men at the Palais Royal. Effigies of Calonne, Loménie and Yolande de Polignac were burned in the streets and one of the Queen was very nearly burned with them. The police warned her to keep away from the capital.

Loménie and the King lost their nerve. The Parlementaires were allowed to return to Paris, after agreeing to extend the income tax for five years and to make nobles and clergy pay it as well, if Louis would withdraw the land tax. Parlement met again on 19 November for another *lit de justice* to endorse emergency State loans; all went well until Orléans rose and, in his timid, stuttering voice, told the King that such registrations were illegal. The Duke was banished to one of his châteaux. In consequence he became a popular hero. As Marie Antoinette observes in a letter to her brother the Emperor, 'From the very first moment of his exile the people forgot the debauchery, the avarice and the swindling of the Duc d'Orléans. All they could see was an illustrious victim of arbitrary power.'

The Queen stood by Loménie loyally all the time he was Controller-General, and plainly had a good deal to do with most of his measures. At the very least he kept her informed about what he was trying to do. Unfortunately she did not realize until too late that he was a man of straw – as has been seen, she had some excuse since nearly everyone considered him to be outstandingly able. Moreover her trusted Abbé de Vermond was constantly singing his praises. She encouraged Loménie by such gestures as sending him her portrait miniature set in diamonds, and giving his niece a position at court. But, as Mme de Staël points out, Loménie, for all his shows of strength, vacillated fatally – 'He tried to be strong but gave way at meeting the slightest resistance . . . arbitrary and constitutional by turn, he showed himself maladroit which ever way he tried.' But the Queen simply could not see this, perhaps because the Controller-General so often did what she told him. She was almost certainly responsible for exiling Orléans and for the arrest of two particularly truculent Parlementaires, and probably for several other of Loménie's actions.

On the whole Marie Antoinette seems to have kept astonishingly calm. By contrast, despite the outlets of his hunting and his hobbies, her husband began to give way to fits of rage and weeping and developed eczema. The reason for the Queen's serenity was almost certainly her children, who were now the centre of her existence. Her friend Mme Vigée-Lebrun painted a portrait of her with them in 1787. She wears a red velvet dress trimmed with sable and looks almost massively maternal; her figure has clearly filled out (we know from Rose Bertin's order-book that at this date she had a bust measurement of forty-four inches). On one side of her is Madame Royale, who was to live until 1851, on the other the Dauphin who was soon to die, and on her lap the future Dauphin who would perish miserably in the Temple. The Queen's expression is sometimes explained as one of gentle melancholy in allusion to Sophie's recent death – the empty cradle in the picture is undoubtedly intended as a memorial. However, in nearly all her later portraits Marie Antoinette wears a similar expression of detached, almost dreamy, composure. Interestingly, many contemporaries considered this portrait of her in the red dress to be the best likeness of her. Mme Vigée-Lebrun had hoped to exhibit it in the Salon at the Louvre in 1788. The government hesitated in view of the Queen's unpopularity but eventually gave permission. Apparently it had the success it deserved, and the King told the blushing artist, 'I don't know much about painting but you have made me love it.' Later, after the elder Dauphin's death, Marie Antoinette could not bear to look at it.

Loménie, despite all evidence to the contrary, still hoped that the privileged classes would co-operate in the end. It is likely that his patroness agreed with him. To frighten the Parlement into a biddable mood, the Controller-General published the new figures for the deficit, which despite all economies had now reached 160 million livres. But the magistrates wanted their revolution. They again refused vociferously to abolish the exemption of nobles and clergy from taxation, and then published an aggressive remonstrance which claimed that the monarchy was subject to laws which had to be approved by the Parlement. Loménie finally conceded that like the Notables the Parlementaires would never yield. No doubt with the Queen's assistance he now

Marie Antoinette and her children, by Mme Vigée-Lebrun

tried to make Louis play the absolute monarch. In Tom
Paine's words, the Archbishop 'by a line of conduct scarcely
to be accounted for . . . perverted every opportunity, turned
out a despot, and sank into disgrace'. In May 1788 the
Parlement of Paris and the twelve provincial Parlements were
all suspended, their members being dispersed at the point of
the bayonet. Special courts were set up to administer their
legal functions, while their powers over taxation passed to
the new provincial assemblies.

The reaction throughout the entire country was one of
fury among every class. There were riots everywhere. Nobles
threatened to bring back the Parlements even if it meant
drawing their swords. At Rennes, the capital of Brittany,
officers refused to fire on the mob. At Grenoble, the capital of
Dauphiné, there was a pitched battle between troops and
rioters in June on the *Journée des Tuiles* (Day of Tiles) when
tiles were hurled down on to the King's men from the
rooftops – one local regiment, including its officers, would
not fight. In desperation Loménie turned to the Church for
financial assistance, but the assembled prelates told him, 'The
people of France are not taxable at pleasure,' and deliberately
reduced their usual contribution to the royal revenues. They
also demanded the restoration of Parlements. Royal authority was beginning to collapse. Then, in August 1788, the
Controller-General discovered that the Treasury was bankrupt. He suspended all payments, raised a little money to
tide the government over the next few days – by floating
bonds and appropriating the funds of the Invalides, the
Comédie Française and the Opéra – and announced that the
Estates General would meet at Versailles on 1 May 1789. The
King dismissed him on 25 August, much to his relief. For as
long as he lived Loménie could never speak of his time as
Controller-General without shaking.

If one may believe Mme Campan, Marie Antoinette was
extremely worried by the decision to call the Estates General.
She realized instinctively that a truly revolutionary situation
might ensue, that 'the people would influence the deputies'
discussion'. With great shrewdness she tried to make Louis

summon it to a place at least 150 miles from Paris, but Necker insisted on Versailles. Mme Campan is borne out by the memoirs of M. Augeard, one of the Queen's household officials, who says that she told him at this time that she blamed the summoning of the Estates Council entirely on the Parlement and the clergy.

Always magnanimous, Marie Antoinette was loyal to Loménie to the end and insisted on a cardinal's hat being obtained for him. In consequence she shared in his unpopularity, incurring still more odium. She must unquestionably take some of the blame for his failure. But at least she had had the courage to support him.

During the last six months the streets of Paris, and of other cities, had rung with shouts for the recall of Necker. France did not realize how illusory, even fraudulent, his apparent success in managing the nation's finances had been. There were those, including Louis, who disliked the man and agreed heartily with Artois that he was 'a fornicating foreign bastard'. His smug rectitude and fashionable intellectual opinions could be extremely irritating. Unfortunately even opponents took Necker at his own face value and accepted the vain old banker's view that he could cope with the situation – practically no one save Calonne had gauged his sheer lack of judgement. Marie Antoinette herself did not like him, but with his experience and his nationwide popularity he seemed to be the only available choice. Again she intervened, forcing the King to appoint Necker Controller-General on the very same day that Loménie resigned. She had serious misgivings nonetheless – 'I tremble when I think that I am responsible for recalling Necker. I seem fated to bring misfortune, and should he fail like his predecessor, or do any harm to the authority of the crown, I shall be hated even more than I am already.' Conscientiously she tried to flatter the new Minister, inviting him to her apartments to discuss privately the problems he was going to face. Meanwhile her gullible husband told Necker, 'I have not known such happiness for years.' He replied oilily that the King would never need to say that again – 'All will be well!'

The Queen was by now an active and important force in French politics. She would make terrible mistakes which contributed to her own destruction, but so did practically every French politician. Inevitably she has been compared to the Empress Alexandra, the consort of Nicholas II of Russia, but save that Marie Antoinette was the wife of a weak ruler confronted by revolution there is absolutely no resemblance whatever. The Queen was far from being a religious maniac – the Abbé de Vermond was hardly a French Rasputin – and, however unpopular, she was never politically isolated. She was always looking for new allies, ready to flatter and persuade, even prepared to compromise. It is all very well to blame her for meddling, but with such a weak and indecisive husband there was little else she could do. Naturally she was determined that her son would one day inherit an all-powerful monarchy; in her limited and un-read experience, benevolent despotisms were best – in Austria the Habsburgs had done more than anyone else for the poor, or thought they had. In the event she took on the entire French Revolution and the forces of progress, and not surprisingly she lost. It was not for want of purpose or lack of courage – she was always what the Scots call 'a bonny fighter'. Of course no one would claim that she was a born politician, but she was certainly not so foolish or lacking in intelligence as is almost invariably assumed. Some outstandingly able men came to regard her as a valuable ally, and not just because she could handle Louis.

Necker, on his return, was cheered in the streets. Some spectators wept. He quickly borrowed enough money – even bankers trusted him – to keep the country running for the time being. Yet he had to admit that there must be direct taxation on all classes. Wearily the King recalled the Parlement of Paris once more, on his Controller-General's advice, but the magistrates still refused to register new taxes, however much modified. They declared stubbornly that any important matters must wait until the Estates General.

The Parlementaires also laid down rules for the coming assembly's composition, insisting that clergy, nobility and

commons should each have the same number of members, to
ensure that the middle classes could be kept safely in check.
But, to the amazement of the 'fathers of the people', the
Parisian mob turned on them. Their popularity vanished
overnight. From his exile in London Calonne wrote to Louis
to say how astonished and alarmed he was to hear of this new
development which was causing riots all over France against
the aristocracy. Some contemporaries thought that the
monarchy was trying to use the commons in its struggle with
the privileged orders – 'The privileged have been so bold as
to resist the King,' wrote Lamoignon, 'and in two months
there will be no more Parlements, nobles or clergy.' It was
the end of the *révolte nobilaire*, though to the very last both
noblemen and priests refused to pay taxes, even during a
second and final Assembly of Notables which dispersed only
in December 1788.

Necker persuaded the King to agree to the doubling of the
Third Estate's membership. Unquestionably he was supported by Marie Antoinette who made a most intelligent
political gesture by announcing that she wanted to be 'Queen
of the Third Estate'. Indeed she may well have been
optimistic about an alliance with the bourgeoisie against
selfish aristocrats. Artois, who had loudly opposed the
doubling of the Third Estate, accused her of allying with the
people against the nobility. The aristocracy began to dislike
her even more – even the toadying Polignac tribe abandoned
her. Losing her brother-in-law and the Polignacs depressed
her deeply, but she was undeterred. We know from Mercy-
Argenteau that at the end of 1788 she was watching events
almost too closely: 'Her Majesty is completely absorbed in
matters concerning the government, the economies, the
reforms and the debates in the Assembly [of Notables].' He
was not at all happy about her involvement because of the
French government's seemingly total lack of policy. 'The
resulting ill will is in large part directed at the Queen, who is
distressed to the point that it is seriously upsetting her.'

There was another and very good reason why she should
be upset. It was only a year since little Sophie had died, but it

was now becoming plain that the Dauphin would follow her. Like so many of his chronically diseased family, he was riddled with tuberculosis which in his case took the form of rickets. His mother wrote to his uncle Josef II that 'He has one leg shorter than the other, and his spine is twisted and sticks out unnaturally. For a considerable time he has suffered from attacks of fever and he is thin and sickly.' Ironically, he had probably inherited scrofula – the 'King's Evil' – from his father, whose 'touch' was supposed to cure it. It is a tuberculosis which sometimes attacks the bones as well as the lymph glands. The disease had begun to show itself early in 1788. Mme Campan tells us how, 'In a few months he declined from rude health into a condition which bent his spine, distorted his face and made his legs so weak that he was unable to walk without being supported like some broken old man.' He suffered from strange delusions and suspected that Yolande de Polignac was trying to poison him, because of her distinctive scent which he found sickening. The unfortunate child was moved to Meudon. All accounts agree that he was a heartrending spectacle. His mother was constantly in tears.

With her own splendid constitution, the Queen must have marvelled at the miserable health of the Bourbons. Save for Louis XIV, no French King had reached threescore years and ten, while innumerable heirs to the throne had died young. Her father-in-law, her mother-in-law and her husband's elder brother had all perished from tuberculosis. The obesity of her husband and of her brother-in-law Monsieur was almost certainly due to a tubercular condition. (Their extraordinary appetites may also have been due to a dietary deficiency induced by tuberculosis.) In those days there were no sulphonamide drugs. Although mercifully she was at least spared the knowledge, her younger son was also to die of scrofula or of tubercular adenitis. With a mother's intuition, she somehow sensed that something was wrong with him, and saw that he had as much fresh air as possible. In 1789 she was to write uneasily that 'the slightest unusual noise has an extraordinary effect on him'.

In her anguish Marie Antoinette turned increasingly to Catholicism. She received Communion much more frequently; this then implied long preparation and long thanksgiving, and even the devout took the Sacrament only three times a year. Her religion would seem very unfamiliar to many modern Catholics. It was not just that her pastors were gentlemanly priests with powdered hair, and wearing fiddleback chasubles. The very Latin Mass they celebrated was not even the Tridentine rite but the Gallican, with prayers for the King rather than the Pope. There were cults of obscure wonder-working Gallo-Roman saints, with pilgrimages, relics and scapulars, distinctive French customs like the distribution of *pain bénit* (blessed but unconsecrated bread) after Mass, and such miracle cures as that performed by her husband when he touched for the 'King's Evil'. There were also ferocious fastings, scrupulous examinations of conscience, vigils, much praying for the souls of departed relatives, and lengthy meditations upon the prospect of death – including watching by deathbeds and coffins or in vaults. It was a most unfashionable creed among intellectuals, not a faith for well-read aristocrats let alone clever bourgeois. All too many thinking members of the French nobility tended to be godless Voltaireans, who sneered at royal piety – it was Robespierre who said 'atheism is aristocratic'. But the Queen's Catholicism was plainly a source of strength to her. Indeed, combined with her lack of fashionable education, it perhaps made her more of a realist than many French intellectuals of the Enlightenment – from her cradle she had been warned against idle dreaming.

Her piety owed a great deal to a Frenchwoman whom some contemporaries later acclaimed as a saint. Madame Elisabeth, her sister-in-law, nine years younger than Marie Antoinette, was devoted to her brothers and their wives, and quite content to remain unmarried so long as she could stay in France. Pretty, not very clever, the Princess liked almost everybody and almost everybody liked her. There was real if undemonstrative affection between Madame Elisabeth and the Queen. Elisabeth spent part of her time at Versailles and

part at her own little château of Montreuil, where she kept a
farm to provide milk for the local peasant children. She had
been very close to her aunt Madame Louise, the Carmelite
nun, who had recently died (in 1787), and obviously thought
of taking the veil herself – she particularly enjoyed visiting
convents. Ladies of the court asked her for spiritual advice
when they suffered bereavement and it is likely that Marie
Antoinette did so too. Yet it would be wrong to think of
Madame Elisabeth as sanctimonious. She was a lively and
cheerful young woman who liked dancing, with a sharp
tongue for those of whom she disapproved and an extraordinary toughness of spirit.

In public the Queen concealed her suffering and showed an
unfailingly brave face. Châteaubriand, presented at court
about this time, saw her return from Mass in the Chapel
Royal and was struck by her seeming gaiety. When he met
her again, 'She gave me, looking at me with a smile, the
gracious bow she had already made me on the day of my
presentation. When she smiled Marie Antoinette showed the
shape of her mouth to such an extent that (ghastly to relate)
the memory of her smile enabled me to identify the jawbone
of the daughter of kings when the unfortunate woman's skull
was dug up at the disinterrment in 1815.'

The winter of 1788–89 was a terrible one, the coldest for
many years. Peasants died of cold or starved because of a
disastrous harvest, while bands of brigands terrorized the
countryside. The Duc d'Orléans made himself popular by
selling some pictures from his gallery at the Palais Royal and
devoting the proceeds to poor relief – his agents ensured that
this was widely known. They also alleged that the King and
Queen had done nothing to help.

Marie Antoinette hurt her reputation still more by
avoiding Paris altogether. She no longer visited its theatres,
and the Parisians never set eyes on her or on her children.
Orléanist pamphleteers continued to attack her. No doubt
they were encouraged by their employer, who had been
bitterly insulted when the Queen refused to countenance any
prospect of a future engagement between her daughter and

his son, the Duc de Chartres (one day to be King Louis-Philippe).

Yet both she and Louis XVI by now gave at least the appearance of sharing the general illusion that the Estates General would usher in a French Golden Age. Mme de La Tour du Pin tells us that the nobility were most optimistic of all, 'laughing and dancing our way to the precipice . . . never had people been so pleasure seeking'. Even the cleverest thought that what lay ahead was merely a matter of ending abuses and the waste of public money. 'France, they said, was about to be reborn. The word "revolution" was never uttered. Had anyone dared to use it, he would have been thought mad.'

Meanwhile, in these early months of 1789, little councils were meeting in every bailiwick of the realm to elect their representative to the Estates General. Orléans had a candidate in each bailiwick where he owned property and where he sent a suitably 'patriotic' proclamation. Marie Antoinette had four more years to live.

[7]
'Voilà la victime'

Les citoyens ridicules et les rois malheureux, voilà tout le
théâtre existant et possible'

Beaumarchais, *Le Barbier de Seville*

Done to death by slanderous tongues

Shakespeare, *Much Ado about Nothing*

'EVERYONE was at Versailles' says Mme de La Tour du Pin,
writing of the days immediately before the Estates General.
'We all waited with much gaiety and without any anxiety – or
open anxiety at any rate – for the opening of the assembly
which was to give birth to a new France.' Indeed with
hindsight one can see that while a revolution was inevitable,
the Revolution as we know it was far from inevitable. All
depended on Louis XVI and on his chief adviser – Marie
Antoinette.

There is a famous engraving of the first session of the
Estates General on 5 May 1789. It met in the *Salle des Menus
Plaisirs* ('The Hall of Lesser Pleasures') at Versailles, a vast,
pillared room twice as long as it was wide and with a high
painted ceiling. The King wearing a cocked hat sits on his
throne on a purple velvet dais, the Queen beside him in an
armchair with the Princes of the Blood on stools. Everyone
else sits on benches, in closely packed rows. On the right of
the hall in scarlet, purple and black are the First Estate, the

clergy of France; on the left in white-plumed *chapeaux*, gold-edged mantles and court swords are the Second Estate, the nobles of France. The Third Estate, the commons of France, in plain black and without a sword among them, are at the far end of the hall facing Louis. Nothing could be more orderly or more decorous. 'Viewing it as an opera, it was imposing,' commented the minister of the United States, Mr Thomas Jefferson, who was present.

The Estates General had never been an established legislative assembly, but was summoned only in times of national emergency. It had not met since 1614. Naturally so momentous a gathering was accompanied by all the pageantry of the *ancien régime*. The day before the opening session there had been a procession through the tapestry-hung streets of Versailles by everyone taking part, to attend a service in the church of St Louis. Each person carried a lighted taper, save for banner-bearers and royal falconers – the latter with their birds on their wrists. Marie Antoinette, walking with her distinctive, majestic step, wore a dress of gold and silver tissue. Mme de La Tour du Pin, sitting in one of the palace windows, noticed that she 'looked sad and cross'. The Queen passed under a balcony where the dying Dauphin lay watching from a day-bed and, barely able to hold back her tears, blew him a kiss. At the very same moment prostitutes from the Palais Royal shouted spitefully 'Vive Orléans!' Marie Antoinette, turning quickly to see from where the insult came, lost her balance, and was only saved from falling by Mme de Lamballe; some spectators thought she was going to faint. But she recovered, setting her face, and went on to the church. Here she had to sit through a hectoring sermon by the Bishop of Nancy, who rebuked the King for allowing extortioners to 'martyr' his subjects. The Queen went red and bit her lip. She was so nervous and upset that when she returned to the palace she snapped one of her diamond bracelets.

The next day, the first session of the Estates, was even worse for her. When Louis entered the *Salle des Menus Plaisirs* he was cheered enthusiastically. Marie Antoinette followed him, this time in mauve and white, to be greeted by a stony silence – no one from the clergy or the nobles, let alone the commons, could summon up a cheer for her. The Comte de Mirabeau – sitting with his inferiors of the Third Estate – muttered to a neighbour, '*Voilà la victime!*' During a short opening speech, delivered in a firm voice, the King was constantly interrupted by applause. He even impressed Thomas Jefferson. Another American spectator, Mr Gouverneur Morris, writes that by contrast the Queen seemed on the verge of tears throughout – 'not one voice is heard to wish her well'. He wanted to cheer her himself but felt it would be improper for someone who was not a Frenchman. Mme de La Tour du Pin remembers that, 'The Queen's great dignity was much commented on, but it was plain, from the almost convulsive way in which she was using her fan, that she was extremely agitated. Frequently she looked towards the end of the hall where the Third Estate sat and seemed to be trying to find a friendly face in the ranks of that mass of men among whom she had so many enemies.' The poor woman would probably much rather have been with her dying son. Instead she had to endure a three-hour speech of notable tedium from Necker, full of statistics and delivered in a droning, monotonous voice. When at last Louis rose to leave there were more shouts of '*Vive le Roi!*' Marie Antoinette rose too. Suddenly there were cries of '*Vive la Reine!*' Surprised, she curtsied majestically to the assembly, to be cheered still more warmly. She responded with a second curtsey and was seen to be smiling slightly on her way back to the palace. But the Estates General had cheered her only because they wanted to please the King.

For the rest of May the Estates were occupied by increasingly acrimonious discussions on procedure. By custom the three estates debated separately, but the commons began to agitate for a single assembly which they could dominate. During this time the Queen was completely absorbed in the Dauphin, who was in his final agony. Public prayers were said in all churches on 2 June, but it was quite clear that nothing could save the by now hideously diseased and deformed child. His mother, in floods of tears, never left his bedside. He died in her arms at 1 o'clock in the morning on 4 June 1789, aged seven and a half. Tradition stopped her attending his funeral – she could not even mourn by his body. Within an hour of the boy's death a deputation from the Estates forced its way into Louis's presence, long before dawn and despite his anguished plea, 'Aren't there any fathers among you?' Marie Antoinette's hair began to turn white although she was only thirty-four; when her miniature was painted a few months later, before giving it to Mme de Lamballe she wrote on it, 'Unhappiness has made my hair white.' She said bitterly of the Estates, 'My dearest little Dauphin is dead and no one even seems to notice.'

The treasury was bankrupt, there were bread riots all over the country, and throughout France the poorer classes were terrified by rumours of plots against them by the Queen, the Austrians or the nobles. But the Estates were wrangling about whether to become a National Assembly or not. By the middle of June the clergy had joined the commons, who now claimed they represented 96 per cent of the nation and that no taxes could be levied without their consent. The nobles still refused to join them. On 19 June Necker went to see Louis who was at Marly. When he arrived the Queen at once summoned the Controller-General and complained that the commons and clergy were 'a pack of madmen and criminals'. Much to her irritation, he insisted that the King dare not resist their demand for a National Assembly. She was not present at the Council meeting which followed, when Necker proposed that the Estates be allowed to form a National Assembly on condition they draw up a two-chamber constitution for France on the English model; he also wanted to abolish qualifications of nobility for posts in the army and legislature. Louis wavered. Then a note came from Marie Antoinette and he at once left the room. Necker told his fellow councillors, 'We've lost!' The King returned to say he would have nothing to do with the proposal.

The Queen's resistance has been ascribed to blind panic and feminine contrariness. Hadn't she hoped for an alliance with the Third Estate? In fact she was perfectly consistent. She had indeed hoped that the monarchy might be able to use the bourgeoisie to bring the privileged orders to heel. But she had even less wish to surrender to a *révolte bourgeoise* than to a *révolte nobilaire*. She realized that a National Assembly dominated by the Third Estate would inevitably start not just a revolt but a revolution, and make the King its puppet. The monarchy had been forced into a corner from which there was no escape. She saw that absolutism would have to be sacrificed. Louis's only chance of saving any of his powers was to accept the *révolte nobilaire*, by keeping the Estates General intact and enlisting the support of nobles and clergy, even if it meant turning himself into a constitutional monarch.

On 20 June the commons and the clergy tried to enter the *Salle des Menus Plaisirs* without the nobles, but were deliberately locked out. They therefore occupied the Versailles tennis court where they took an oath not to disperse until a constitution had been established. It was a direct challenge to Louis. Necker pleaded with him not to resist and to embitter the Third Estate who were 'speaking for all France'.

Marie Antoinette insisted that her husband stand firm and fight the bourgeois – interestingly, Monsieur, that shrewdest and subtlest of politicians, supported her. The King decided to take her advice. On 22 June the three estates were summoned to the *Salle des Menus Plaisirs*. In his address he told them that, in effect, he was going to become a constitutional monarch; no taxes would be levied without the assent of the Estates General, while all privileges would be guaranteed. He also told them that they must continue to debate separately, that there could be no question of having a National Assembly, and that if the commons would not cooperate he would consider himself the only true representative of the French people. Finally he ordered them to leave the hall, and left himself.

But the Third Estate stayed stubbornly where it was. One account says that the King thought of ejecting them at the bayonet point but then changed his mind and muttered

'*Foutre*, let them stay.' Significantly Necker had avoided accompanying Louis to the session – the Queen attributed his absence to 'treason or criminal cowardice'. She urged her husband to dismiss the Controller-General and to use troops on the so called National Assembly. Everyone knew it, and mobs surged through the streets of Versailles and round the palace itself, yelling that Necker must stay. Alarmingly, the *Gardes Françaises* refused to fire on them. The Controller-General, always a glutton for applause, walked smugly back to his house through cheering crowds, assuring them he would keep his place. The air rang with shouts of '*Vive M. Necker!*'

The King took refuge with his hounds in the depths of the forest and Marie Antoinette played with her children. They were still reluctant to admit how serious the situation had become. Yet the entire country was in uproar. Arthur Young, who was in France at the time, gives us some idea of it. He says on 9 June that in the previous week nearly ninety-two new political pamphlets had appeared on sale at the Palais Royal, that as many more were coming out, not to mention those appearing in the provinces; the vast majority of them 'are in favour of liberty and commonly violent against the nobility and clergy'. The diarist notes with astonishment that the government is doing nothing to stop them. 'Is it not wonderful, that while the press teems with the most levelling and even seditious principles, that if put into execution would overturn the monarchy, nothing in reply appears, and not the least step is taken by the court to restrain this extreme licentiousness of publication . . .?'

Beyond question the Orléanist faction was ultimately responsible for much of the uproar. Since the previous year it had had a proper party manager in the person of the Duke's talented private secretary and man of affairs, Pierre-Ambroise Choderlos de Laclos. A former gunner captain in his late forties and the author of that elegantly immoral tale of vice among the nobility *Les Liaisons Dangereuses*, whose promotion had been blocked by lack of quarterings and whose military career had been soured by aristocratic

superiors, Laclos was the archetypal Orléanist. He owed his
appointment to Freemasonry, being recommended to the
Duke by his lodge. Just like a modern political agent he tried
to give Orléans an attractive public image and his party a
credible manifesto. It was Laclos who had suggested the
distribution of bread in the Duke's name during the winter,
with such gratifying results. It was Laclos too who was
responsible for the public letters from Orléans to his
bailiwicks with advice about elections to the Estates, and
about *Cahiers de Doléances* – or lists of grievances – which they
sent to the Estates for discussion; the wording was un-
mistakably anti-monarchist in tone, all but revolutionary.
Laclos's prompting may well have been behind the Duke's
challenge to Louis in the Parlement of November 1787.
Under Laclos's skilful management the Palais Royal became a
centre of political debate of the most extreme sort. Young
records that 'the coffee houses in the Palais Royal present yet
more singular and astonishing spectacles; they are not only
crowded within, but other expectant crowds are at the doors
and windows, listening *à gorge déployée*, to certain orators, who
from chairs or tables harangue each his little audience: the
eagerness with which they are heard, and the thunder of
applause they receive for every sentiment of more than
common hardiness or violence against the present government, cannot easily be imagined.' Laclos's aim was to project
his master as an alternative monarch, a true Prince of the
Parisians who would be a King for the new France (as
Orléans's son Louis-Philippe would try to be forty years
later). Unfortunately for Laclos, the Duke was timid,
inarticulate, undecided, and basically frivolous; as Mirabeau
put it later 'depending on him is like building on mud. But he
is admired by the mob, he loathes the King, he loathes the
Queen even more, and if he needs courage we'll give him
some.' Their candidate's inadequacies did not discourage the
Orléanists from doing their best to start a revolution and
from trying to discredit Louis XVI and his advisers – in
particular Marie Antoinette. Probably few enemies did her
more harm than Laclos.

The King at last decided to take action, accepting that a
coup d'état was unavoidable. Alas, he was not exactly a
Bonaparte. On 27 June he attempted to gain time by ordering
the clergy and nobles to sit with the commons 'for the safety
of the State'. There were bonfires in Paris to celebrate the
commons' victory. But Louis had given orders for troops to
move up and surround Versailles and the capital. Within a
few days the secret was out. In his gutter paper *L'Ami du
Peuple* Jean-Paul Marat told the Parisians that soldiers were
coming. Soon they could see Besenval and his Swiss
encamped on the Champs de Mars on the left bank, while
other Swiss and also German regiments set up tents in the
gardens of Versailles. By 8 July M. de Mirabeau was rallying
his fellow deputies and drafting resolutions to tell the King
he must withdraw his troops. Thomas Jefferson helped
Lafayette draw up a declaration of human rights inspired by
the American Declaration of Independence. On 11 July
Jefferson wrote to the English radical Tom Paine that the
National Assembly were ready to 'set fire to the four corners
of the kingdom, and to perish with it themselves, rather than
to relinquish an iota from their plan of a total change of
government'.

On the same day that Jefferson wrote to Tom Paine, Louis
XVI struck (if 'struck' is the right word). Necker was
dismissed and banished. His successor as Controller-General
was the septuagenarian Joseph-François Foullon, an administrator of great experience and ability but with an
unfortunate name for avarice and callousness. At a time when
many Parisians were starving someone – perhaps Laclos –
cunningly spread the damning rumour that Foullon had said,
'If the *canaille* haven't any bread, they can eat straw.' The
Maréchal Duc de Broglie, France's most famous general,
summoned from Alsace, was appointed Minister for War;
Jefferson describes him as 'a high-flying Aristocrat, cool and
capable of every mischief'. The real power behind the new
administration was the Queen's candidate, Louis-Auguste,
Baron de Breteuil, a tough ex-soldier and diplomatist, who
became Minister for the Royal Household, or Minister of the

Interior. Even so royalist an historian as the Duc de Castries succumbs to contemporary propaganda and portrays him as a brutal thug. In fact when Breteuil had been Minister for the Royal Household from 1783–88 he had shown himself both merciful and imaginative in reforming the penal system; he had closed the horrible dungeons at Caen, shut the prison at Vincennes and proposed that the Bastille be demolished. Moreover he had kept Paris calm and never allowed riots to get out of control. He had all the marks of a genuine strong man and was an excellent choice to carry out a *coup d'état* – but the King would not give him a free hand.

Next day, 12 July, was a Sunday. In the afternoon a howling mob, bearing wax busts of Orléans and Necker (looted from a shop window) as standards, roared into the Place Louis Quinze (now Place de la Concorde) and attacked royal troops with stones and bottles. The latter had to give way as they had strict orders from Louis that they were on no account to shed blood. This was not just a rising by the starving workers, but by all Paris – proletarians, middle class, liberal nobles, and even capitalists. The bankers closed the Exchange. The Palais Royal resounded to countless rousing speeches. By Monday a *milice bourgeoise*, soon to become the National Guard, was being enrolled at the Hôtel de Ville with the Marquis de Lafayette as its Colonel. Street-fighting continued sporadically all over Paris. Gunsmiths were broken into and there was a desperate search for arms throughout the capital, while shops were plundered and religious houses were sacked. The Assembly sent a deputation to the King to demand that he withdraw his soldiers at once.

Yet, according to Mme de La Tour du Pin who was at Versailles, she and the other courtiers had no idea that anything particular was happening. 'The court put complete trust in the small army gathered on the Grenelle plain and on the Champs de Mars.' A few months afterwards Tom Paine informed Edmund Burke that Louis and his ministers had 'counted with certainty on the Troops under M. Broglio: at the time it was certainly known by *some* that those Troops would not act against the People'.

On Tuesday 14 July the mob surrounded the fortress prison of the Bastille in the centre of Paris. They managed to storm this symbol of royal absolutism after it had been shelled by mutinous *Gardes Françaises*. (Ironically, the King had already approved plans for the Bastille's demolition.) The governor was torn to pieces and his head stuck on a pike. Besenval could do nothing. Broglie did not bother to send him any instructions from Versailles, where his officers were now warning him that many of their men would not fight. In despair Besenval decided to move his troops out of Paris, a disastrous decision. This was the moment when Louis XVI finally lost his authority. Yet no one informed him of the fact until the next morning, when at his *lever* the Duc de Liancourt gave him the news of the fall of the Bastille and, on being asked if it was a revolt, is said to have given the famous answer, 'No, Sire, it is a revolution.'

The King at once went to the National Assembly to announce that the troops would be withdrawn from Paris. He also said that he had full confidence in the Assembly. His words of recognition and surrender were cheered again and again, and he was applauded wildly by the crowd as he walked back to his palace. A vast mob swarmed into its courtyard, shouting '*Vive le Roi!*' Even Marie Antoinette was hailed ecstatically when she made a tactful appearance with her children on a balcony. She herself had no illusions about what had happened, burning large quantities of secret papers and packing all her jewels into a single small trunk the same evening.

A royal council was held the following morning, which she attended. Provence and Artois still wanted to resist but were told that even the Swiss were growing mutinous and could not be relied on. The possibility of fleeing to Metz and the protection of the frontier regiments was also discussed, but Broglie – by now hopelessly demoralized by Louis's weakness – said that the countryside was too unsafe for such a journey. In the end they decided that the only possible course was to recall Necker and reappoint him Controller-General.

That night the greatest in the land fled secretly. All the Princes of the Blood left – Artois through a secret door – except the wily Provence, who was far from convinced that the situation was irredeemable. Broglie and Breteuil, who had no doubts whatever, went too, as did even the faithful Abbé de Vermond. Very wisely the Polignacs departed *en masse*; they knew only too well that the Paris mob had howled for their blood on many occasions.

Marie Antoinette was distraught at losing all her closest friends, even if there had been some coldness in recent months. She was particularly upset at having to part with Yolande, whom she ordered to go for her own safety. The Duchess left at midnight, disguised as a chambermaid and sitting on top of the coach like a servant. As the horses were about to set off into the darkness, a note was pressed into her hand which came from the Queen who dared not be present – 'Farewell, my dearest of friends. It is a dreadful world.' The note was accompanied by a purse of 500 *louis d'or* for her travelling expenses, with a message that Marie Antoinette knew they would need every penny. At Sens Yolande and her husband were recognized by a postillion but he was good-natured enough to keep their secret – they might well have been torn to pieces. They eventually reached Switzerland and safety.

The Queen had every reason to fear for her own life, indeed even for that of the King himself. There were more rumours that armed rioters were marching on Versailles; the English ambassador, the Duke of Dorset, heard that as many as 50,000 were ready to set out. Very courageously Louis, who certainly never lacked physical bravery, decided that the only way of defusing the situation was to accede to a request by the National Assembly that he should visit 'his good town of Paris'. His wife thought he would never come back alive; he himself plainly had misgivings. They took Communion together, and he appointed Provence Lieutenant-General (Regent) of the Realm, in case he should not return. Then, with a scanty bodyguard, he set out at ten o'clock in the morning of 17 July for the Hôtel de Ville. Marie Antoinette locked herself in her apartments with her children – most of the friends who would normally have comforted her had fled. 'A terrifying silence filled the palace,' says Mme Campan; 'Fear was everywhere.' The Queen actually drafted a speech which she meant to make to the National Assembly if Louis was made a prisoner – 'Do not let those whom God hath joined together in heaven be put asunder on earth.' From time to time she wept.

But at six o'clock a page arrived to say that the King was coming home. Tom Paine tells us that in Paris 'The Croud [sic] was immense, but orderly and well arranged, and everyone armed with something. – Those who had no Muskets or Swords, got what they could, – Scythes, Sickles, Carpenters Chissels and Iron Spikes fixed upon Sticks, Blacksmith's with Sledge Hammers, and in short every thing and any thing that could be got. When the King alighted at the Hôtel de Ville, he had to pass through an Alley of Men, who crossed them over his head under which he had to pass, impressed perhaps with the apprehension that someone was to fall upon his head.' However the visit went off smoothly, though he was made to put into his hat a red, white and blue cockade (soon to become the badge of the Revolution). Thomas Jefferson, who watched the visit, writes that it was 'an *amende honorable*, as no sovereign ever made, and no people ever received'.

A citizen army escorted Louis back to Versailles. Marie Antoinette threw herself into his arms, weeping. However Mercy-Argenteau adds that when she saw the vulgar favour in his *tricorne* she recoiled, saying 'I did not know I had married a commoner.'

Nevertheless she had had good reason to be frightened. On 22 July old Foullon, who had briefly replaced Necker, was caught by the Paris mob and hanged on a *lanterne*. His head was hacked off and the mouth stuffed with straw – in allusion to his alleged jibe that *canaille* ought to eat straw – and carried on a pike in triumph through the streets.

It was not just Paris and Versailles that were in turmoil, but all France. Within a week of the Bastille's fall, mobs stormed and destroyed the Bastilles at Bordeaux and Caen, and the Hôtel de Ville at Strasbourg. There were bloody riots with much fighting at Lyons, at Rennes, at Rouen, at Saint-Malo, and at Saint-Germain just outside Paris, where they hanged all the millers. A municipal revolution was taking place everywhere. In the countryside peasants armed with pitchforks and cudgels were storming châteaux and abbeys to burn their masters' deeds – and sometimes the house and the master as well – while the lanes were full of workless, starving labourers. There were also strange and terrible rumours of armies of brigands, or of revengeful landowners and Royalists. Mme de La Tour du Pin thought this widespread phenomenon – the '*Grand Peur*' – incomprehensible 'unless one accepts the existence of a gigantic network stretching to every corner of France'. But the principal cause was undoubtedly misery born of hunger and the scarcity and prohibitive cost of bread.

Admittedly a few Orléanist agents were probably spreading tales of Austrian invasion. On 28 July Mme de La Tour du Pin saw a man on horseback telling terrified country people that the Austrians were only three hours away, pillaging and burning. It was widely believed that many aristocrats wanted the Emperor to march into France from his Belgian territories and restore order. His sister was more than ever the nation's bogey-woman.

Even so, at Versailles there was little change in the ritual of court life apart from the conspicuous absence of certain faces. The Queen appointed the Marquise de Tourzel as governess in place of Yolande de Polignac. On 24 July she wrote a letter to the new governess about her charges, often quoted but too revealingly personal to omit. 'My son is two days short of being four years and four months old. I won't describe his physique or appearance as in any case you are soon going to see him. His health has always been good, though even in his cradle it was noticed he was very nervous and upset by the slightest sudden noise . . . Because of delicate nerves he is always frightened by any noise to which he isn't accustomed and, for example, is afraid of dogs after hearing one bark near

him.' She describes him as thoughtless and hot-tempered but
also good natured, even affectionate, and as having too
much self-importance which, however, may be a help to him
one day if carefully managed. 'My son cannot read yet and
finds his lessons very difficult, but is much too scatter-brained
to concentrate. He has no sense of conceit and I want that
to continue.' Marie Antoinette shows herself surprisingly
imaginative about bringing up children. 'My children are
taught to trust me completely and to tell me themselves if
they do anything wrong. So when I reprimand them I can
look hurt and upset instead of angry . . . exercise taken by
little children playing and running about in the open air is far
healthier than making them go for long walks which tire
their backs.'

Meanwhile the Revolution gained momentum. On 1
August there was a meeting of tailors outside the Louvre,
demanding better wages to meet the astronomical price of
bread. The Queen's apocryphal remark about cake, now
widely circulated, must have been very much in their minds.
The National Assembly began to demolish the old society.
On the night of 4 August in a single sitting the nobles
voluntarily and emotionally relinquished feudal privileges
and the clergy followed them, disclaiming all manorial rights
and dues, all *capitaineries*, all fines and claims, all game laws,
all tolls and tithes, all immunities. The Assembly then
insisted on giving the renunciation legal force by incorporat-
ing them in decrees, which were presented to Louis in the
Hall of Mirrors at Versailles on 13 August – much to his
horror. Secretly he thought that both nobles and clergy had
gone mad. The Assembly now set about debating and
drafting a 'Declaration of the Rights of Man and of the
Citizen' which it approved on 26 August. This too was
presented to the King and received no less politely. He
managed to postpone formal assent to both decrees and
declaration.

However August 1789 was a comparatively calm month
for the royal family. The Queen spent much time at the
Trianon and the Hamlet and there were some court balls. On

25 August, the Feast of St Louis, as was the custom representatives of the City of Paris were received by her. They included the new Mayor, officers of the National Guard led by Lafayette, and a delegation of fishwives. 'The Queen was not in court dress,' Mme de La Tour du Pin informs us, 'but sparkled with diamonds and other precious stones . . . To the right and left Duchesses in court dress sat on their *tabourets* while behind her stood her entire household of ladies and gentlemen.' She snubbed the Mayor, Lafayette and his officers and even the fishwives. All left very annoyed. 'The officers of the National Guard, who might have been won over by gracious words, went away in a thoroughly bad mood to spread their feelings all over Paris, increasing all the ill will being stirred up there against the Queen, mainly at the Duc d'Orléans's instigation.' It may have been unwise of Marie Antoinette not to hide her resentment at what had happened in July, but it was natural. In any case she was becoming a little more confident about the future. She wrote to Yolande in Switzerland that affairs seemed to be improving though she dared not hope for too much. 'But you can be sure no troubles will ever daunt my determination or my spirits.' Even Mercy-Argenteau was impressed by her 'greatest courage' of which 'much is required if she is not to be saddened, or indeed disgusted, by so many injustices and misfortunes'.

Alas, by the end of August Paris had again grown menacing. Extremists demanded that the King should leave Versailles and move into his capital. By his abortive *coup* Louis had forfeited much of his popularity and reputation for impartiality, which had hitherto been his strongest asset. Nonetheless he still personified France. Sixty years later the Goncourt brothers would write 'in those days the King was the popular religion, just as the nation is today'. Tom Paine claimed as late as 1791 that 'The Monarch and the Monarchy were distinct and separate things; and it was against the established despotism of the latter, and not against the person or the principles of the former, that the revolt commenced, and the Revolution has been carried.' In the autumn of 1789 it still seemed essential that the King must co-operate if the new constitution was to be valid. Reformers believed with Paine in the 'natural moderation of Louis XVI', that he could be won round. They also suspected, correctly, that the Queen was influencing him against them. The only way to counter-act her influence was to bring him to Paris.

At first only extremists were prepared to compel him. On the night of 30 August several hundred Parisians set out for Versailles, led by a liberal nobleman, M. de Saint-Huruge. Almost at once they were stopped and dispersed by National Guards, but the National Assembly heard the news with consternation. Even Necker, who had returned to become Controller-General once more, was shaken. A committee set up by the Assembly agreed with him, as did his fellow ministers, that the King must leave Versailles and move further away from the capital. Louis refused. Yet all the time he was sitting on a time-bomb, since he was still trying to avoid signing the August decrees and the Declaration of the Rights of Man. On 14 September, with almost unbelievable tactlessness, he sent openly for the reliable Flanders Regi-ment and ordered it to march from the northern frontier. The Parisians were convinced it had been summoned not just to protect the royal palace but to attempt another *coup d'état*. They knew that the King had other soldiers available as well – the household troops and also a detachment of light horse at Rambouillet.

The Flanders Regiment, a thousand strong, reached Versailles on 23 September. Louis and Marie Antoinette were delighted, feeling that they were safe at last. On 29 September the Queen presented both the Flanders Regiment and the household troops with new colours. The following day there was a church service in which the flags were blessed, and the celebrations continued until 1 October. That afternoon the officers of the household troops – Body-guards, Musketeers, Horse Grenadiers, Swiss – gave a dinner to the officers of the Flanders Regiment in the Versailles opera house. Around a horseshoe table on the stage over 200 officers sat down at three o'clock to a cheerful and lengthy meal, sumptuously prepared by the royal chef, while other ranks sat drinking happily in the pit. Toast after toast was announced by trumpeters in the intervals of a rousing concert played by the royal orchestra. The atmosphere suddenly became highly emotional when the orchestra played the aria *O Richard, ô mon Roy* (from Grétry's opera *Richard Coeur de Lion*), with everyone in tears and officers drawing their swords to salute. By then the royal family were present in a box, Marie Antoinette having persuaded Louis to come as soon as he returned from hunting. The Dauphin, in the care of a Swiss officer, actually walked the entire length of the horseshoe table between the enraptured diners, beaming at his cleverness in not upsetting any glasses – though much to his mother's anxiety. The royal family retired when the cheering grew a little too wild. There were shouts of 'Down with the Assembly!' Some of the Queen's ladies took white ribbons from their hats and handed them out to make white cockades.

The news of the banquet aroused furious anger in Paris. It was said that the officers had trampled the red, white and blue cockade underfoot and that Marie Antoinette had personally given a white cockade to everyone present; that not only had there been shouts of 'Down with the Assembly!' but that there had also been shouts of 'Down with the Nation!' The Parisians' fury grew still more intense at news of another banquet of the same sort, given by the officers of the household troops on 3 October, when black Austrian cockades as well as white ones were distributed. Marat's newspaper *L'Ami du Peuple* trumpeted that every citizen should prepare for battle. On Sunday 4 October the speeches at the Palais Royal were even more frenzied than usual, Camille Desmoulins – not for the first time – standing on a table in a café and telling his audience that the Parisians must fetch the King from Versailles and put him in the Tuileries. It was noticed that the women present were particularly loud in their condemnation of the Queen and were threatening to 'put matters right to-morrow'. This Sunday was also a day when bread vanished from the shops in Paris – the shortage caused riots, one unfortunate baker being hanged by an enraged crowd. Rumours circulated that the dearth of bread was because the court was hoarding flour at Versailles, and there were yells of 'Cut the Queen's throat!' Large numbers of women, many well dressed, with powdered hair, announced their intention of marching to Versailles.

Early on the morning of Monday 5 October crowds of women began to collect in the Place de Grève, summoned by church bells. Among them were men in female dress, including the liberal Duc d'Aiguillon and a considerable number of Orléanist supporters (though not Orléans himself, as royalists later claimed). Choderlos de Laclos's team of agents was busy offering money and brandy to any woman who would join in a march to Versailles. As on the previous day some of the mob were expensively dressed with elaborate coiffures, and not all of these were prostitutes, though the majority were unquestionably the poor and wretched, fishwives, servants, or washerwomen from the floating laundries on the Seine – crazed by hunger and harrowed by starving children. It began to rain but, fortified with Orléanist brandy, the women assembled in the Place Louis Quinze in the early afternoon. They chose a man to lead them, Maillard – one of those who had stormed the Bastille – and somehow acquired two cannon, and horses to pull them. Nearly 6,000 strong, armed with kitchen knives, broomsticks, skewers, spits, sickles, pitchforks, and the odd sword or pistol, they set off through the now pouring rain to march the ten miles to Versailles.

Meanwhile the National Guard of Paris was also mustering excitedly. Their commanding officer – that hero of the American war and an old bugbear of Marie Antoinette, the ridiculous Lafayette – was told by his men that they were determined to join the women. Lafayette did his best to dissuade them but they grew threatening. Eventually he received an order from the Hôtel de Ville to take them to Versailles. Accordingly at six o'clock that evening he rode out from Paris at the head of 15,000 National Guardsmen, who were accompanied by a rabble of several thousand other

Parisians armed with pikes and a few old muskets.

Mme de La Tour du Pin informs us that no one at Versailles expected anything out of the ordinary to happen that day, although they had heard of the previous day's riots. The King was hunting as usual. After lunch, as she was driving in Madame Elisabeth's garden, she saw the Duc de Maillé ride past at full gallop. He shouted to her 'Paris is marching here with cannon!' Mme Campan confirms that the court was in no way apprehensive and that having finished his hunting Louis was indulging in some shooting at Meudon. As for Marie Antoinette, 'The Queen was by herself in her gardens at the Trianon, which she was seeing for the last time in her life. She was sitting in her grotto, absorbed in sad reflections, when she received a note from the Comte de Saint-Priest – the Minister for the Royal Household – begging her to return to Versailles at once.'

The army of women reached Versailles at about half-past three, wet through and covered in mud. Inflamed by large doses of brandy they were shrieking 'Bread! Bread!' or else screaming what they intended to do to the Queen – 'We'll cut off her head . . . rip her heart out . . . fry her liver . . . make her guts into ribbons.' Some of them were nearly ridden down by the King and the royal hunt returning at full gallop. Fortunately Saint-Priest had closed the great iron gates (which had not been shut since Louis XIV's time). The household troops, together with the Flanders Regiment and a few local National Guardsmen were drawn up in front of the château, behind the railings, in full battle order. As Louis passed them, the men of the 'Flandre' cheered him and shouted '*Vive le Roi!*' He ignored them, went straight to his room and shut himself in. Meanwhile the entire palace was in a state of confusion and panic. Finally the Captain of the Guard managed to see the King and ask him for orders. 'Against women!' laughed Louis, 'you are joking.' At last Saint-Priest, after a long argument, convinced him of the seriousness of the situation and persuaded him to withdraw to Rambouillet, only a few miles away, and to wait there to see what the National Assembly would propose. 'Sire, if you are taken to Paris tomorrow, you will lose your crown,' said the Minister. Marie Antoinette ordered her ladies to pack – 'We leave in half an hour.'

While Louis had been trying to make up his mind, he had received a delegation of five women. Their spokesman, a seventeen-year-old artist's model called Louison Chabry, whispered simply 'Bread, Sire,' and then fainted. She was revived with wine in a gold cup and a flask of smelling-salts. The King kissed her on both cheeks and promised to do something about the famine.

But throughout the evening obstacle after obstacle prevented the royal family from leaving Versailles – the carriage-horses' harness was cut, some of the women climbed into the palace courtyard, the local National Guardsmen fired the odd shot at their officers, the household troops were attacked with stones and bottles. As on so many occasions, Louis delayed for too long. Within half an hour of telling her ladies to pack, the Queen had to tell them they were staying. Her husband, muttering 'A fugitive King! A fugitive King!' thought of flight for a second time and then changed his mind once again. At midnight Lafayette and the Paris National Guard arrived, to reassure him. 'Sire, I am come to offer my head in place of your Majesty's. If my blood must shed, then let it be in the service of my King instead of by torchlight on the Place de Grève.' (The Place de Grève was used for executions.) Lafayette positioned his men all round the palace and then went to sleep on a sofa. Marie Antoinette, who had remained impressively calm while her courtiers 'paced the length and breadth of the palace rooms without exchanging a word', went to bed at two o'clock in the morning, quite exhausted. She told her two ladies-in-waiting to go to bed themselves, 'imagining that there was nothing to fear, at any rate that night'.

At about six o'clock the Queen's ladies – who despite her instructions had not gone to bed but remained sitting outside her bedroom – heard 'shots and the most horrible yells'. A band of armed women had found an open gate into a courtyard and stormed up a staircase, killing two of the household troops. Another of the royal guards, Miomandre de Sainte-Marie, tried to hold them off alone and shouted to the ladies outside Marie Antoinette's room, 'Save the Queen!' They bolted the door on the brave guardsman, who was cut down only a few moments later, and rushed to Marie Antoinette's bed screaming, 'Get up Madame! Don't stay to dress yourself – run to the King's apartments!' Dressed in a night-gown, hearing behind her shrieks of 'Kill the bitch!' and pikes battering on her door and then the noise of her rooms being sacked, the Queen fled barefoot down the corridors. She had to bang on the doors of her husband's apartments for five minutes before she was let in. He was not there, having gone to rescue her, but soon joined her. From his bedroom they listened to axes crashing against the doors of the beloved *oeil de boeuf* room. Suddenly the uproar ended. Horrified by the harpies, many of whom were drunk and half naked, the National Guardsmen had forgotten their anti-monarchical sentiments and driven the women out with their bayonets.

Even so Versailles was still surrounded by a shrieking rabble, and the harridans continued to occupy two court-yards from where they were yelling threats and shouting *'Vive M. d'Orléans!'* The palace itself was full of far from reliable National Guardsmen with their rowdy friends from Paris. From one of the courtyards someone saw Marie Antoinette looking out of a window and there were howls of 'Damned whore'. There were also yells for the King to show himself.

Louis went out on to the balcony to be met with shouts of *'Vive la Nation!'* and, more reassuringly, *'Vive le Roi!'* Then there were less amiable cries of 'The Queen to the balcony!' Her ladies blenched but she insisted on going out, with rumpled hair and a white face 'that somehow kept its dignity' and holding her children by the hand. The latter were terrified and began to cry. When they all appeared on the balcony there was a roar of 'The Queen alone! No children!' She sent them in. For a good two minutes she stood there motionless while the mob shouted 'Shoot her! Shoot her!'

and aimed their guns at her. At last she curtsied gravely. This piece of cool courage was rewarded by a great shout of '*Vive la Reine!*' at which she went back into the palace.

But then the mob began to cry 'To Paris! To Paris!' Marie Antoinette said grimly to Mme Necker, 'They are going to force the King and I to go to Paris, carrying our guardsmen's heads on the end of their pikes.' Sure enough, Louis had to return to the balcony with Lafayette and promise that he would go to Paris with his family whom he entrusted to 'the love of my good and faithful subjects'. The 'good and faithful subjects' howled their applause and fired their guns into the air to express their appreciation. They began to bellow for the Queen again.

Lafayette asked her what she was going to do. She replied, 'I know perfectly well what is in store for me but my duty is to die at the King's feet with my children in my arms.' 'Come with me, Madame,' said Lafayette. 'What, to the balcony, Sir? Can't you hear their threats?' When he and Marie Antoinette appeared, the howls became more menacing than ever. Always a man with a sense of theatre, Lafayette bent and kissed her hand ostentatiously. The howling died down and he was able to announce that, 'The Queen has been misguided, but she swears she will no longer be so. She promises to love her people, to be united with them just as Jesus Christ is with his Church.' The mob responded with cheers. Lafayette did not seem to have realized how much he had humiliated Marie Antoinette. She went in to dress – she was still in her night-clothes – and to pack.

That afternoon Louis XVI and his Queen and their children left Versailles for ever. It was half-past one. Marie Antoinette would never again see the palace which had been her home for nearly twenty years, nor indeed the Trianon or the Hamlet. They rode to Paris in a coach drawn by six horses in the midst of an extraordinary procession. It numbered more than 30,000 people. First came the National Guardsmen, straggling along with loaves of bread stuck on their bayonets, then a band of drunken harridans riding on cannon and waving bottles, and then the royal coach. The triumphant Lafayette rode immediately in front of the coach, around which danced women and ruffians with the heads of murdered guardsmen on their pikes, chanting 'We are bringing back the baker, the baker's wife and the baker's boy and we won't go short of bread any more.' Inside it the King held his handkerchief up to his face to conceal the fact that he was crying, while the Queen's face showed 'the marks of violent grief'; from time to time the terrified Dauphin leant out of the window begging the mob to spare his mother – '*Grâce pour Mamun!*' Behind the royal coach trudged the dejected household troops and Flanders men, without their arms and shamefacedly wearing the revolutionary cockade. Behind them followed nearly 200 carriages containing almost the entire court and at least a hundred deputies from the National Assembly. Of those who were there, Mme Campan says 'Great God! What a procession!' while Mme de La Tour du Pin calls it 'a horrible masquerade'.

The royal family did not reach the Hôtel de Ville until six in the evening, when it was already growing dark. They were received exultantly by Bailly, the Mayor of Paris, who solemnly presented Louis with the keys of his capital and then took him to the window to show to the waiting Parisians by the light of guttering *flambeaux*. The crowd outside was 'of the better sort', many of them respectable bourgeois and very different from the mob which had invaded Versailles. They cheered their King and Queen heartily. Eventually Louis and his family were allowed to leave and go to the Tuileries, which they at least reached at ten o'clock.

Their new home had not been lived in by royalty since Louis XV had left it as a boy in 1722. It had been used as 'grace and favour' accommodation for royal pensioners, who were now hastily ejected. There were not enough beds, sheets or candles for the royal family, let alone for the household, while some of the windows were broken and the Dauphin's door would not shut – his sister had to sleep on a sofa. Marie Antoinette installed herself in an apartment formerly occupied by the Comtesse de La Marck. It was hardly what she and her children had been accustomed to. 'Isn't it ugly here, Mama,' said the Dauphin. His mother replied soothingly, 'Louis XIV was happy enough here – you shouldn't ask for more than he did.' Nevertheless Mme de Tourzel watched by the overwrought child's bed all night.

The Queen wrote to Mercy-Argenteau that she could hardly believe what had happened, that it would be impossible to exaggerate 'what we have seen and have suffered'. What she did not say in her letter to him was that she was the only member of the royal family who had been in real danger of death – of a terrible death. Everyone who saw her was impressed by her dignity and courage and by her ability to communicate courage to others.

She had a single source of strength outside herself. Fersen was in Paris. He had returned to Versailles at the end of September and actually rode in the dreary procession to Paris. 'I went to Paris in one of the coaches which followed the King,' he told his father in a letter. 'The journey took us six and a half hours. God forbid that I should ever again see such heartbreaking sights as those of the last two days.' He tried to join the court at the Tuileries on the evening when it arrived, but M. de Saint-Priest asked him to stay away in order to avoid any scandal. Fersen complied. But he remained within reach.

[8]
The Tuileries: Act One

Calumny kills people better than anything and it is
by calumny that they will kill me

Marie Antoinette

The King is heavy, inert, inexperienced, timid,
without resources

Edmund Burke

LOUIS and Marie Antoinette soon refurbished the Tuileries. Cartloads of furniture came from Versailles. The King's new apartments were on the first floor, overlooking the Seine, as were those of the children and Madame Elisabeth. The Queen's were on the ground floor together with the dining-room – a private staircase to the King's floor was specially built, to which Marie Antoinette herself and the Dauphin's governess, Mme de Tourzel, alone held keys. Much has been made of the discomfort of the Tuileries – of dark passages which had to be lit by oil lamps during the day – yet Axel von Fersen, no stranger to courts and accustomed to the lavish splendours of Gustavus III, was surprised by the luxury of the Queen's apartments. Moreover the court ceremony of Versailles continued as though nothing had happened, with all the elaborate rituals of *lever* and *coucher* and dining in public. Household troops paraded every morning in the gardens to the sound of stirring military music. The royal chapel saw services just as impressive as those at Versailles.

Indeed many Frenchmen – perhaps most – thought the Revolution was over. (The word 'Revolution' was not used until much later.) The presence of King Louis in Paris was both a symbol and a guarantee of reform. All that remained was for the Assembly to make a new constitution and enact decrees for a new society without privilege. Foreign observers were not so sure. On 10 October Edmund Burke wrote to his son about 'the portentous State of France – where the Elements which compose Human Society seem all to be dissolved, and a world of Monsters to be produced in the place of it – where Mirabeau presides as the Grand Anarch; and the late Grand Monarch makes a figure as ridiculous as pitiable'. A month later Burke pointed out grimly that the new French government had little hope of solving the country's basic problems – 'a publick Bankruptcy seems the only remedy for the distempers of their Finance, and a civil war the only chance for producing order'. He suspected rightly that the King and his ministers, and indeed the Assembly, had neither the ability nor the strength to cope with so desperate a situation.

Like many others Burke must have been puzzled by Louis XVI's withdrawal from politics. For nearly four months the King left the Assembly to its own devices. Almost certainly this was in part due to a nervous breakdown. The events of 5 and 6 October had shattered his self-confidence and self-esteem – personally the bravest of men, he was plainly terrified for his wife and children should the mob indulge in another outburst of the same sort. For all the pomp and circumstance he was a prisoner of the Parisians; the Tuileries was 'protected' by the National Guard under Lafayette, who answered to the Assembly. The latter – renamed the Constituent Assembly – was now installed in the Manège (riding school), within full view of the King's windows, and proudly flying the new tricolour. He had to stop hunting and was restricted to the odd ride in the Bois de Boulogne, a serious deprivation for a man used to hard exercise all his life; he continued to eat with his customary gluttony, growing even heavier. His one relaxation was a specially installed smithy, where he spent most of the day constructing locks. Yet his lack of political initiative was not entirely due to depression and loss of nerve, as will be seen.

In the circumstances his wife's dominance over Louis had become stronger than ever. Far from being daunted or shaken, Marie Antoinette was developing real strength – her extraordinary courage during that dreadful night at Versailles was not an isolated display. Where her husband was muddled and indecisive, she was purposeful and determined. Her sole ambition was to save the throne of France for her son. She failed, but it is unlikely that any other woman in her situation could have succeeded. In the months to come it was she who took the political initiative and looked for allies. A born Queen, she was scarcely a born politician yet she nevertheless showed herself far from inept.

Even so, in the winter of 1789–1790 she seems to have been just as inactive politically as her husband. For besides being angry and alarmed, she was plainly bewildered by the situation in which the monarchy found itself. No one, progressive or conservative, understood what was happening or could foresee the future course of the Revolution. Among the very few in her own circle who could provide at least a plausible explanation was Louis himself. She admired her husband's intellect if not his judgement. Undoubtedly she listened to him.

We can make a fair guess at what was in Louis XVI's mind. He had a deep respect for David Hume's *History of Great Britain*, which he read constantly – apart from devotional works, it was the last book he looked at before his execution. Hume's account of the English Civil War seemed a blueprint of France's situation: a financial crisis had forced Charles I to summon, against his will, a revolutionary assembly which usurped his authority; the English King had tried to recover it by military means, but having failed, he then waited for his enemies to fall out, in order to ally with the strongest, and he nearly succeeded – he did not succeed because he intrigued too much. Yet Charles had been correct in his assessment of the basic strength of his position. '"You cannot be without

me," said he, on several occasions: "You cannot compose the
nation but by my assistance." ' Hume (Ch. X) goes on:
'Distractions every where, terrors, oppressions, convulsions:
from this scene of confusion which could not long continue,
all men, he hoped, would be brought to reflect upon that
antient government under which they and their ancestors had
so long enjoyed happiness and tranquillity.'

An additional reason for Louis's obsession with Charles I
was the knowledge that he was the martyr's direct descendant, a fact frequently overlooked by his biographers. Charles,
through his daughter Henrietta, Duchess of Orléans, was the
grandfather of Maria Adelaide of Savoy who married the
Duke of Burgundy, Louis XVI's great-grandfather. The
King was plainly horrified at having such a forebear – people
like Turgot, who dared to compare him with his ancestor,
savaged a very raw nerve indeed. As Louis's reign pro-
gressed, so did the resemblance to Charles I, until the final
tragedy.

Louis must also have read and reread Voltaire's account of
the Fronde in *Le Siècle de Louis XIV*. This French Civil War,
which lasted from 1647 to 1652, 'began in Paris as it had
begun in London, over the question of a little money'.
Voltaire describes the total collapse of royal authority and the
humiliation of the French monarchy. 'Any man of importance, or who hoped to become important, tried to make his
fortune out of public ruin though public welfare was on
everyone's lips . . .' The government seemed bound to fall
but the rebels could never unite, which saved it. 'The people
were like a stormy sea whose waves are driven this way and
that by a hundred contrary winds.' Eventually the Fronde
blew itself out. Louis XVI believed that if he waited long
enough, this second Fronde would also blow itself out. As
Lord Acton puts it, 'Monarchy transformed itself into
anarchy to see what would come of it.'

The King may well have read to Marie Antoinette
passages in Voltaire about the trials of Anne of Austria,
Queen Mother of France, during the Fronde. 'The Queen
could not appear in public without being insulted . . . she

found herself driven from her capital by a fickle and angry people . . . everywhere she went she heard filthy jokes about her, bursts of spite and vileness which besmirched her chastity.' Marie Antoinette would have found this all too familiar.

Probably she too agreed that as little political action as possible should be taken for the time being. Even so Mme de La Tour du Pin observed how difficult the Queen found it to conceal her frustration. 'If displeased she showed it only too plainly, heedless of consequences, which did considerable harm to the royal cause.' Two days after her arrival in Paris, representatives of the city and the National Guard asked her to go to Paris theatres to show that she and the King enjoyed being in their capital. Marie Antoinette replied that she was much too upset by recent events and felt that an entry into Paris preceded by the heads of guardsmen killed in front of her door was hardly something to celebrate – she would visit the theatre later, when she had recovered from her distress. 'This display of resentment, while natural enough, was peculiarly unfortunate and made the Parisians even more hostile towards her.'

It was almost certainly her idea that Louis should enlist unofficial political advisers. The first was the Marquis de Lafayette, fortyish, long-nosed and sandy-haired, still very much the great nobleman despite his liberal views, who had become a popular hero by bringing the royal family to Paris. For nearly a year this condescending and enormously rich grandee dominated the political scene, wooing the Patriot party in the Assembly. His intention was to be (in Georges Lefebvre's words) 'the George Washington of France, to rally King and nobility to the Revolution and the Assembly to a strong and energetic government'. He regarded himself as both saviour and mentor of Louis and Marie Antoinette, who had to listen tactfully to interminable and unconvincing advice. In reality neither was impressed by a posturing windbag whose instincts were essentially those of an actor rather than a politician. The Queen had regarded Lafayette as a not very pleasant joke ever since his clownishly awkward dancing had diverted her friends – who did not admire his aversion to duels, even if it was on grounds of principle. The spectacle of this 'simpleton Caesar' parading on a white horse in front of her during the dreadful journey from Versailles had not lessened her dislike. He had some small successes, such as eliminating Orléans by sending him on a fool's errand to London, but his hopes of becoming Prime Minister were blocked as early as November 1789 when the Assembly prohibited deputies from accepting ministerial posts. Thomas Jefferson, who had gone home, feared that he would not survive, while the new American Minister, Gouverneur Morris – who shared Marie Antoinette's opinion of him – prophesied his downfall. Morris too was not an admirer of the marquis. Even so, Lafayette had considerable power and, as commander of the National Guard, was custodian of the Tuileries. Louis and the Queen were forced to pay flattering attention to his lectures while secretly despising him. Marie Antoinette commented, 'M. de Lafayette's thirst for popularity dooms him to join indiscriminatingly in every fashionable madness.' Yet it was she who made her husband act with such uncharacteristic subtlety in his dealings with Lafayette.

The other important figure of the Revolution's early days was a much more formidable and indeed alarming figure. Honoré Requetti, Comte de Mirabeau was a political genius who could dominate the National Assembly at its stormiest. Châteaubriand saw him 'in the midst of a session in frightful uproar . . . at the rostrum, sombre, ugly and motionless; he put one in mind of Milton's Chaos, impassive and expressionless amidst disorder'. However Mirabeau was also unsavoury; his house was usually full of duns and whores – he was even suspected of incest with his own sister – and he was so venal that even faithful admirers feared the court might buy him. In addition Mirabeau, politically speaking, was fundamentally flawed; he was a genuinely great man and knew it in circumstances which he did not realize were beyond his control. He might be able to dominate the Assembly for the moment but he could not hope to direct the

course of the Revolution. There was more than a little truth
in Burke's gibe – 'the great Anarch'. To the Queen he seemed
an horrific figure, a blustering liberal who was also a vicious
libertine. Moreover he was repellent in his person, with a
hideously pock-marked face on an outsized head over a gross
body ruined by debauch. Yet, as in so many other ways, he
resembled Charles James Fox across the Channel in posses-
sing a compellingly attractive personality.

At the end of 1789 the largest party in the national
Assembly was that of the Patriots, those committed to
building a new France on the Rights of Man. There were also
the *Monarchiens* who wanted an 'English' constitution with an
upper as well as a lower house and to leave the King the
power to veto any legislation. But even before the move from
Versailles the Assembly rejected a bicameral system and
refused to let Louis keep more than a delaying veto. The
'Blacks' or counter-revolutionaries were those who wanted a
complete return to the *ancien régime*. (The name 'Black' may
have been taken from the colour of the Queen's cockade.)
More and more disillusioned *Monarchiens* began to join them.
However most Frenchmen continued to support the Revolution and the Patriots, who were helped by the promise of a
good harvest in 1790 which did indeed materialize. In many
ways the year was to be a much more peaceful one than 1789,
even if there were localized *Jacqueries* and if discipline in the
army was breaking down.

Monsieur nonetheless saw possibilities. At the beginning
of 1790 the Marquis de Favras, a fire-eating professional
soldier and a convinced Black, proposed to him that the King
should leave France as the first step in a counter-revolution.
Almost certainly Monsieur gave him money, and perhaps
even the Queen herself encouraged him. But the plot was
betrayed at a very early stage and in February 1790 Favras
was arrested, tried and hanged – the mob shouting 'Dance,
nobleman, dance!' Mme Campan claims that Marie Antoinette knew nothing about the plot, though she admits that
'the Queen did not hide from me how alarmed she was at
what the unfortunate man might confess'. She undoubtedly

sent money to his wife and son. In the event Favras died like a
hero, revealing nothing. Lafayette made himself splendidly
useful for once by leading Louis to the National Assembly on
4 February to swear loyalty to the emerging constitution. In
consequence the royal family were allowed to spend a
summer holiday out of Paris, though not too far away – at
Saint-Cloud.

Meanwhile, far from solving the problem of the deficit, the
Revolution had increased it. Necker kept the country's
finances afloat on little more than a day-to-day basis.
Growing anarchy resulted in the collection of less and less
taxes. The introduction of a new paper currency of *assignats*
produced soaring inflation. The financial wizard of the 1780s
was now seen for the fraud that he was. It was obvious that
Necker must go, something for which Marie Antoinette had
long hoped in vain.

On 10 May 1790 Mirabeau, the 'Lion of the Revolution',
wrote to Louis XVI pledging himself to support the
monarchy. While he did so for money and advancement, he
was convinced that the crown was still the key to the
situation. In his letter Mirabeau also stated that he had not
hitherto been aware of 'the strength and intelligence of Maria
Theresa's daughter' and of how much he could count on her.
In a second letter he declared: 'The King has only one man to
support him – his wife. Her sole guarantee of safety is the
restoration of royal authority. I dare to believe she would
take scant pleasure in life without a crown on her head and
am absolutely convinced she will lose her life if she does not
save her crown. The time is coming, and not too far away,
when she may have to find out what a mother and son must
do with power, something which her own family have
experienced.' In the meantime Mirabeau urged patience,
moderation and not too much optimism. It is revealing that
this essentially political animal should openly appeal to Marie
Antoinette. Moreover he was trying to win her by flattering
her as a statesman, not at all what one would expect from so
confirmed a womanizer.

The Queen has been criticized for taking so long to accept

Mirabeau's offer of assistance. This is a naive simplification. The King's attempt to pair him with Lafayette may well have been at her suggestion. When the two fell out she showed herself ready to back Mirabeau as the better bet, despite her contempt for his ignoble combination of public idealism and personal corruption. Mme Campan encapsulates him in an unusually apt phrase which she may have heard from the Queen – 'Mirabeau, the mercenary democrat and venal royalist'.

He insisted on a private audience with her. This has been variously attributed to the residual snobbery of a renegade aristocrat or the lustfulness of a pathological libertine. It is quite possible that the basic motive was much simpler – a working partnership with Maria Theresa's daughter might make both a new France and the fortunes of Mirabeau. It may even be that her long refusal to meet the man was because of an intuitive understanding of what he wanted and a determination to exploit it to the utmost.

Mirabeau was perfectly sincere. This great tribune of the people, who once bellowed, 'I am a mad dog from whose bite despotism and privilege will die', had been horrified by the October Days of 1789. From then on he was genuinely convinced that France's salvation lay in the monarchy alone. Furthermore, long before his letter to Louis he told a friend that the Queen 'has extraordinary strength of mind and a man's courage'. Nevertheless Marie Antoinette can scarcely be blamed for suspecting that M. de Mirabeau was 'not to be trusted' and a 'fine rascal', even though his friends in the Assembly thought him a political genius. She considered that 'his whole existence is nothing but deceit, cunning and lies'. After all, he was largely responsible for the terrifying situation in which she and her family found themselves.

However from the spring of 1790 Mirabeau was in Louis's pay. His debts were settled, he had a pension of 72,000 livres a year and he was to have a further million when the National Assembly was dissolved and the royal authority restored. The payments were of course secret and he never visited the Tuileries, communicating with the King only by letter – the go-between was the Comte de La Marck.

Mirabeau insisted on meeting the Queen. He clearly believed that she was the key to the situation and might even replace Louis. In 1789 he had seriously considered forcing the King to abdicate and make Philippe d'Orléans Regent, though he speedily recognized the latter's worthlessness, and, as has been seen in his second letter to Louis, had written those extraordinary words 'she may have to find out what a mother and son must do with power'. Marie Antoinette refused to see him. But on 12 July the National Assembly enacted the Civil Constitution of the Clergy, which deprived the Pope of his jurisdiction in France – the Church's property had already been nationalized and its religious orders dissolved – plunging the King into an agony of conscience. It was intensified when secret papal briefs arrived, declaring that the Civil Constitution would never be accepted by Rome. Under the new laws Louis could not exercise a veto, but he could at least try to prevent further anti-clerical legislation. Perhaps unconsciously he realized that this was the final parting of the ways between the monarchy and the new France, though it was to be a long time before he would admit it. Ironically, the godless Mirabeau's advice became important as never before. The King begged his wife to see the man.

At eight o'clock on the morning of Sunday 13 July, M. de Mirabeau, his hat over his eyes and muffled in a cloak, arrived in a chaise driven by a nephew disguised as a coachman, at a small gate into the park of Saint-Cloud. Before he entered he gave a letter to his nephew to deliver to the National Guard should he not return – he did not quite trust the Queen. He was met and conducted to a private garden. Then he heard footsteps. It was Marie Antoinette coming to meet him, alone. Later she told M. de La Marck how horrified she was by Mirabeau's hideous face. She recovered and, according to Mme Campan, informed him that she might be ill advised in consulting a man who had sworn to destroy monarchy but that 'a Mirabeau' was different. Apparently he was deeply flattered by 'a Mirabeau'. Nobody knows what they dis-

cussed, though it seems he begged her forgiveness for being a
principal architect of the Revolution – an apology accepted
'with an affability which charmed him'. It is also likely that he
warned her that her husband must be stronger if the
monarchy were to survive. What is certain is that she
enslaved this habitual exploiter of women. At the end of the
meeting he knelt to kiss her hand and, weeping, declared,
'Madame, the monarchy has been saved!' When he returned
to his carriage, he told his nephew in a voice shaking with
emotion, 'She is very great, she is very noble and she is very
unfortunate, but I am going to save her.' Henceforward the
Queen had no more faithful supporter. 'Nothing will stop
me,' he wrote shortly afterwards to La Marck. 'I will die
rather than not make good what I have promised.'

Mirabeau did his magnificent best. He thundered at the
National Assembly and the political clubs in such a way that
he seemed only a Patriot, indifferent to left or right. Even so
that evilly brilliant observer Marat realized that the man had
gone over, and even the most trusting wondered how he
could afford to give such lavish parties for his whores or buy
Buffon's wonderful library. Yet it was impossible to pin
down so skilful a politician and many people continued to
believe him.

In August he submitted a carefully thought-out plan to the
Tuileries. The King must first build up a proper party
organization, with funds and propaganda to attract ad-
herents. He should then leave Paris for a base in the provinces
– Rouen or Compiègne perhaps – from where he could
appeal to the nation as a whole. If necessary there would have
to be a civil war. But, as has been seen, the one step which
Louis could never be made to take was to start a civil war, and
in this he seems to have convinced his wife – no doubt she too
remembered Charles I. So straightforward a woman could
scarcely be expected to feel much confidence in such a
monstrous cynic, however much he might have assured her
of his devotion. She wrote angrily to Mercy-Argenteau that
Mirabeau's plan was 'mad from start to finish', and at that
stage she may well have been right.

Her strange champion continued to pose as a tribune of the people in the Assembly. He advised the King to give official posts to Jacobins – 'a Jacobin minister does not always stay a Jacobin'. His cynicism reached new heights in November when he roared at the Assembly that it must prosecute priests who would not take the oath to the Civil Constitution, while advising Louis that persecution of this sort would serve perfectly to rally all good Catholics behind the Crown and 'provoke resistance to the Assembly'. The King and Queen found it impossible to trust such a man, especially when it was obvious that he would do nothing which might damage his own popularity. However, they continued to pay him and to read his reports – at least they believed his warnings of disaster. It is not true, as is often alleged, that Marie Antoinette preferred Lafayette's advice. Admittedly she gave the latter frequent audiences, but this was simply because his military duties frequently brought him to the Tuileries. In fact she far from discounted Mirabeau and hoped to make use of his valuable talents when the monarchy regained power.

It says volumes for the growth of the Queen's political sense that she even hoped to make use of the talents of the scandalous but brilliant Bishop of Autun, M. de Talleyrand. There were rumours, though there is no direct evidence, that during 1790 agents of the court approached him and offered large sums of money for his assistance. When the Assembly considered offering him an official post, Marie Antoinette asked her doctor, M. Vicq d'Azyr, to try to rally support for the Bishop. News of this leaked out and caused so much ill feeling that it blocked Talleyrand's appointment.

The adviser who had most influence on Marie Antoinette was of course Axel von Fersen, who was living discreetly at Auteuil – not too far away from Paris or Saint-Cloud. She must certainly have discussed Mirabeau with him and he no doubt shared her distrust, even if he agreed that the royal family must escape from the capital. What survives of Fersen's correspondence with the Queen has suffered from the censorship and destruction by his great-nephew, Baron Klinckowström, a fanatical monarchist who venerated the memory of Marie Antoinette. Fersen's correspondence with his sister contains what appear to be many references to the Queen, though of course in these he was the soul of discretion. Most of those who have studied the strange romance are obsessed with the question of whether the couple ever slept together, a question which fascinated some of their contemporaries. With his usual vulgar omniscience Napoleon said, '*Fersen a couché avec la Reine*', but at the time he himself was an obscure and half-starved young gunner officer with no means of knowing. Someone who had at least the possibility of being better informed was the Minister for the Royal Household, the Comte de Saint-Priest. A former Grey Musketeer and a Knight of Malta, with a distinguished career in the army and in diplomacy behind him, Saint-Priest seems very much a *grand seigneur* of the old world, yet he was also a constitutionalist and a firm ally of Necker, which can hardly have endeared him to Marie Antoinette. Nor did he have much reason to like her – she had tried to replace him. In his memoirs he claims that Fersen was always at Saint-Cloud during 1790 and that he was nearly arrested by a guard in the small hours of the morning. Saint-Priest says he at once warned the Queen that such visits might damage her reputation seriously, but that she simply did not care. Saint-Priest also told his wife who was then in London, in a letter, that Fersen was exposing 'a certain person' to public contempt.

However, there is some reason to suspect that Saint-Priest was not telling the truth. He had even more reason to dislike Fersen than the Queen, since Fersen was Mme de Saint-Priest's lover. Moreover Fersen told his sister categorically in a letter of 28 June 1790 that he had not been to Saint-Cloud – although he indicates in the same letter that he may have been seeing Marie Antoinette at a secret, unidentified rendezvous. On the whole it is likely that Fersen did not go to Saint-Cloud but kept in touch by letter. Judging from the references to '*mon amie*', which he makes to his sister, it was plainly an emotional correspondence. On 4 April he writes, 'She is the most perfect being I know'; on 10 April, 'poor woman, she is an angel in her courage'; on 28 June, 'her courage is beyond everything'.

In the present writer's view the relationship always remained platonic. Fersen was unquestionably a sensualist, who found it amusing to seduce a friend's mistress, but it is more than probable that less distinguished females satisfied his physical needs. Post-Freudian biographers all tend to ignore Marie Antoinette's intensely devout personal religion which, as with her mother, was the real source of her strength. Nor is it irrelevant that while she was at the Tuileries the supremely respectable Campan was accused of taking a lover (most untruthfully) and that the Queen asked her sternly to give the man up – whatever Marie Antoinette was, she was not a hypocrite. On the other hand the lack of physical consummation does not mean that she did not love Fersen passionately.

Yet danger must have brought her increasingly close to her husband. On 28 June Fersen lamented, 'Matters here grow worse every day and God only knows how it will all end. The King and Queen are deeply unhappy.' In June titles and the traditional laws of inheritance were abolished. The steps against the Church have already been mentioned. On 14 July, the first anniversary of the storming of the Bastille, Louis had to take a public oath at a 'Feast of the Federation' in the Champs de Mars – 'I, the King of the French, do swear and declare that I will use all powers delegated to me by the state's constitutional law to maintain the constitution decreed by the National Assembly.' Mass was celebrated at this revolutionary coronation by Talleyrand, Bishop of Autun, the very man who had proposed the nationalization of the Church's property.

The Queen, tricolour ribbons in her hair, watched ostentatiously from a balcony of the École Militaire with her son. '*Chou d'amour*', as she called him with characteristic exuberance, had undoubtedly become the most important person in her life. She wrote to his former governess, the exiled Yolande de Polignac, how he and his sister 'are nearly always with me and are my consolation'. Louis-Charles had

by now grown used to the Tuileries, where he played happily
in the gardens. A fortnight before the ceremony in the
Champs de Mars he received 1,500 Bretons who had marched
down to Paris to swear their own allegiance – to his father.
He had been picking flowers on the palace terrace. 'The
pretty boy gave a flower as long as they lasted to every
Breton', says an English lady who was watching, 'and then
gathered lilac leaves, and for fear they should not last, tore
them in two and gave half a leaf apiece to the rest.'
Kucharski's portrait of him is of a charming and apparently
healthy child, yet even without the Revolution Louis-Charles
was already doomed. When he died four years later he was a
rickety little wreck, covered with ulcers and tumours. It is
inconceivable that his perceptive mother did not fear secretly
that he might have within him the seeds of the disease which
had killed his brother – in her letter to Mme de Polignac she
speaks significantly of daily walks 'which do him much
good'.

Marie Antoinette's own brother, the Emperor Josef, had
died in great pain but with much dignity at the beginning of
1790. 'He died in a manner worthy of myself,' she said
proudly when told of his death. Nevertheless 'the Queen's
grief was not excessive', Mme Campan tells us; 'she knew he
watched our troubles as Sovereign of Germany rather than as
brother to the Queen of France'. The new Emperor was their
brother Leopold II, until now Grand Duke of Tuscany, who
was one of the most gifted of all Habsburgs, flexible,
imaginative and far-sighted. But he would reign for only two
years. While she had been intimidated by Josef, Marie
Antoinette had at least understood him. She was not used to
corresponding with Leopold or asking his advice. He would
of course show himself a loyal brother but he had strange
ideas and even sympathized with liberals. In any case he was
preoccupied with putting his inheritance in order. The
change can only have increased the Queen's feeling of
isolation.

Almost all her biographers are impressed by Kucharski's
most regal Marie Antoinette of a year or so later (1791–92). It

Marie Antoinette in 1791, by Kucharski

portrays a notably mature face, puzzled but strong and determined. It is not the face of an introvert nor does it reveal insecurity, yet it is plainly that of someone who has thought a good deal. Not even the Queen's worst enemy could accuse such a woman of shallowness or frivolity. The worries and trials of her position were bringing out all her best qualities. The portrait does indeed look like that of a daughter of the Empress Maria Theresa.

The political situation was so bewildering that many people again thought that the 'Revolution' was over. In reality the Feast only made matters worse, feeding the general enthusiasm for change, in particular in the army. Mutinies on a serious scale broke out in garrisons all over France, stirred up by local political clubs. After a pitched battle, one at Nancy was put down by General the Marquis de Bouillé, who executed several men and sent forty Swiss to the galleys. His action was greeted with fury and, as so often, the Queen was blamed. There was a further rash of filthy pamphlets and this time – most ridiculously of all – she was actually credited with sleeping with Lafayette. At the Opéra the Parisians savagely booed an aria from *Iphigénie* in praise of a queen.

There were fresh fears for Marie Antoinette's life. A certain M. Rotondo announced he was going to kill her and got as far as the inner gardens of the Tuileries where she was known to take a daily walk; only the fact that rain had kept her indoors saved her. The Queen's doctor, M. Vicq d'Azyr, warned Mme Campan to guard against poisoning, giving her several antidotes and telling her to change Her Majesty's sugar each day. Marie Antoinette caught Campan changing the sugar and told her not to bother. 'Not a grain of poison will be used on me,' she said. 'The modern age employs calumny. Calumny kills people better than anything and it is by calumny that they will kill me.'

The Queen must have been heartened by increasingly vocal public sympathy, on however limited a scale. Nobles who remained in Paris made a point of being at the Tuileries to parade their loyalty, while at the theatre ladies wore bunches of royal lilies in their hair and even sported white

cockades. Many of them must formerly have enjoyed all the
nasty gossip directed at the Queen. Now they were loyal
enough. Mme Campan records an odd scene which occurred
at Saint-Cloud in the summer of 1790. One afternoon while
she and Marie Antoinette were at their needlework they
suddenly heard voices outside the château and, looking down
from a balcony, saw a group of about fifty people, 'women
both young and old, smartly dressed in country costume, old
chevaliers of St Louis, young Knights of Malta, and a few
priests'. In hushed tones they cheered the Queen – 'Courage,
Madame, good French people suffer for you and with you –
they are praying for you.' Then the little crowd went away as
quietly as possible.

In fact reactionaries throughout France were gathering,
especially in the south-east. A 'Plan of Languedoc' came to
nothing, though in May and June it caused bloody fighting at
Montauban and Nîmes. Much more serious was a scheme for
a rising in early December at Lyon. The 'French Salon' – a
club of 'Blacks', or extreme royalists – contacted the King,
proposing that he escape and join the rising. He refused. In
the event the plot collapsed and the ringleaders were arrested.
A detachment of noblemen from the Auvergne riding to
Lyon were warned in time and crossed the frontier instead.
Abroad an increasing number of *émigrés*, Artois at their head,
were urging foreign governments to invade France and put
down a movement which threatened the entire established
order of Europe.

Louis was incapable of profiting from any movement in
his favour. As Edmund Burke said of him, in a letter in mid-
1790, 'the King is heavy, inert, inexperienced, timid, without
resources'. Monsieur, who was determined to hang on till the
last possible moment and who spent his evenings in game
after game of whist with his brother, told Mirabeau that
Louis's weakness and indecision were barely credible, and
compared his character to 'oiled ivory balls which one tries in
vain to hold together'. To be fair, the King genuinely saw
himself as the father of his people and was horrified at the
thought of shedding their blood in a civil war. Marie

Antoinette, infinitely more virile, as Mirabeau said, and hampered by no such scruples, must have argued endlessly with him. She meant to save her children and their inheritance.

But events were forcing Louis's hand. As has been said he had already been deeply disturbed by the Assembly's Civil Constitution of the Clergy. Only at the end of August did he consent to sign it, though steps to make the priests swear allegiance to it were not taken until the following year. In September 1790 Necker, that discredited apostle of the Enlightenment, finally resigned in despair and went home to Switzerland. His protégé Saint-Priest also despaired and left for London. Lafayette – who was after all a professional soldier – had lost much of his popularity by supporting Bouillé's repression of the mutiny at Nancy; the Queen nevertheless continued to listen to him with exquisite courtesy, though long before Nancy she had observed, 'I see clearly that M. de Lafayette wishes to save us, but who is going to save us from M. de Lafayette?' Mirabeau was still trying to serve the monarchy by thundering at the Assembly, though he was increasingly suspect.

The last months of 1790 were characterized by rancour and uproar, made worse as the *assignats'* depreciation caused a vicious price rise. The bourgeoisie paraded their newly won equality with aggressive panache, its women wearing 'Liberty hats' and 'Constitutional jewellery'. *Le Mariage de Figaro* was not allowed to be performed in Marseilles theatres because of its emphasis on social distinctions.

In the autumn Edmund Burke published his *Reflections on the Revolution in France* and a French translation appeared almost at once. Premature and overdrawn, it immediately became a bible for counter-revolutionaries while infuriating progressives. Alas, Burke was to prove a true prophet. His famous lament for the indignities suffered by Marie Antoinette in 1789 – 'such disasters fallen upon her in a nation of gallant men' – provoked Tom Paine's graceful but fatuous riposte, 'He pities the plumage, but forgets the dying bird.'

By October 1790 at latest Marie Antoinette had persuaded

her husband that he must escape from Paris. Mirabeau was left out of the plan, the chief adviser being Fersen. While the King and Queen ignored Mirabeau's warning – in the scheme he had submitted in August – that Louis must on no account go near the frontier, they followed his advice in asking General de Bouillé for help. Bouillé was the right man. Although he had put down the Nancy mutineers with such severity, he was so popular with his troops that they confirmed him in his command by an election; his army was an oasis of order in a desert of increasing indiscipline. The General, originally a convinced Constitutionalist who had at first welcomed the Revolution, was growing uneasy; even so Louis had enough sense to reassure him that there was no intention of seeking assistance from any foreign government after the escape. Most unfortunately the King and Queen did not take up Mirabeau's suggestion that they should engineer Bouillé's transfer to a command near Paris – though the General might well have found his new troops less loyal and amenable. Instead they decided on a long, unescorted, secret journey to Bouillé's headquarters at Metz. Fersen began making the arrangements in December.

Funds variously estimated at between 12,000 and 120,000 francs were provided by a foreign power, the Order of Malta. The Knights' *chargé d'affaires* in Paris, the Chevalier d'Estourmel – who seems to have supplied the money – must have done so with the approval of the Prince and Grand Master at Valetta, His Most Eminent Highness Fra Camille de Rohan. (Ironically, Rohan was a nephew of the unhappy Cardinal of the Diamond Necklace.)

As early as 1789 Louis had written privately to his cousin Charles IV of Spain repudiating all concessions to the constitutionalists. He had also sent the Abbé de Fontbrune to ask both the Spanish King and the Emperor for money. As soon as the decision to escape was taken, the exiled M. de Breteuil was given full powers to negotiate with foreign governments. However the French King and Queen regarded most *émigrés* as a dangerous embarrassment. Marie Antoinette had no desire to be rescued by an army of revengeful nobles, the very people who were responsible for the monarchy's troubles. She and her husband intended to set up a new royal government at the little fortress town of Montmédy, not far from Metz and easily protected by Bouillé's army. The Assembly would have to obey Louis when he was supported by a congress of foreign powers. But, as Georges Lefebvre emphasizes, 'The Queen if not Louis thought monarchs who committed themselves to a congress would not hesitate to order an invasion should the Assembly balk.' Already, as in the previous year, the peasants of Champagne and Lorraine lived in dread of Austrian troops.

Events increasingly confirmed the Queen's opinion that France was no longer governable. Relations between Church and State reached breaking point in January 1791 when bishops and priests were ordered to swear allegiance to the Civil Constitution of the Clergy; all save four prelates (among them Talleyrand) refused as did most priests; within three months schismatic pastors were being installed forcibly in parishes throughout France, the vast majority of clergy remaining non-jurors. When in February 'Mesdames Tantes', Adelaide and Victoire, quietly departed for Rome they were pursued by National Guards and arrested in Burgundy, being only released by a special decree forced through the reluctant Assembly by Mirabeau. At the end of the same month several hundred noblemen armed with court- or hunting-swords descended on the Tuileries, on a pretext of protecting the King and Queen but intending to take them to Metz; Lafayette arrived and made Louis order them to surrender to the National Guard.

The old aunts had not fled simply because they knew of their nephew's intention to escape. It was also because they wanted to practise their religion in freedom – they were too pious to have anything to do with schismatic State priests or to deny the Pope's authority. They tried to persuade Madame Elisabeth to go with them, but Louis's sister preferred to stay with her brother even if it meant martyrdom. Mirabeau spent an entire night trying to bully the King and Queen's confessor, the curé of Saint-Eustache, into taking the oath to the State. Louis and Marie Antoinette thereupon found another non-juring confessor, but concealed his identity. The action of the President of the Assembly, as Mirabeau now was, shows how dangerous he thought the monarchy's attitude towards the new State Church.

A further alarm was the death of Mirabeau at the beginning of April – characteristically, he slept with two whores on the very last night of his life. Death may have saved him from imminent political defeat, as he was clearly beginning to lose his hold on the Assembly. He had grown increasingly ill, with bloodshot eyes bulging horribly out of a ghastly yellow face. During his last days the King sent constantly to his house to find out how he was. On his deathbed Mirabeau admitted how horrified he was at having contributed to such general ruin, and told Talleyrand despairingly, 'My friend, I take with me into the grave the last shreds of the monarchy.' Marie Antoinette was surprised to find that she was saddened by the news of his death; she now knew quite enough about politics to realize just how useful he could have been – indeed she wept. Such was the atmosphere that she wondered if he had been poisoned. But not even 'a Mirabeau' would have been able to save either the monarchy or the French Revolution itself.

By March 1791, if not earlier, the Queen was making her own preparations to depart. It has to be admitted that she showed herself not altogether practical in insisting on having complete new sets of clothes made for herself and the children, together with special dressing cases and other travelling equipment – though in fairness it must also be said that she had never had to be practical in her life. Unfortunately the Tuileries was full of spies – on 21 May a 'woman belonging to the wardrobe' would actually go to the Hôtel de Ville and report that the royal family was planning to escape. However, long before then Paris was full of alarming stories about the King's intentions, and also of an Austrian invasion. It had been noticed that the Queen's brother, Emperor Leopold, was beginning to mass troops in Belgium.

Mirabeau's forebodings about the royal family's recusant attitude on the religious question were dramatically confirmed barely a fortnight after his death. On Sunday 17 April – Palm Sunday – it was noticed that Louis did not go to Communion as usual, and the National Guardsmen refused to present arms as he left the chapel. When he announced his intention of leaving for Saint-Cloud the next day, for his summer holiday, there was uproar; Marat, in *L'Ami du Peuple*, shrieked that the King was leaving early in order to perform his Easter duties 'unconstitutionally'. Louis took no notice and sent his household ahead. However when he and Marie Antoinette got into their carriage to leave on 18 April, the National Guardsmen mutinied, refusing to allow the horses to be put in and shouted insults. Perhaps understandably the normally staid bourgeois who composed that corps were terrified that this was the first step in a counter-revolution, which would take away their new privileges and bring back the detested nobility. They regarded the King and Queen as hostages in case of intervention by angry foreign sovereigns. After two hours, during which Lafayette had alternately begged and abused his men, the royal family descended and went back into the palace.

As they did so Marie Antoinette told the mutineers in a loud voice, 'You must admit that we are no longer free.' She was not entirely displeased by such insulting treatment, even if on 20 April she wrote to Mercy-Argenteau 'our lives are no longer safe'; she says in the same letter 'what has just happened confirms us more than ever in our plans' – which, in plain language, meant that it had forced her pitifully indecisive husband to make up his mind when to go. Moreover she hoped that, when they did escape, the memory of the ugly scene in the Tuileries courtyard might do something to justify their action in the eyes of their more rational subjects.

With typical consideration the Queen realized that after her flight her ladies and gentlemen might be in considerable danger, and she told them to leave Paris, giving them money for travelling expenses. Among them was Mme Campan, in whom she confided her political plans. If Campan is telling the truth – Marie Antoinette would certainly not have bothered to deceive her – then they show sound political sense and even moderation. 'She assured me that the King was going to the frontier solely in order to negotiate with the Assembly, and would leave France only if his proposals and suggested programme did not have the effect he was hoping for. She was relying on a large group in the Assembly, many of whose members were, so she said, completely cured of their earlier enthusiasms.' The Queen did not conceal her obvious intention of going to Brussels to visit her brother Leopold but this does not mean that she wanted Louis to accompany her. She seems to have grasped that intervention by foreign troops was thoroughly undesirable – at any rate at this stage.

[9]
'This delicate operation'

I am quite aware of all the dangers and unpleasant
possibilities . . . but I would prefer to perish while
trying to save myself rather than let myself be crushed
and utterly destroyed through doing absolutely
nothing

Marie Antoinette

I can say nothing of my state of mind; we exist, that is
all

Marie Antoinette

ON 20 JUNE 1791 Louis XVI worked in his study,
apparently with his usual painstaking attention to detail,
giving his household their orders and receiving members of
the Assembly. He looked as amiably bovine and phlegmatic
as ever. After attending Mass the Queen was seen walking
with her children in the gardens of the Chaussée d'Antin. As
usual she and the King were joined at supper by Monsieur
and his wife. 'Don't upset me,' Marie Antoinette said to the
former, 'I don't want people to notice that I have been
crying.' At 11.15 p.m. she retired to bed. Her husband had
already made his ritual *coucher* and had said goodnight to his
courtiers.

Louis XVI waited till his *valet de chambre*, who was a spy,
had left the room. Then the King, going out through another
door, waddled down the corridors to a secret closet from
whence he emerged as a valet himself, in livery and a brown

wig – in the service of the Baronne de Korff (a Russian friend
of Fersen's), Marie Antoinette's alias. He had no trouble in
leaving the Tuileries, despite sentinels, or in reaching the
Place du Petit Carrousel. Here Axel was waiting in a quiet
corner with a large cab, disguised as its driver. Alas, there
was no sign of the Queen.

Marie Antoinette, dressed as a governess, had first been
delayed by a sentry on duty at the top of the staircase by
which she intended to leave the palace. Fortunately the man
was marching up and down and eventually she nerved herself
to dash on tiptoe to the bottom of the stairs when his back
was turned. But then she and her escort – one of the
Bodyguard, M. de Malden – lost their way in the rabbit
warren of streets just outside the Tuileries. Midnight was
striking when at last they reached Fersen's cab in the Place du
Petit Carrousel, with the 'coachman' and 'valet' in an agony
of suspense. Madame Elisabeth, Mme de Tourzel and the
children had arrived long before. This lost half-hour would
be the ruin of all their plans. Yet Fersen then proceeded to
waste still more time by taking too discreet a route and then
failing to find the berlin in which the 'Korff' family were to
travel. It was almost two o'clock in the morning before he
did so, a few miles outside Paris on the road to Metz. Shortly
after, the Count and his passengers said an emotional good-
bye to each other, Fersen abandoning the little party to seek
his own safety in Brussels.

The failure of the escape has been in part attributed to the
berlin. This vehicle resembled a private and luxurious stage-
coach, a vast 'six-in-hand', green and yellow outside with
cushions and curtains of white taffeta within, taking six
people inside and three on top. Like a careful mother, Marie
Antoinette had insisted on special equipment for the long
journey, including cooking stoves and two leather chamber-
pots. It should be emphasized that a not inconsiderable
number of families, bourgeois as well as noble, possessed
such conveyances. In the words of Mme de Tourzel, 'there
was nothing remarkable about it, despite what has often been
said. It was simply a large berlin, very like my own, though

made more expensively and with an unusual amount of conveniences inside'. The doors did not bear the royal arms, as has frequently been claimed. Even so, not only was it accompanied by a smaller carriage carrying ladies-in-waiting but the disguised members of the Bodyguard who drove it wore livery which, if not exactly regal, was certainly eye-catching among less fortunate members of society. Worst of all was the fact that its six horses had to be changed at least every fifteen miles. It was slow as well as conspicuous. Two fast light carriages would probably have ensured success – Monsieur, who fled the same night, used a more modest vehicle and had no trouble in reaching the Belgian frontier and safety.

Yet the King did not even tell his coachmen to drive fast, although there was a long and dangerous journey ahead. The berlin would have to cover many miles before it reached Montmédy and General de Bouillé and his army. Admittedly, at Pont-Sommevesle, just after Châlons-sur-Marne, a troop of hussars under the Duc de Choiseul would be waiting, and this escort would be reinforced as they went further into territory under Bouillé's command. But Pont-Sommevesle was more than a hundred miles from Paris and Montmédy was well over two hundred.

However, Louis was bursting with optimism about the success of 'this delicate operation' (Fersen's words). After leaving Meaux – towards six a.m. – he told his wife, 'I shall be a new man once I've got my arse in the saddle again', a favourite phrase of his great predecessor Henri IV. Having eaten an enormous picnic breakfast, he then read her the letter which he had left behind for the Assembly. In it he stated that he had been forced to make many concessions against his will and that useless sacrifices had been imposed upon Frenchmen, including loss of property, danger to their lives 'and anarchy suffered throughout the realm'. He, the King himself, had lost his freedom – he complained of the insult done to him at Easter, when he had been prevented from going to Saint-Cloud. Nevertheless he insisted in his letter that he had no intention of leaving France, but was simply removing himself from the troubled air of Paris.

Marie Antoinette was far from being so sanguine. A month earlier, writing to Mercy-Argenteau about the projected escape, she had admitted that she was only too well aware 'of all the dangers and unpleasant possibilities' in the event of failure, though prepared to risk them rather than let herself be destroyed by doing nothing. But she had sufficient self-control to joke with Viennese acidity, 'I wonder if M. de Lafayette's head is still on his shoulders?' It was about eight a.m.

This was the hour when the royal family's absence was discovered. When Lafayette rushed to the Tuileries he found it surrounded by a furious crowd which roared at him – a National Guard called Danton bellowed at him, 'We want the King or your head.' It soon stormed into the palace. At nine a.m. there was an emergency session of the Assembly, which ordered Louis's arrest – though the document used a more tactful word. Jacobin extremists moved a motion that he had abdicated by running away and asked if there was any point in having a successor. Pictures of the King and Queen were torn down throughout the capital. Mme Roland, the future heroine of the Girondins, wrote breathlessly, 'with cannon roaring amid wild commotion', that 'the King and Queen have fled; the shops are all closed, everything is in uproar. Lafayette is almost certainly implicated. This means war.' At noon agents left Paris in pursuit of the fugitives. One, Bayon, soon found the way they had gone – all too many people remembered the berlin and its occupants – and rode after them like the wind. He himself was followed by M. de Romeuf, an aide-de-camp to Lafayette, with the warrant for Louis's arrest – though secretly intending to prevent it at all costs.

Meanwhile the berlin was trundling along at a leisurely pace. The King could not be stopped from talking to peasants about the harvest while the horses were being changed. When one of the bodyguard respectfully advised him to keep out of sight, he replied fatuously, 'I sense that my journey is safe from any accident. We are out of danger.'

When they reached Chaintrix at two o'clock that afternoon, Louis was recognized by the posting-master, a devout monarchist, who insisted on giving the royal family a meal. Still more time was lost when the harness broke and had to be repaired. When they set off again at three p.m. they were two and a half hours overdue at Pont-Sommevesle, which was still three hours away. Incredibly, Louis still felt no sense of urgency.

Matters were very different at Pont-Sommevesle. Here Choiseul's hussars had attracted some most unfortunate attention. The excuse for their presence was that they were there to guard a consignment of government bullion which would arrive shortly. The local peasants did not believe it, suspecting that they had come to collect the rents of the local landowner, the Duchesse d'Elboeuf. Soon an angry mob gathered, several hundred strong and armed with pitchforks. At four a.m., when the 'bullion' was three and a half hours overdue, Choiseul's nerve broke. He led his cavalry off in the direction of Varennes, and sent a message to other detachments behind him that there was no sign that the 'bullion' would arrive today and that they would be given 'new orders tomorrow'.

Only half an hour after Choiseul's withdrawal the berlin left Châlons without incident and Marie Antoinette cried, 'We are saved'. But when they arrived at Pont-Sommevesle at six p.m. they found no sign of the expected escort and, for the first time, began to feel uneasy. However, the peasants had also left and at Sainte-Ménehould, not far on, there would surely be another reliable detachment of Bouillé's men. But here too M. d'Andoins had told his men to fall out after receiving Choiseul's message, and when the berlin arrived only half an hour later he was too nervous of the local National Guard to reassemble them. At the next village, Clermont, the escort-commander, Colonel Damas, had also dismissed his men and also decided against reassembling them. After all, just beyond the next post, Varennes, General de Bouillé's troops were waiting in sufficient strength to deal with any opposition. The berlin rolled on. It reached

Varennes at ten-thirty p.m. Safety lay a mere few hundred yards away, just beyond the other side of the little town.

But at Pont-Sommevesle the posting-master Drouet, an aggressive *petit bourgeois* of classic revolutionary mould, had recognized Louis XVI. One account says that he did so from the face on the gold *louis d'or*. He had galloped through the forest, ahead of the berlin, to alert the municipality and its National Guard that the King was escaping and would try to pass through their town. First he had the bridge which led out of Varennes blockaded by a wagon-load of furniture, then he and the National Guardsmen waited by a narrow arch over the main road. It was precisely eleven p.m. when the berlin went under the arch and was halted. The local officials accepted the Baronne de Korff's passport and were ready to wave her on, but Drouet insisted that her party must wait until daybreak. Soon a man who had lived at Versailles confirmed Drouet's recognition.

Louis's better, if rarely exhibited, qualities now showed themselves and nearly saved the day. Emotionally he explained to the little local dignitaries why he had escaped from Paris, 'where I might have been murdered', embracing their leaders and obtaining a promise to escort him to Montmédy the following morning. He was not being excessively optimistic – for once – in hoping that Bouillé's soldiers would burst in at any moment. But at five a.m. Bayon, the Assembly's agent, came instead, followed a few minutes later by M. de Romeuf who, in tears produced the warrant for the royal family's arrest. By now a crowd estimated at several thousand had come into the town and were shrieking, 'Bring them back to Paris!'

Also in Varennes was Choiseul. He had his hussars and a number of spare horses. With considerable enterprise he had forced himself into the house where the royal family were confined and told the King that it was still possible for him to escape on horseback – Louis holding the Dauphin on one mount, Marie Antoinette and the rest of the party on others. His hussars would cut a way through. The King, always a sentimental idealist, had refused with the words, 'One would have to possess the soul of a monster to shed one's subjects' blood.' It was then that Bayon and Romeuf appeared on the scene.

General de Bouillé was so near that he arrived with the Royal German Regiment on the river bank opposite Varennes at seven-thirty-five a.m. Louis knew that the General must be near, though he did not realize that the river at the other end of the town was too deep to ford and that the blockaded bridge would appear a formidable obstacle. He played for time, asking for a meal – which he found impossible to eat. A lady-in-waiting gallantly pretended to have an epileptic fit, without making much impression. The Queen tried to persuade the wife of the town's law officer, Mme Sauce, to make her husband delay their departure; the woman, horribly frightened, replied that she didn't want M. Sauce's head cut off, and that anyway the King would be mad to give up a job worth 24 million a year. (In the event poor Sauce's head was cut off, for allowing Louis to burn some papers.) Outside, not only had the entire National Guard of the district gathered by dawn but also a shrieking mob, 10,000 strong – the latter had just torn a local nobleman, M. de Dampierre, off his horse and clubbed him to death in a ditch for coming to pay his respects to the King. Bayon went out again and again to harangue it, returning each time to say slyly that he could not control such bloodthirsty peasants much longer.

At last Louis gave in, and at about seven-thirty a.m. the dejected little party climbed back into the berlin. Five minutes later General de Bouillé arrived with the Royal German Regiment on the river bank opposite Varennes. Helplessly he watched his King and Queen depart – he did not know that there was another, unblocked bridge across the river, just a little way along, over which he could easily have intercepted them. Then Bouillé grimly turned his horse's bridle and rode off into exile.

Despite the yells of the mob which accompanied them, brandishing pieces of M. de Dampierre on pitchforks, Marie Antoinette fell asleep. She had travelled many miles over rough roads in a vehicle with iron-shod wheels and since then had been kept up for a second night running, while in any case she must have been exhausted by excitement and fear. However, the Queen quickly awoke again, to find herself in a procession even more dreadful than that from Versailles in October 1789. This time it would take four days to reach Paris, and in stifling hot weather. Moreover Mme de Tourzel says that the mob's feet raised so much dust on the road that it seemed as though the berlin was travelling through a fog – it caked the faces of those inside as well as outside. From moment to moment there were fresh howls of hatred, and once a man leant through the berlin's windows and spat in Louis's face. The three members of the Bodyguard, who were now handcuffed together on top, were in constant danger of being dragged down and cut to pieces. The party did not get to bed until they reached Châlons at two o'clock in the morning after leaving Varennes. Next day another mob arrived from Rheims, loudly demanding the Queen's liver. At Épernay a man tried to shoot her and she was jostled and threatened, singled out as the real villainess of the plot to abandon such loving subjects. Nevertheless she still had quite enough courage to preserve her dignity, insisting on hearing Mass in the mornings, and always lowering the blind before eating, despite howls of disapproval, and not raising it until she wished to throw the bones out of the window; seemingly to herself, she remarked, 'We will show spirit to the very end.'

We know how Marie Antoinette behaved from the account of M. Jérome Pétion. He was one of three deputies sent by the Assembly to meet the returning party en route, which they did an hour after the berlin had left Épernay. One of Pétion's companions, the former Marquis de Latour-Maubourg, was a man of the right but the other, M. Barnave, was a progressive like Pétion – so much so that he was popularly known as '*Le Tigre*'. Maubourg chivalrously got into the little carriage to protect the ladies-in-waiting, but Pétion and Barnave insisted on travelling inside the berlin although there was no proper room. Even so, although the manners of Pétion left much to be desired – he was constantly asking Madame Elisabeth to refill his wine glass – Barnave was deeply embarrassed at sitting next to the Queen. With her quick intuition, she soon sensed that this handsome young man with the retroussé nose might be won over. Indeed, as it turned out he was not only a romantic but no longer a progressive. She teased him, joking to Pétion, 'Do tell M. Barnave to stop gazing out of the window whenever I ask him questions.' The 'Tiger' was enslaved by such condescension. Nonetheless, during the journey, although he spoke a good deal to her, apart from the occasional remark Marie Antoinette appeared to listen to him without much interest and even with indifference – or so it seemed to the watchful Pétion, not the only man to underestimate her.

At Meaux she somehow managed to talk to Barnave alone. He told the Queen that the monarchy had been so badly defended that he had often felt like offering his services. Later she surprised Mme Campan by the excellent opinion she had formed of Barnave on the road from Varennes, although he had previously been regarded by the Tuileries as a dangerous extremist. This extraordinary new friendship was to have important political consequences.

The return to Paris was still more terrifying than anything already experienced on the journey. Even Louis XVI was apprehensive, constantly assuring the deputies that he had never had any intention of leaving France. More subtly, the Queen begged their protection not for herself or her husband but for the three fettered members of the Bodyguard on top of the berlin. At the outskirts of the capital yet another howling mob had gathered, including a large female contingent who hurled themselves on the National Guardsmen now accompanying the party and whose threats were mainly aimed at Marie Antoinette – the air rang with shouts of 'Bitch! Slut! Whore!' When, in an attempt to arouse sympathy, she held her son up to the carriage window, women screamed, 'Everyone knows the fat pig isn't his father!' Some of the mob climbed on to the berlin, even on to the horses. Then the National Guardsmen started to quarrel with each other, drawing their swords and bayonets.

Eager to defend his newly discovered heroine, Barnave leant out and warned the Guardsmen's Colonel, 'You will answer with your head for the royal family's safety!' The Dauphin began to cry, while the King looked so bewildered and dazed as to seem drunk. Somehow the National Guardsmen shook off their frenzied rabble and entered Paris. It was Saturday afternoon, and within the city walls a strange calm prevailed. The royal party was driven towards the Tuileries by a roundabout route through menacingly silent crowds; instead of presenting arms, soldiers reversed them as though on a funeral parade and not a single man raised his hat as his sovereign passed – placards warned 'Whoever cheers the King will be flogged: Whoever boos him will be hanged.' However, just before the berlin reached the palace, uproar again broke out and a determined attempt was made to pull down the three members of the Bodyguard, who were mistaken for 'friends of the Queen' – they were only saved by the escort's bayonets. At last the party drove into the Tuileries courtyard and safety.

Inside, the berlin was met by M. de Lafayette in a plumed hat, riding a splendid charger and beaming idiotically, who asked smugly for Louis's orders. The King replied, laughing, 'I'm much more at your orders than you are at mine.' With less dignity he also told him that during his outing he had come to realize that all France shared Lafayette's opinions. Marie Antoinette – whose very bonnet was clogged with dust – did not even try to hide her irritation and ignored the man as she swept into the palace. Within she was greeted by lines of bowing courtiers, as though she had never left, and the evening meal was ready as usual.

Nonetheless the Queen saw immediately that she was surrounded by even more spies than ever. She at once wrote to Mme Campan. 'I am dictating this from my bath, into which I have just thrown myself, to refresh myself at least physically. I can say nothing of my state of mind; we are alive, that is all.' It was a reasonable comment. Yet, with her usual concern for a friend's well-being, she warned Campan not to come back to Paris until she received a letter from her indicating that it was safe. When Mme Campan returned a month later, she noticed with horror how her mistress's already whitening hair had turned 'as completely white as that of a woman of seventy'.

Marie Antoinette also wrote to Fersen, telling him not to worry. 'Don't be disturbed, I'm going to be all right. The Assembly wants to treat us well.' (Barnave must have reassured her.) She also warned her friend not to write to her or to come to Paris as his part in the escape was known. The following day she again wrote to him, but this time she begs him to write – 'I want to know desperately that you too are all right.' She repeats that he must not worry about her. 'I can only tell you that I love you . . . I cannot live without writing to you. Good-bye, most beloved and most loving of men. All my heart goes out to you.'

Fersen had been waiting in Brussels. When he received news of the royal family's arrest at Varennes, he was plunged into the deepest anguish, sending frantic letters to his father and to his King – even the jealous Gustavus III was roused to fury against the French. But for several months, with tactless if justifiable caution, he dared not write to the Queen. No doubt his curious temperament luxuriated in such misery. As will be seen, his silence hurt the poor woman deeply at a time when she needed as much support as possible.

Yet Marie Antoinette never blamed her most self-centred of lovers for the failure of her attempted escape. According to Mme Campan, the Queen said it was all the fault of Baron de Goguelat, one of the three members of the Bodyguard; he had underestimated the length of the journey, he had mishandled the hussars at Varennes, and he had foolishly told her excessively humane husband that cutting a way through their captors meant bloodshed. Consciously or unconsciously, she was trying to exonerate the real culprit, Axel von Fersen. He cannot be blamed enough. Responsibility for overall planning had been his, he had countenanced the berlin and ostentatious liveries and – fully aware of Louis XVI's indecisiveness and inability to deal with the unexpected, as he had seen at Versailles in October 1789 – he had not stayed with the party.

The position in which the French monarchy found itself was scarcely promising. By trying to escape, Louis had antagonized, even disgusted, most Frenchmen. 'Here will be a whole nation disturbed by the folly of one man,' wrote Tom Paine, and of 'a wretch who has dishonoured himself'; by now the English Jacobin was referring to 'Louis Capet'. The Constituent Assembly suspended the King and appointed seven committees to investigate the affair. Although one of those Americans who love royalty, Mr Gouverneur Morris informed President Washington: 'It would not be surprising if such a dolt as this were to lose his throne.' For the time being Louis and his family were prisoners in the Tuileries. It was a decorous confinement, during which full court ceremonial was observed, though officers entered the Queen's bedroom several times a night to make sure she was still there.

Yet Louis XVI had reason to hope that he would survive as King, if not as absolute monarch. The Assembly had not finished drafting its new Constitution and a majority of deputies could not imagine France as a republic – even Pétion, during the return from Varennes, had admitted that the French were not ready for one. And no substitute monarch was available. Orléans was in Paris again, but completely discredited. (Officially changing his name to 'M. Philippe Egalité' impressed nobody – everyone knew that in London he had forgotten all about the Revolution and spent his time on whores, gambling and horses and in drinking himself into a stupor.) The committees of investigation were instructed to find that the King had been 'abducted' and was therefore innocent. Most deputies hoped he would accept the Constitution when it was ready and obediently play his new role as constitutional monarch. After all he had been taught a harsh lesson.

If only Louis XVI had possessed a spark of leadership and the capacity of forming a King's party, he might well have exploited such a situation. He might even have regained most of his powers, as the guarantor of the bourgeois Revolution. He did nothing. Napoleon commented afterwards that retaining Louis as the sovereign was 'entrusting the ship in the midst of a tremendous storm to a pilot no longer capable of sailing her, was asking the crew to mutiny in the name of the public safety, and inviting anarchy'.

But if the King was incapable of action, his wife was ready to take his place. Through a trusted courtier, General the Chevalier de Jarjayes – husband of one of her ladies – she swiftly contacted her promising new acquaintance, young M. Barnave. In a careful letter, with names in cypher, written less than a week after her enforced return to the Tuileries, Marie Antoinette told the Chevalier: 'I want you to get in touch with [Barnave] for me and tell him how taken I was by his talents, which I recognized at once during the two days he was with us, and that I would very much like to hear from him what we ought to do.' Like the calculating woman she had become, she added, 'After considerable thought since our return about the man's strength, ability and intelligence, I have reached the conclusion that it would be of the utmost value to start a correspondence with him, always of course on the understanding that I am completely frank about my own views.' As instructed, Jarjayes showed the letter to Barnave, who was enraptured. Like Mirabeau before him, he promised he would save both Queen and monarchy. Like Mirabeau too, it seemed no idle boast. Barnave's faction was then perhaps the most influential in the entire Assembly.

The flight to Varennes and its failure had in fact doomed the King and his consort, but this was not apparent until the middle of 1792. At the time Marie Antoinette herself clearly recognized it as a disaster, though far from irredeemable. As always she refused to admit defeat. Moreover in the midst of the débâcle she had managed to recruit a most valuable ally. All the terrors and humiliations of the dreadful journey back had impaired neither her courage nor her determination.

10

The Tuileries: Act Two

Une femme bien discrète, en verité

Beaumarchais, *Le Mariage de Figaro*

We tried, Madame

Antoine Barnave

DURING her last year at the Tuileries Marie Antoinette tried to transform herself into a professional politician. She was of only average intelligence and pitifully handicapped by lack of education and experience, even more by having such a woefully inadequate dummy for a husband. Her friend Fersen had no political judgement whatever and was far too wrapped up in his neuroses. In fact both men were liabilities rather than supports. She had to rely entirely on herself. Yet at home she manipulated the enslaved Barnave to considerable effect and others as well, showing herself both practical and flexible, while in foreign affairs, controlling or bypassing the impossible Louis, she evolved a policy which was at any rate coherent. If she was not exactly a Talleyrand, it is grossly unfair to dismiss her efforts as 'female meddling'. And her coolness was always remarkable in a situation which deteriorated with horrifying rapidity.

For more than a year after the return from Varennes there was a semblance of monarchy, of '*démocratie royale*'. There

were convinced Constitutional Royalists even among the
Girondins – the rising party, ostensibly republican. Many
politicians continued to regard the Crown as the key to
France.

By the time the indomitable Campan returned to her
mistress at the end of August 1791, the harsher restrictions
on the royal family had been relaxed. The doors were no
longer locked on them, while the King was treated with
much more respect. This was largely due to the knowledge
that the Assembly had nearly completed its wonderful new
Constitution, of which there were great hopes. During her
semi-imprisonment the Queen had actually found some
encouragement, discovering a surprising number of secret
sympathizers among the National Guards, who tried to make
life in the Tuileries less disagreeable by ignoring the
restrictions as far as possible. Nonetheless Marie Antoinette
was still very shaken. Much of her sorrow was due to
Fersen's strange silence. However, her mind was also full of
another man.

M. Antoine Barnave was a Protestant lawyer from
Dauphiné, who had been prominent in French politics since
helping to organize the uproar at Grenoble in 1788. A good
deal of his revolutionary sentiments stemmed from being
snubbed by the local nobility. Although a bourgeois, he had
the manners of a nobleman (indeed the Grenoble Parlement
had waived its noble qualifications to let him join) and was
romantically good-looking, despite his snub nose and stocky
build. He was still only thirty. If her interest in him was
principally political, the Queen certainly found Barnave
attractive. She astonished Campan by the enthusiasm with
which she spoke of him – 'respectful delicacy . . . considerate
. . . full of talent and feeling'. She did not even blame him for
being a revolutionary. 'Understandable pride' had naturally
made him want to change the system which blocked the
career of a young man of his gifts simply because he was a
commoner and a Protestant. He had not betrayed the
monarchy like so many liberal nobles whose duty was to
defend the Crown. Such traitors could never be forgiven. But

'if we ever regain power, Barnave's pardon is written in our heart'.

Marie Antoinette meant what she said. Had the Bourbon monarchy been restored in the way she wanted, Barnave's talents might well have made up for his lack of quarterings. Time and again she returns to her detestation of the French nobility. She disliked them all, whether conservative or liberal: they were equally to blame for starting the Revolution. It is often forgotten how many aristocrats were liberals until the final destruction of the constitutional monarchy. Up to the very end, a surprising number of the most famous names of old France were to be found at the Tuileries – la Rochefoucauld, Noailles, Choiseul, Rohan-Chabot. (Some of their descendants are still discreetly rich and eminent in modern France.) It is not without significance that she made no new friends among them. By now she had an almost personal feud with the great *noblesse* of France.

Barnave was the leader of a trio of influential and ebulliently radical deputies who were popularly known, even by Marie Antoinette, as the Triumvirs. His two allies, MM. Alexandre de Lameth and Duport, were at first inclined to dismiss the Queen as frivolous and unstable but were swiftly converted. Through her they hoped to control the King.

As a result of Varennes a republican element had emerged in the Assembly which demanded the abolition of the monarchy. At the same time the right announced, in a suicidal gesture, that while Louis was a prisoner they could not sit in the Assembly. Only left-wing moderates remained to defend the Crown, among them the Triumvirs. Barnave made a magnificent speech in support of the monarchy, which won the day – he made the particularly telling point that, 'If people want to go on destroying, what aristocracy will there be left to pull down, except ordinary property owners?' He then wrote to Marie Antoinette, insisting she must co-operate with the Constitutional Royalists, and must be seen to do so by persuading Emperor Leopold to accept the Constitution when completed and by persuading Monsieur and the *émigrés* to return to France. 'Any other path leads to ruin.' He warned her that if she did not support their policy the Triumvirs would have to abandon her. Meanwhile he maintained his reputation as a progressive by telling the Assembly that the property of *émigrés* should be confiscated if the owners did not return before a specified date.

Marie Antoinette sent Barnave a second letter. Yes, she would write to the Emperor. On the other hand, *émigrés* had already had too much of their fortunes taken from them – it seemed unlikely they would return. She was anxious about Louis's position under the new Constitution. Would he be 'inviolable'? Barnave replied, reassuring her about the King's proposed status and promising her that the Triumvirs' policy was bound to succeed, though repeating that if Louis did not support it the Triumvirs would have to oppose him 'for their own safety and for the public good'.

On Sunday 17 July the Jacobins staged a huge demonstration in the Champs de Mars, demanding an end to monarchies. Lafayette and his men were waiting for them. Someone shot at him with a pistol, whereupon his men opened fire, killing fifty of the crowd. It was the first time since the Revolution had begun that troops had dispersed a Parisian mob. The Jacobins were terrified and their leaders went into hiding.

This made Marie Antoinette believe that the Constitutional Royalists were well in control of the situation, and that there was nothing to fear from republicans. On 20 July she wrote another shrewdly flattering letter to Barnave, asking to be in closer touch with the Triumvirs and requesting regular advice on matters of State. Delighted, he replied, repeating his earlier demands and his perfectly sincere opinion that 'the Revolution must be brought to an end'. She reciprocated with a further letter, asking for a draft to be sent to the Emperor at Vienna and suggesting a meeting with the Triumvirs. Barnave forwarded a draft, reiterating that the monarchy must on no account depart from his group's policy – if she supported it she would again be Queen of France in the most real sense, with the 'homage of a mighty people'. She answered that she thought his draft excellent and, after copying it, would have it delivered to Vienna. She added that she was impressed by Barnave's frankness.

The Queen herself was being considerably less than frank. She sent the letter drafted by the Triumvirs to Vienna, but at the same time wrote to Mercy-Argenteau telling him to advise the Emperor to ignore it. For this she has been accused of abandoning the monarchy's last hope. In fact she was behaving like any other politician – what can be forgiven in a Talleyrand or a Napoleon is condemned in a Queen. Much of this prejudice may be ascribed to her sex. Even before the Revolution Frenchmen disapproved violently of queens or royal mistresses – the only women who had any political power – interfering in matters of State; Catherine de Medici, Anne of Austria and Mme de Pompadour had all been detested for doing so. France had never had a female absolute monarch, like those in the Empire, Russia or Sweden, since the Salic Law made it impossible for a woman to become head of State. The French of the 1790s disliked all female politicians; writing of Mme Roland, Georges Lefebvre says that 'active participation by a woman in politics was at that time ridiculed and her presence only weakened her party'. Indeed Marie Antoinette was the one serious female politician of the entire revolution, Mme Roland being merely a pretentious little salon intriguer. The Queen demonstrated a far more realistic assessment of the situation than the Triumvirs. She saw from the first that even if she had wanted a constitutional monarchy, it could not possibly succeed. In August she told Mercy-Argenteau that France was on the verge of complete anarchy, incapable of producing a government which could restore order. 'The army is lost, no money is left,' she explained, 'and there is nothing to restrain the armed rabble.' The only salvation was intervention by foreign troops. Until it came she would try to temporize by appearing to support the Constitutional Royalists. However, she could not see that ironically she was making her husband take the course of negotiating with both sides which had been the ruin of his *doppelgänger* Charles I. Yet if it was a policy of despair, it was at least a policy.

It had to be admitted that such a policy was also a terrifying gamble. She knew very well that the chances of failure were extremely high. But it is likely that to some extent she was both a fatalist and a pessimist – the loss of her father and her sister at an impressionable age, the miseries of her early married life and, above all, losing two children, together with the suspicion that her surviving son was diseased, can scarcely have inclined her to optimism. On the other hand she never allowed herself to be overwhelmed for one moment by either fatalism or pessimism, countering them by an unquenchable hope which she derived from her increasingly intense spiritual life.

It is only fair to point out that Marie Antoinette genuinely liked Barnave. She believed that he had a role to play not merely in the immediate present, but also when the monarchy had recovered its proper position. Her liking for him nearly made her betray her hand. Having offered the Triumvirs the bait of her husband's full support in return for strengthening his powers in the new Constitution, and having seen them swallow it, she saw very clearly that, since they had now cut themselves off irreparably from the republicans, they could not hope to survive without Louis. The same day that she wrote to Mercy-Argenteau about the desperate condition of France, she had also sent a letter to Barnave threatening to withdraw royal support for the Triumvirs if they did not make good their promise of insisting on 'the monarch's just and lawful rights'. Barnave and his friends were thunderstruck by her tone, replying that she was being most unfair and reminding her that she had asked them for an alliance. She quickly backed down, with flattering diplomacy. Reassured, the Triumvirs finalized the Constitution, sending a copy to her. She told Mercy-Argenteau what she thought of the document – 'an impractical absurdity' – while soothing Barnave by declaring most untruthfully, 'there are very real advantages in the Constitution for both King and monarchy'. She also made a show of co-operating by preparing a tactful speech for Louis to deliver when he gave his public assent.

In fact by now she was increasingly urging the necessity of an 'armed congress' of foreign powers intervening to restore her husband's authority. Three days before her letter to Barnave approving his Constitution she had again expressed her true feelings to Mercy-Argenteau, with brutal realism. 'What we must do is to trick them and make them trust us, so that one day we will be able to defeat them.' She admitted she was beginning to find the strain almost unbearable – 'It is simply not possible to go on living like this.' What alarmed her was not the burden of pretending to support Barnave and his allies, but the prospect – which Barnave was incapable of seeing – of a much more radical revolution.

Beyond question her attitude towards the *émigrés* was far more objective than that of the Triumvirs, who hoped for their repentance and return as a useful public relations exercise. She knew they would never come back and indeed she had nothing but contempt for 'the cowards who have abandoned us', for traitors who had precipitated the Revolution, and who would only try to impose the oligarchic neo-feudalism of the *revolte nobilaire* if they managed to return. She spoke bitterly of a 'confused and selfish' party at Coblenz, of 'evil talk and evil ambitions', and nowadays referred to her brother-in-law Monsieur as 'Cain'. She was desperately anxious that these people should not accompany the longed-for army of intervention and salvation, writing to Prince Esterházy that 'their appearance in this country would mean our losing everything'.

If Axel was far away, Marie Antoinette was now able to find support from her own sex. She had been woefully lacking in female company. Despite her loyalty and trustworthiness, Campan was really no more than an upper servant, while the women friends of her youth had by now decamped *en masse*. Such ladies-in-waiting as Mmes de Tourzel, de Mackau and de La Roche-Aymon were unquestionably devoted but scarcely kindred spirits. However in the autumn of 1791, to her surprise and delight, she received a letter from Marie de Lamballe announcing her wish to return to court. The Princess had long ago left France for the safety of

London and was now comfortably installed among fellow refugees at Aix-la-Chapelle. The Queen, as has been seen, had no illusions at all about the dangers which threatened the royal family. Although obviously longing to see her again, she wrote to Marie that she must on no account come back. Mme de Lamballe was now in her forties, very middle-aged in appearance and oddly spinsterish for a widow, just as silly as ever; still excessively nervous and timid, still capable of fainting at the sight of a plate of prawns, she continued to shriek like a peacock when frightened. She herself was hysterically alarmed about the monarchy's future, panic-stricken by more and more apocalyptic forecasts from the *émigrés* around her. She realized perfectly well that the new France had no room for princesses – it is not impossible that she had a premonition of the horrible fate which awaited her. Nevertheless she possessed quite extraordinary courage. She made her will, then crossed the frontier and went straight to the Tuileries. Marie Antoinette received her rapturously, installing her in a flat in the Pavillon de Flore.

For all her silliness Marie de Lamballe must have been an enormous strength and comfort to the Queen, especially as her sister-in-law could occasionally be tiresome. While spiritually a tower of strength, Madame Elisabeth's political views were those of the blindest reaction. Marie Antoinette wrote wearily that she 'is most indiscreet, surrounded by intriguers and so slavishly obedient to her brothers over the frontier that it is quite impossible for us to discuss affairs without quarrelling all day long'. This was certainly an exaggeration, since both women were clearly devoted to each other, but plainly there was some reason to grumble. It also underlines how much more practical and realistic the Queen had become in her own views.

At long last the Assembly, momentarily dominated by a strange alliance between Barnave and Lafayette – formerly bitter enemies but now friends by necessity in a new grouping of the right called the Feuillants – completed its Constitution. With hindsight one can see that it was doomed from the start. The three functions of sovereignty –

legislative, executive and judicial – were kept entirely separate from one another. The 'Legislative Assembly', as it was to be called, provided none of the ministers, let alone a Prime Minister, so that it had no way of influencing the government apart from being as noisy as possible in its disapproval. Understandably the Left began to complain, loudly. On the other hand the King could neither summon nor dissolve the Assembly, even though he was able to veto, if only temporarily, any measures it might pass. Most impractical of all was a clause which forbade any deputy of the Constituent Assembly to seek re-election to the new Legislative Assembly – not only did this deprive the new chamber of what political experience had been gained since 1789, but it ensured that its membership would be much further to the Left.

Marie Antoinette was absolutely correct in assuming that the new Constitution was unworkable. It simply could not provide the firm government needed to deal with social and administrative chaos which was compounded by apparently insurmountable economic problems – the inflation was by now approaching astronomical heights. The King's lack of power meant that the executive was all but defenceless against a *coup d'état* and a fresh Revolution, as events would demonstrate only too quickly. The Queen's rejection of Barnave's policy had, alas, been more than justified.

Nonetheless the Constitution was acclaimed with joy. The majority of Frenchmen thought it would bring the Revolution to an end while consolidating all the gains of the last two years. Barnave, gracefully persuasive, succeeded in coaxing the Constituent Assembly to free Louis from the restaints which he had been under since Varennes. Save for a dogmatic minority, the deputies were only too willing. As for 'the representative of the people', as the King was now styled, he had no alternative but to accept the Constitution, however unhappily and insincerely – privately, like his wife, he thought it 'monstrous'. The farcically embarrassing ceremony of his oath to uphold the Constitution took place at the Manège on 14 September 1791. Marie Antoinette and her children watched from a box. To Louis's inexpressible humiliation the deputies remained seated when, bare-headed, he swore his allegiance and then addressed them. Even so his speech, carefully vetted and revised by Barnave on the Queen's instructions, aroused wild applause which lasted for several minutes and included shouts of '*Vive le Roi!*'

That night loyal crowds swarmed in the Tuileries gardens, which were illuminated by a magnificent firework display. When the King and Marie Antoinette drove down the Champs Elysées, they were heartily cheered. A few days later they were applauded with no less euphoria at the Opéra during a performance of Gluck's *Psyche* and later at the Théâtre Français after a performance of *La Gouvernante* (which at the Queen's request had replaced the tactlessly named *La Coquette Corrigée*). However when Marie Antoinette went to Grétry's *Les Evénements Imprévus* at the Théâtre Italien, the house was packed with Jacobins – at the words 'Ah, how I love my mistress' the singer curtsied to her, whereupon there were indignant yells of 'No mistress, no Queen', and a riot broke out which had to be quelled by the National Guard. Marie Antoinette was cheered as she left, but it was the last time she ever went to a playhouse.

It will be remembered that Mme de La Tour du Pin had criticized the Queen for failing to conceal her resentment in 1789. She had learnt a lot since then. No one who saw her smiling graciously at the Manège or at the theatres could have guessed at just how much rage and grief she was hiding. After swearing loyalty to the Constitution, Louis XVI had wept when he returned to the Tuileries, throwing himself into a chair and covering his eyes. 'Why did you have to come to France to see me humiliated?' he asked his wife, who burst into tears and flung her arms round him. She actually thought of trying to escape to Vienna that same night, though after the fiasco of Varennes she quickly admitted the impossibility of such an idea.

Nevertheless she continued to make Barnave believe that she was ready to co-operate with the Feuillants. Now that her apartments were no longer guarded she received him secretly; the first time he came he turned back on seeing a suspicious acquaintance in the courtyard, so that she waited for two hours in vain in one of the palace corridors. The young man's infatuation was confirmed when at last he saw her. In October she assured him in a letter that 'I have been completely frank and always will be, since that is my character. I know how to overcome my prejudices . . . not to make any mental reservations.' Later she agreed that Barnave should read all her letters. If one cannot entirely admire the deception, it is impossible to deny the resourcefulness of this woman derided as feather-brained by so many historians.

She wrote letters of whose existence Barnave never dreamt. Mme Campan tells us that the Queen spent the whole day writing, adding that 'her temper was in no way spoilt by her misfortunes and never for a moment did she seem in a bad mood'. The letters, principally to Mercy-Argenteau and her brother, sometimes as long as thirty pages, were written in cipher or in lemon juice or invisible ink, and were dispatched to Brussels in biscuit or chocolate boxes, or inside hats. She dwelt obsessively on the need for foreign intervention. She did not necessarily want France to be occupied by foreign troops – she thought the French might be willing to restore the old monarchy in return for Louis's mediation to prevent the threatened invasion.

Leopold, too clever by half and still very much the Enlightenment intellectual, was distinctly unsympathetic. He would not accept that the Constitution was unworkable, that France was trembling on the brink of a second, far more radical, Revolution which might spread to his own domains. He temporized ostentatiously, signing a 'Declaration' at Pillnitz at the end of August with the King of Prussia; the two sovereigns proclaimed their intention of helping Louis restore the French monarchy – but only if all the other leading powers joined them, which was of course an impossible condition. Those French politicians who supported the Constitution were irritated, but were also reassured that they had nothing to fear from Leopold II.

Her brother's obvious reluctance to invade France and

save her made Marie Antoinette suspect with justice that the major European powers would prefer to see a weak French republic rather than a strong French monarchy. If Mme Campan is to be believed, the Queen was especially suspicious of England, to the verge of hysteria. 'I never speak the name Pitt without feeling that death is behind me,' she said at this time. 'That man is France's mortal enemy and he is taking a terrible revenge for the misguided support which the Versailles government gave the American rebels. He would like to ensure his country's control of the sea for ever by destroying us.' She was not at all reassured when the secret envoy whom she had sent to the English Prime Minister returned with the message that Pitt would not allow the French monarchy to fall. Not for nothing was Britain known as *perfide Albion*. The poor woman was bewildered. She was staking everything on foreign intervention but it seemed further away than ever.

In fact both the Emperor and the English were hopelessly confused about what was happening in France. At the beginning of 1792 Edmund Burke noted that the 'imprisoned court' were intriguing with the Feuillants in 'a manner beyond all their former dissimulation', but clearly even such a sharp and well informed observer did not understand the course events were taking. On the other hand it is equally plain that Burke did not like what he could see, 'a mingled Scene of Crime, of Vice, of disorder, of folly, and of madness'. No doubt Emperor Leopold was of the same mind, but he appears never to have lost hope that the new Constitution might be modified in a conservative direction. He had naturally no objection to a weak France, going so far as to declare: 'We cannot possibly spend our money and our blood on restoring France to her old strength.' In any case he had other concerns – designs on Bavaria in the west, on Galicia in the east.

By now Marie Antoinette was in contact with Axel. She had never been able to understand his callous silence. She had managed to communicate with Esterházy – busily succouring *émigrés* – and send a message to tell 'HIM that vast distances of miles and countries can never separate hearts'. She also sent Esterházy a ring, together with one for Fersen. 'Give it to HIM on my behalf. It is his size. I wore it for two days before wrapping it. Say that it comes from me. I do not even know where he is. It is frightful not to have news of those whom one loves, not even to know where they are.' Fersen's ring was inscribed *Lâche qui les abandonne* – 'A coward to abandon them' – and bore the three lilies of France. It meant not so much that Axel had deserted her, as that he had deserted the French monarchy. At the end of September a letter at last arrived from Fersen, who was in Vienna trying unsuccessfully to persuade the Emperor to invade France and save his sister. A fresh correspondence began between them. In October, on almost the same day that she was writing to Barnave to assure him of her co-operation, she was telling Axel she had not 'joined the madmen, and if I'm friendly with some of them it is only in order to make use of them. They disgust me far too much'. He replied that she must not even think of trying to win them over – it would disgrace her 'for ever'. Fersen's advice was not entirely disinterested. He had just noted in his journal that, 'They are saying here [Vienna] that the Queen is sleeping with Barnave and allowing herself to be ruled by him.' Such cool objectivity may well imply that he did not believe so silly a rumour, though he may have suspected that Marie Antoinette was at least attracted to Barnave, which was very likely true.

The Legislative Assembly and its new deputies had their first sitting at the Manège on 30 September 1791. They were a completely inexperienced body, dominated by the Left and in particular by the party later known as the Girondins who wanted to take the Revolution much further. Yet there was still a semblance of loyalty to Louis, whose new position as constitutional monarch was curiously modern – men like Lafayette, the Comte de Narbonne-Lara and the Vicomte de Noailles, grandees of the *ancien régime*, genuinely believed the Constitution was going to work. In January 1792 Burke, although recoiling in horror at the humble origins of the Assembly's deputies, was to admit that 'The French pride themselves on the Idea, however absurd, that theirs is a Démocratie Royale.' All the same there were republicans in the Assembly who began to grumble about the retention of monarchy and to show that they wanted radical change – there were egalitarian debates complaining that the King was still addressed as 'Sire' or 'Majesty'. Of such people's attempts to make trouble Barnave said contemptuously that they were men 'who grow big and fat on public disorder, just like insects on carrion'.

Barnave still continued to advise Marie Antoinette, although no longer a deputy. He agreed with the Queen that Louis must demonstrate that he was still King, whereupon, on Barnave's advice, she made Louis use his veto in December to block two resolutions of which he particularly disapproved – one in November condemning to death all *émigrés* who continued to serve in the army of the Princes after 1 January 1792, and another in December decreeing that all non-juring clergy would be imprisoned if they did not take the oath of allegiance. By doing so he antagonized the greater part of the Assembly, who knew very well who was behind him. Marie Antoinette was christened *Madame Veto*. All the old hatred of her revived at once. She wrote to Fersen 'We live in a hell.'

Undeterred, she redoubled her efforts to find allies. It is probable that she speedily succeeded in winning over the new Feuillant Foreign Minister, Antoine de Lessart, a nonentity from Guyenne who had been a protégé of Necker and also the new Naval Minister Bertrand de Molleville. Though there is no proof, it seems almost certain that Lessart was engaged in some sort of secret correspondence with Vienna on the Queen's behalf, and one may infer that secretly he both knew and approved of her policy. He was to pay for it with his life.

One ally whom Marie Antoinette definitely did not want was 'Philippe Egalité', who returned to Paris at the end of 1791 and came to court to offer his support. Poor trusting Louis XVI received his treacherous cousin with delight, claiming that Orléans was perfectly sincere and 'he will do

everything he can to undo the mischief done in his name'.
The Queen knew better – Egalité was more trouble than he
was worth, the most broken of reeds. According to Bertrand
de Molleville, in the ante-room several courtiers spat in the
Duke's face. They were not rebuked by Marie Antoinette
when she heard of it.

During the winter of 1791–92 she wrote indefatigably to
the great European powers, to her brother Leopold, to the
Kings of Prussia, Spain and Sweden and to Catherine the
Great of Russia, begging them to form the armed congress
with which to dictate to France. Fersen went from court to
court to arouse interest in her plans and to stress the need for
swift action. On 3 December, at her dictation, Louis penned a
formal letter to the King of Prussia, pleading with him to
implement the Queen's plan and warning him that if he did
not, the Revolution would spread throughout Europe.
Indeed in the Assembly the Girondins were ranting almost
every day about 'foreign tyrants' and claiming that every
throne in Europe was tottering.

Ironically, the politicians of the Left seemed to be helping
Marie Antoinette. At the very end of 1791, on 30 December,
the ex-Orléanist Jacques-Pierre Brissot – the son of a cheap
eating-house keeper and a former lawyer's clerk and
pamphleteer who had seen the inside of the Bastille – made a
speech in the new Legislative Assembly, calling for 'a new
crusade for universal liberty', which was applauded enthusiastically by other radical deputies. They did not realize,
as she at once saw, that by advocating war with the Emperor
he was playing straight into the Queen's hands. Meanwhile
the increasingly alarming deterioration of the country's
finances made the Feuillants still more anxious to avoid a
war.

Much to Marie Antoinette's anguish, Emperor Leopold
still hoped for peace, even if he was angered by France's
recent annexation of Papal Avignon – a flagrant breach of
international law. However even his patience was tried by an
ultimatum in Louis XVI's name to the Electors of Triers and
Mainz, which aggressively demanded that they disarm the

émigrés. Asked to mediate, Leopold sent a distinctly unhelpful letter which was read to the Assembly on 31 December, the day after Brissot's speech calling for a crusade for 'universal liberty'. The Emperor gave unconvincing assurances in his letter that he would see *émigrés* were disarmed, but at the same time threatened that imperial troops would defend Triers in the event of a French invasion. French pride was outraged. There was uproar in the Assembly and in the Paris streets, although watching from across the Channel Edmund Burke thought Leopold was merely blustering. It was plain that before long the Girondins would oust the Feuillants and declare war.

Barnave, a broken man, gave way to despair. Popular rumour was by now saying that he had sold himself to Austria. For the first time the hitherto unthinkable possibilities of defeat and death burst in on his mind. Later, before he was guillotined, he was to admit ruefully that it was much easier to start a Revolution than to end one, that Louis XVI's only chance of survival had been to transform the monarchy into a constitutional system or a military dictatorship at the beginning of his reign – a chance lost by delaying until change was forced upon him. Barnave paid two more secret visits to Marie Antoinette at the Tuileries. On the third and last occasion, at the end of January 1792, when he was about to leave Paris for his native Dauphiné, he told her that he now realized his views were not hers. 'We tried, Madame,' he said wistfully, referring to his efforts to build a constitutional monarchy. He added, 'I can see little hope for the plan you have decided to follow. You are too far away from your allies, though I fervently hope that my gloomy prophecy doesn't come true.' He ended, 'I am certain to lose my head for trying to help you in your misfortunes and for the services I tried to do you. As my sole reward, I request the honour of kissing your hand.' The Queen was in tears as she gave it to him, and always remembered him with affection. Barnave was correct in both his predictions – he went to the scaffold only two weeks after Marie Antoinette.

The life led by the doomed royal family in the Tuileries

was made increasingly miserable by the menacing crowds which demonstrated ceaselessly outside the palace. Guardsmen on duty at the gates were insulted every day, and there were constant shouts of 'Death to the King!' and 'Kill the Queen!'. There were also fears that an attempt would be made to poison them. Marie Antoinette was by now all too well aware of the importance of discretion in matters of religion. She made her Easter duty for 1792 at a service conducted by candlelight before dawn by a non-juring priest. She continued to attend daily Masses in the Chapel Royal celebrated by State clergy who had taken the obnoxious oath, but did not communicate. It is likely that with Madame Elisabeth she went to other secret services.

At five-thirty p.m. on 13 February 1792, wearing a wig for disguise but bringing his dog Odin with him, Axel von Fersen returned to Paris for the last time. He immediately contacted the discreet M. de Goguelat and two hours later was with the Queen in her apartments. 'I went to her rooms by the usual route,' he notes in his journal. 'Did not see the King.' There follow two words, '*Resté là*' – 'stayed there' – which have been inked out, not by Fersen but by the prurient Baron Klinckowström. These are interpreted by both cynics and romantics as implying that he slept with her, but it is unlikely – it was more prudent for him to stay than to risk slipping past the guards again, and they had a vast amount to talk about. The following night Axel saw Louis and tried to persuade him to attempt an escape once more. The King refused. 'He is restrained by his scruples,' Fersen records, 'because he is an honourable man.' Louis had given his word that he would not leave Paris. Axel left the Tuileries at nine-thirty p.m. that second night. He never saw Marie Antoinette again.

A month later both Fersen and the Queen were dealt a serious blow. On 16 March Gustavus III of Sweden, one of their staunchest supporters, was assassinated at a masked ball in the Stockholm opera house by Captain Jacob Johann Anckarström, as part of a plot organized by the King's brother. (The murder was the inspiration of Auber's opera,

'*Un Ballo in Maschera*', and later of Verdi's opera of the same name.) Axel, his friend since boyhood, wrote to Marie Antoinette, 'It is a very cruel loss.' This was an understatement – Gustavus had been the one allied sovereign who was so far enthusiastic about invading France 'to throttle the Hydra in its lair'.

The Queen had already suffered an even more alarming bereavement. On 1 March 1792 the Holy Roman Emperor Leopold II had died suddenly and unexpectedly. He was the one man in Europe who might have averted the war about to break out, but the Paris mob danced in the street at the news. When she heard it Marie Antoinette wept, exclaiming that he must have been poisoned. (Edmund Burke thought so too.) Nevertheless she at once sat down with Campan to draft a letter to the new Austrian ruler, her nephew Franz II, an undistinguished young man whom she had never met, quite unlike her brilliant brothers, but 'in whom I see the pupil of Josef II'. By this she meant that she thought him more likely to go to war than his father, Leopold.

Louis XVI, with almost somnambulistic ineptitude, now chose to dismiss Narbonne from his post as War Minister for criticizing the Naval Minister, Bertrand de Molleville, who was regarded as a slavish royalist. Narbonne wanted war and was the only Minister respected by the Assembly. The Girondins raged and the terrified Feuillants resigned *en masse*.

In came Girondin ministers bent on war. They were encouraged by the wife of the new Minister for the Interior. Mme Roland was a blue-stocking intoxicated by politics, a *petite bourgeoise* of the most envious sort, whose abilities and beauty have been grossly exaggerated, notably by Thomas Carlyle, but who was unquestionably to do considerable harm and help to ruin her husband's party.

The Girondins had long been suspicious of M. de Lessart, the former Foreign Minister whom with some justice they suspected of being a tool of the Queen. In the process of bringing down the Feuillants they impeached the unhappy man on a charge of treason, and Lessart was sent to a prison at Orléans to await trial. (When he was being brought back to

Paris for the trial later that year, he was recognized en route at Versailles, his escort was overpowered by the mob and he was strangled with a rope.) The impeachment was clearly intended as a warning for Marie Antoinette. She and the King were so alarmed that they burnt a large number of papers.

The new Foreign Minister, and all-but-Prime Minister, General Dumouriez told Louis that he had no choice but to declare war on Louis's nephew, the King of Hungary and Bohemia – he had not yet been crowned Emperor – which he did formally on 25 April. Dumouriez and the Girondins – and also, predictably, Lafayette – believed that the war would strengthen the régime by distracting attention from France's domestic miseries.

The General informed the King of the French plan of campaign, whereupon the Queen promptly sent a letter to Mercy-Argenteau at Brussels, informing him exactly where the French would strike. 'An attack in Savoy and another in the country round Liège. M. de Lafayette's army will be used for the latter attack. This was decided by the Council yesterday.' Shortly afterwards she warned Breteuil that Dumouriez was negotiating to detach the Prussians from the Austrians. Already, in her letter of 1 March, she had told her nephew that the French intended to invade the Austrian Netherlands.

Understandably this has earned Marie Antoinette accusations of treachery, of betraying her husband's subjects. Admittedly her attitude would be hard to justify in the modern world, but in her day it was valid enough. Like almost all contemporary rulers she saw a kingdom as a fief, a personal estate held directly from God, a point of view retained by the Habsburgs until the end of their empire in 1918. Coming from a multi-national state as she did, she had no sense of nationality. To her, Europe was divided horizontally by class, not vertically by nationality (an attitude far from extinct in the twentieth century). Rulers owed assistance to each other, and especially in waging a just war on rebels who had withdrawn their allegiance not merely from their King but from their God.

The royal family's new mentor, General Charles Dumouriez, was a career soldier and a nobleman of sorts (his real name being du Périer du Mourier). A red-faced cavalryman in his fifties, something of an adventurer who in his time had been in the Bastille, he had a cheerful, jolly manner, loved popularity and knew how to make himself extremely agreeable. According to Mme Roland, he joked about everything – except himself. He was in fact a complete *faux bonhomme*, totally without principles or loyalties, a compulsive, amoral, intriguer consumed by ambition. What Dumouriez wanted was power and he expected to get it by ingratiating himself with the Queen. He speedily obtained an audience, to tell her that 'even if he had put the red bonnet [of Revolution] so firmly on his head that it came down over his ears, he never would or could be a Jacobin', that 'the Revolution had been allowed to spread to the rabble who thought of nothing but plunder . . . giving the Assembly a great army only too ready to pull down what was left of an undermined throne'. He then seized Marie Antoinette's hand and, kissing it passionately, cried, 'Let yourself be saved!'

The Queen had trusted Barnave, she had trusted Mirabeau, she had been prepared to trust even Talleyrand, but she did not trust this man. She at once recognized that he was thoroughly dangerous. She also saw that while he had come to realize what she had known from the beginning – that the Constitution was unworkable and by weakening the Crown had made it impossible to stop the Left taking over – he wanted to establish a limited monarchy which he himself would control. Nor was she impressed by his conviction that the French army could easily defeat the Austrians, Prussians and Sardinians in a brief and glorious campaign.

She told him with brutal frankness, 'Monsieur, you may be all-powerful just now but it is only because of your popularity with the people, who soon smash their idols. Your survival depends on your performance.' She finished, 'Neither the King nor I can tolerate all these amendments to the Constitution. I must make it quite clear that you will have to

row your own boat.' The General understood immediately
that she would never co-operate with him, could never be
used to manipulate Louis. As soon as he had gone, she told
Campan, shaking, 'One can never trust a traitor's promises.'

Events proved her right. By the summer Dumouriez was
actually encouraging an attack on the Tuileries. The English
historian, John Wilson Croker, who knew the General well
in later years, was convinced that 'having by his presumption
led the King into greater difficulties, he very suddenly and
shabbily abandoned him, and secured himself for a time in
command of the army, where his successes and personal
glory only served to accelerate the catastrophe of his
unfortunate master, and to delay for a few months his own
proscription and exile'. Moreover, as Marat prophesied from
the first, Dumouriez would eventually betray the Revolution
and try to march on Paris before defecting to the Austrians.
Yet many biographers condemn Marie Antoinette for her
handling of him, for 'letting slip the last opportunity' and
'walking blindfold towards the scaffold'.

If the Queen could see through Dumouriez, she was
bewildered by most of the other Girondins. The new
ministers were nearly all typical bourgeois of the *ancien régime*,
people of a sort she had never before met socially. She must
have found them quite incomprehensible, with their agonizing sense of inferiority, their gnawing envy and resentment.
Aggressively bad manners shocked her far more than any
outbursts of Revolutionary zeal. Mme Roland (who had
never recovered from being sent to eat in the pantry when she
visited a château in her youth) saw that her husband behaved
with peculiar offensiveness, making him attend audiences in
uncouthly improper clothes – clumsy, laced shoes and a
round hat – and speak with studied disrespect. Even so,
fearful of the impending deluge, many Girondins had
substituted an insincere and watered-down monarchism in
place of their former republicanism.

During the next six months the war was shamefully
mismanaged by the Girondins. As Marie Antoinette had
always expected, the undisciplined mob which was now the

French army was driven back from Belgium with contemptuous ease, much to its government's astonishment. Lafayette, who had emerged from a brief retirement at the end of 1791 to command the army in the north-east could not tolerate a situation in which three regiments at once deserted to the enemy, while another force turned tail and ran after murdering both its prisoners and its general. He reported that there was no alternative but to try to make peace. Everyone in Paris blamed the débâcle on the 'Austrian Committee' at the Tuileries – in Vergniaud's words, 'a palace where counter-revolution is being planned, where they're planning to re-fasten all the horrors of slavery on us'. Brissot undertook to prove that the Committee really existed. Marat's newspaper, *L'Ami du Peuple*, trumpeted daily that the Revolution was being betrayed and that the soldiers must shoot their generals. The guards at the Tuileries gates were now insulted all day long and beneath the palace windows the mob shouted for an end to monarchy more noisily than ever.

Louis collapsed. He fell into a state of hopeless despondency which amounted to physical debility – for ten days he did not speak a single word, even to his wife or children. Eventually the Queen, aware that the final crisis was almost on them and that he must be ready to act, forced her husband to pull himself together by making a scene, both threatening and affectionate, in which she told him it would be better for them to go out and die fighting the mob rather than be 'murdered on the palace floor'. She at last succeeded in rousing him but, as so often before, his new-found firmness was disastrous.

The Assembly had passed two decrees which the King found peculiarly distasteful. First, that all non-juring priests were to be deported from France. (He had already refused to let them be imprisoned, in December 1791.) Second, and much more alarming, that a military camp of 20,000 volunteers should be set up outside the walls of Paris. This made Louis especially uneasy since the Assembly had just deprived him of the 'Constitutional Body Guards', which he had been given only a few months before. Though he still had his magnificently faithful Swiss, the Paris shopkeepers of the National Guard who formed the bulk of his protectors were clearly thoroughly unreliable. Even Louis was angered by an insolent letter from Roland, delivered in person, which had been dictated by Mme Roland and which warned him peremptorily to sign the decrees or face a new revolution.

On 15 June the King vetoed the two decrees. He did so at his wife's insistence. Afterwards Marie Antoinette bitterly reproached herself – her whole plan had been to give the Austrians and Prussians time to reach the Tuileries, but instead she precipitated the long-dreaded crisis. (It was exactly the same error she had made in July 1789, when she had persuaded Louis to get rid of Necker.) He also dismissed his Girondin ministers, who refused to countersign the veto, though he tried to keep Dumouriez. Always ready to betray anyone, the General was quite prepared to stay but the Assembly was in such an ugly mood that he hastily resigned and took a command at the front. By now the Queen expected the worst. Her letters show that she considered the royal family's chances of survival 'exceedingly remote'.

The Girondins decided to frighten Louis into obeying them, and to teach Marie Antoinette a lesson. It was planned in Mme Roland's *salon* and set in motion by representatives of the faubourgs of Saint-Antoine and Saint-Marceau – wretched, poverty-stricken districts. These announced that on 20 June their 'citizens' would plant a Tree of Liberty at the Tuileries, and also present petitions for the vetoed decrees to both King and Assembly. The urban proletariat, who would gain least of all from the Revolution, was once again on the march as the tool of bourgeois politicians who could not even conceive of socialism. The Girondin Mayor of Paris, Pétion – the same man who had ridden with the royal family on its way back from Varennes – saw that the National Guards at the palace were not reinforced. Louis's loyal Swiss could not possibly reach it in time from their barracks in the Paris suburbs.

On 20 June young Lieutenant-Colonel Bonaparte, on a visit to Paris, saw 'a ragged crowd' which, according to his friend Bourrienne, he estimated at about 5–6,000. They were 'screaming the coarsest insults and converging rapidly on the Tuileries, a mob obviously made up of the dregs of the faubourgs'. He told Bourrienne, 'Let's follow this rabble,' and was an eye-witness of what happened. In the palace Mme Campan saw them approaching, led by a popular brewer Santerre – 'monarch of the faubourgs' – and a butcher, Legendre. They were armed with pikes, hatchets and clubs, and dragging cannon. 'Clad in the filthiest clothes, all looked quite terrifying and the foul steam rising from them infected the very air itself.' One man carried a bullock's bloody heart nailed to a pole with the inscription 'aristocrat's heart'. However, although shouting 'Down with the veto!' they were in a light-hearted mood to begin with, singing and dancing – largely due to drink provided by Girondin agents.

The mob presented its petitions to the Assembly at the Manège, then seemed ready to go home. But as it was marching past the Tuileries, it was irritated at seeing the palace gates closed and cannon in the courtyard. Its mood changed at once, whipped up by men who had been bribed with Santerre's free beer.

Soon the gates had been forced in and a yelling multitude burst into the palace garden. Within a few minutes they were storming into the palace itself and surging up the stairs, still dragging their cannon with them. They then began to break down doors. The King was in a large room used for receptions – known as the *oeil de boeuf* like its predecessor at Versailles – and ordered its doors to be opened. He stood on a window-seat to meet his guests, protected by a few benches in front of which stood six loyal and remarkably brave soldiers. The intruders howled at him – one or two tried to reach him with their pikes, but were warded off by the soldiers. Above the uproar the butcher called Legendre bellowed at Louis, 'Listen to us, Monsieur, it's your job to listen. You're a traitor, you've always tricked us and you're still tricking us. But watch out – you've chalked up a heavy debt and we ordinary people are tired of being treated like fools.' There were more shouts that the King must withdraw his veto.

Louis never lacked physical courage and, after throwing

the biggest of the mob out of the window – the man had attacked him – said calmly, 'I won't be forced and I can't be frightened.' However, with a show of good humour he put on a red bonnet which had been thrust at him. To show his 'fraternal' feelings he also drank heartily from a bottle of red wine which was offered to him – 'People of Paris, I drink to your health and to that of the French nation.' These amiable gestures were cheered loudly. At last, after a nerve-racking two hours, the Mayor of Paris appeared and made a soothing speech to the crowd, asking them to disperse. Louis then made the inspired suggestion that they might like to see the State apartments, whereupon the *sansculottes* were swiftly transformed into gaping sightseers.

During his ordeal the King had appeared on a Tuileries balcony wearing the red cap. 'The poor driveller,' said Bonaparte, watching outside. 'How could he let such a rabble get in? If he had only mown down five or six hundred with his cannon, the rest would still be running.'

Meanwhile Marie Antoinette, her children and some of her ladies had had an even more frightening experience. The first they knew of the mob's entrance was the noise of shouting and running feet and the crashing of doors being broken down with axes – then, from the floors above, the sound of cannon rumbling along and splintering delicate wooden inlay. The Queen had every reason for fear. A large group of rioters were searching for her, yelling that they wanted her blood. 'So they want to kill me,' she whispered when she heard them. But as the axes crashed on the doors of her own apartments, she decided she would simply walk through them and go to her husband's side. Mme de Lamballe held her back, whereupon Marie Antoinette told her, 'I've nothing to fear – at the worst I'll be killed.' After more waiting in a secluded passage she again announced her intention of going to the King, explaining that the mob needed a victim. Fortunately she was stopped by a gentleman who appeared as if from nowhere, the Chevalier de Rouge-ville. He gently dissuaded her and took her into the Council Room, which was still empty. A large table was placed in

front of a window embrasure, in turn protected by Rougeville and a few loyal soldiers, Marie Antoinette and her little
party being installed in the window and the Dauphin seated
on the table. Then the doors were opened.

Suddenly the astonished rioters, still sightseeing, saw the
woman for whom they had searched in vain. Santerre asked
the soldiers to draw back and let the crowd have a good look
at her. The Queen had put on a tricoloured cockade which a
National Guard had given her, but when someone rudely
pushed a red bonnet on to her head she at once snatched it off
and made her son wear it instead. The rabble filed past the
table, sometimes shouting insults at her – 'You vile woman!'
She stood and watched them calmly throughout, her head
held very high, though it was noticed that she was white-
faced and her eyes were bloodshot. Some of those who
passed her carried threatening placards – one read '*Marie
Antoinette à la lanterne*' (a *lanterne* was a street lamp-post and,
with the rope used to haul up its lamp, a favourite
revolutionary instrument for lynching). But at the end of the
queue came the intrepid Madame Elisabeth, to reassure her
beloved sister-in-law.

By eight o'clock that evening the mob had departed more
or less calmly, leaving behind a palace carpeted in broken
glass and splintered furniture, and Louis still wearing his
ridiculous red hat. If there had been a plot to kill him it had
failed, as had the Girondins' scheme of frightening him into
withdrawing his veto. But the royal family knew the mob
would return sooner or later. Even Pétion, the Mayor, was
horrified by the whirlwind which he had helped to unleash.
Everyone, Royalist, moderate or radical, saw that the
monarchy was doomed. It was simply a matter of time. The
Tuileries was like a vast condemned cell, the entire court
expecting a bloody death.

At the front Citizen Lafayette was appalled by the latest
outrage in the name of the movement he had done so much to
create. With his usual conceit he came and hectored the
National Assembly, demanding that the ringleaders of the
mob of 20 June be punished. Unfortunately he forgot to

bring his troops. He was abruptly deflated when a deputy remarked mildly that, since the General was in Paris, he presumed the Austrians had been defeated. Lafayette returned to his army to plot a *coup d'état*, which in any case he had been planning since the spring. Before he left he obtained an audience at the Tuileries and told the King and Queen they must try to escape from Paris. Already forced by Louis's scruples to reject Fersen's plan, and with harrowing memories of the Varennes débâcle, Marie Antoinette was certainly not prepared to risk her life by entrusting it to someone like Lafayette. (Later, Napoleon endorsed her unflattering opinion of this mountebank's capacities.) Predictably, historians continue to blame her for losing another 'last chance' of survival.

In any case the King would never have agreed to leave now, and she refused to desert him – let alone her children. The Landgravine of Hesse-Darmstadt offered to smuggle the Queen out of Paris by herself since she was in the most danger, but Marie Antoinette declined with grateful dignity. Her fatalism was asserting itself. Yet she still hoped.

Although the royal family had rebuffed Lafayette so firmly, they had few illusions as to what lay ahead. The Queen wrote to Fersen, 'I am still alive but only by a miracle. The 20th was a dreadful day. It is no longer just myself who's threatened with death but my husband as well, and they don't even try to hide it. He was strong enough to save us for the moment, but it can happen again at any time.' She adds that Axel mustn't worry about her – 'Rely on my courage.' She also informed Vienna by code that the situation was 'deteriorating with terrifying speed', begging that all friendly sovereigns be informed and asked to intervene as quickly as possible. Again and again she sent messages to say allied intervention must not delay any further. By mid-July she was beseeching Axel to tell Mercy-Argenteau that a single day's postponement could be fatal for her and her husband – 'the band of murderers is growing every hour'. In the streets outside the Tuileries the crowd lynched anyone suspected of being a Royalist.

Marie Antoinette explained the King's inaction to Mme

Campan. In Louis's view, she said, the French Revolution was still conforming almost exactly to the upheavals of seventeenth-century England. He was constantly reading the life of Charles I so as not to make the same mistakes. (Few men have been more the victim of a sense of history – 'Louis XVI was determined to put up with everything because Charles I put up with nothing,' says Tocqueville.) She confided, 'I begin to fear the King may be tried. As for me, I'm a foreigner so they'll simply murder me. But what's going to happen to my children?' She cried a little. Campan observes that the Queen's tears were unusual – although she had suffered from fits of hysteria 'in happier days', she was much calmer now that she was facing danger.

The miasma of venomous hatred infected even the Tuileries. In the corridors National Guards often shouted 'Down with the veto!' when the royal family passed, while in the Chapel Royal the orchestra played the ferocious revolutionary tune *Ça ira* – whose words include '*Les aristos à la lanterne*' – and choristers sang insulting texts from Scripture in place of the royal anthem. Some courtiers never slept, for fear an assassin might penetrate the palace – on at least one occasion an unknown man came into Marie Antoinette's bedroom and had to be thrown out. The garden was full of hawkers selling pornographic prints of her. Filthy songs about her were sung beneath the windows with more savage zest than ever. The mob was only copying its betters, who for over twenty years had branded *l'Autrichienne* as the source of all French evils.

One of the more respectable songs – sung to a jaunty popular dance tune, the *Carmagnole* – explains why the Parisians so hated the Queen. It was because they feared her, the woman who was turning the King against them, who at the head of Austrian troops and revengeful aristocrats was going to massacre everyone in a new St Bartholomew:

> *Madame Veto avait promis*
> *De faire égorger tout Paris.*
> [Madame Veto had promised
> To cut the throat of all Paris.]

All the poorer classes, and even many of the upper bourgeoisie, genuinely believed that their lives were threatened by a bloody counter-revolution which was being plotted by Marie Antoinette. Their fears were tirelessly inflamed by men of the Left. Threatening proclamations by Monsieur and Artois, at Coblenz with the *émigré* army, increased such terrors.

Louis and the Queen expected that an attempt would be made to assassinate them during the celebrations for Federation Day on 14 July – the third anniversary of the storming of the Bastille. Devoted courtiers produced two bullet-proof vests, but Marie Antoinette refused to wear hers. 'If the revolutionaries murder me, it will be a piece of luck. They will release me from a truly wretched existence.' In the event the celebrations in the Champs de Mars went off peacefully enough and the royal family returned to the Tuileries without being molested. But there was an alarming incident. The Mayor, Pétion, had been suspended on 7 July for his failure to prevent the outrage at the Tuileries by a group of moderate deputies led by Talleyrand and the former Duc de la Rochefoucauld d'Enville. He was reinstated six days later and the crowd cheered him to the echo, shouting 'Pétion or death' when he appeared in the Champs de Mars. The Queen smiled at Talleyrand and his friends when she saw them from her box, to show them how grateful she was for their protest. The smile was greeted with howls of execration. Talleyrand was abused as 'a court favourite' – he himself records that 'the Queen's friendly looks, as we passed below the balcony where she sat with the King, turned the mob against us'. Next day la Rochefoucauld left Paris in disguise, but was recognized at Gisors and stoned to death.

More and more anxiously Marie Antoinette waited for the invasion. A far from soothing letter arrived from her sister, Archduchess Maria Christina, explaining that everyone was concerned for her safety but telling her to be patient – to act too quickly might put her in danger. Her nephew Franz also had much more pressing business in Germany, notably his coronation at Frankfurt as Charlemagne's heir and the Holy

Roman Emperor, an event which was attended by Monsieur and Artois, and such old friends as Yolande de Polignac and Calonne.

At last the allied commander, the Duke of Brunswick, was ready to march. On 25 July, before setting out, he issued a manifesto at Coblenz. This document has frequently been cited as a classic example of the Queen's lack of political sense. While it is perfectly true that she urged the allies to issue a manifesto, she certainly had nothing to do with its wording. It was drafted by Fersen – soothing his nerves by sleeping with Mrs O'Sullivan – and by the Marquis de Limon, a former Orléanist. They ignored her instructions 'not to say too much about the King, not to give an impression that your principal purpose is to support him', and not to mention any interference in France's internal affairs. Instead the manifesto threatened all members of the National Assembly, National Guards and Paris district councils with being held personally responsible – 'on pain of losing their heads and of military execution without hope of reprieve' – for anything which might happen to the royal family. Furthermore, any inhabitants of French towns and villages who dared to try to defend themselves against Brunswick's troops would be shot and their houses burnt. At first the Duke refused to sign the incredible document (oddly enough, he had considerable sympathy with the Revolution and even with Jacobins) but eventually he allowed himself to be persuaded; he regretted signing it for the rest of his life. Predictably, when it was published in Paris a week later it sent the French nearly mad with rage. Louis protested frantically, though with a peculiarly unfortunate lack of conviction, that he was completely loyal to the 'Nation'.

It was now not so much a race against time as the last lap of the race. Marie Antoinette knew it only too well. She showed understandable irritation with Axel's letters, which were full of fatuous advice such as telling her to hide in the cellars if there was another attack on the Tuileries, or suggesting whom the restored monarchy should appoint as its ministers. (Plainly Fersen saw an important role for himself in the new

France.) She wrote back on 1 August, 'Among all our dangers it is not very easy to concentrate on choosing ministers . . . just at the moment our chief concern is to escape the assassins' knives and to fight off the plotters who surround a throne on the verge of collapse. The factions no longer bother to hide their plans for murdering the royal family. At their two most recent evening meetings they merely disagreed about the method. I won't go into it in detail. I will simply say that if help doesn't come speedily, only providence can save the King and his family.' One notes with interest that she clearly had excellent spies. She also seems to have been kept informed about the route which Brunswick's army intended to follow, and when they ought to reach the various towns on the way. Mme Campan, who tells us this, adds that the Queen was plainly very worried about what might happen before Brunswick arrived in Paris.

In the event the Duke set out on 1 August and was known to be on his way, but his troops did not cross the French frontier until 19 August. Brunswick, a hero of the Seven Years' War, had the reputation of being a superb commander. Unfortunately, he was rather too careful of his reputation and moved with ponderous slowness. If the French had been cowed by his manifesto – as it was they were merely angry – they would still have realized that it would take him many weeks to reach Paris. Moreover the Left was greatly encouraged by the arrival of 600 sansculottes from Marseilles, who marched into the capital on 6 August, three-quarters of them drunk, singing a new song which quickly became known as the 'Marseillaise'.

The Left – or the 'Mountain' as the extremist Jacobins were called at this time – decided that now was the moment to overthrow the monarchy, the Legislative Assembly and the Constitution. They planned, with great skill, to seize the Hôtel de Ville and install a genuinely revolutionary Commune which would control not just Paris but all France. There would also be an attack on the Tuileries to overthrow the 'executive'. The gullible mob and the men from Marseilles were whipped into a frenzy by tales of royalist plans for massacre, of impending foreign invasion and, above all, of the devilish woman and her Austrian Committee.

It is certain that the spies to whom Marie Antoinette refers indirectly in her letter to Fersen warned her the assault would come on Friday 10 August – the feast of St Lawrence. The previous day ended in a sweltering summer night. Just before one a.m. those at the Tuileries heard the tocsin ring out, the signal for the attack on the Hôtel de Ville. Most unfortunately the Marquis de Mandat-Grancey, Commander of the National Guard and of the Tuileries, a dauntless and experienced soldier, was caught at the Hôtel de Ville and murdered on its steps, his corpse being thrown into the Seine – harpies ran through the streets waving his head. Nevertheless, the palace was far from defenceless.

Realizing that the crisis had come, the Queen had not bothered to go to bed, lying on a sofa or wandering from room to room. At two a.m. she heard a glorious sound – the fifes and drums of the Swiss, who were marching into Paris from their barracks through the Porte Maillot. By three a.m. 900 red-coated troops, professionals to their fingertips, had taken up positions at the Tuileries under two excellent commanders – the Marquis de Maillardoz from Fribourg and Baron de Bachmann from Glaris. By their side were not only 2,500 National Guardsmen but 200 *Chevaliers du Poignard* – 'Knights of the Dagger' as the Parisians called them. These were faithful noblemen, including Marshal de Mailly, eighty-four years old, the septuagenarian M. de Malesherbes and, in Mme Campan's words, 'a few who figured ridiculously enough among what was then known as the *noblesse* but whose devotion ennobled them'. Marie Antoinette had hot drinks served to all the defenders. An eye-witness, Count Roedeer (the chief law officer of Paris), says she 'made no display of heroics, did not pose or strike attitudes. I saw no rage or despair, no thirst for revenge.' He testifies that she was an inspiration to all. Alas, she was not in command.

Louis XVI, who always hated bloodshed, lost his nerve. No doubt, like everybody else in the palace he had not slept for a week. He dozed a little, rumpling his clothes and flattening his wig, then roamed silent and dejected along the corridors. In contrast his womenfolk's resolution was unshaken. 'My sister, come and see the dawn,' said Madame Elisabeth to the Queen, and together the two friends watched a blood-red sky. Eventually the King was told that he ought to review the National Guard, some of whom – only a few – were muttering to each other, 'Do we fight or don't we?' A bedraggled Louis went down into the courtyard where they were drawn up and was greeted by drums beating the general salute. He stammered, 'We're told an attack is coming . . . mine is every good citizen's cause . . . of course I love the National Guard.' Such a performance did not inspire confidence. There were cries of '*Vive le peuple!*' which soon became yells of 'Fat pig!' 'My God, they're booing the King,' gasped the naval minister, Duboucharge, who was watching from a window. Marie Antoinette flushed and sighed tearfully, 'It's all over – reviewing the troops has done irreparable harm.' Her husband's final rousing order was, 'Don't fire until you're fired on.' In reality most of the National Guardsmen were loyal – some aggressively so, such as the Grenadiers of the Fille-Saint-Thomas battalion.

At seven a.m. the main body of the mob arrived at the Tuileries, where their comrades had already trained three cannon on the palace. Half an hour later Roederer completed Louis's demoralization by telling him, 'Your Majesty has only five minutes. The one place where you will be safe is the Assembly.' The Queen protested, 'But we have troops.' Roederer insisted: 'All Paris is marching.' The King muttered dully, 'We will leave.' Marie Antoinette argued, 'Surely we can't abandon all these brave men who have come to the palace to defend their sovereign?' Any man with a spark of leadership would have been able to rout the largest mob with such a garrison, as Napoleon confirms. But it was useless arguing with Louis. Escorted by loyal National Guards, the royal family passed between two amazed, contemptuous lines of Swiss and noblemen on their way through the Tuileries gardens to the Manège. 'We will soon be back,' cried the Queen defiantly. The King said nothing, apart from remarking that the leaves were falling early.

The mob now attacked. Their amateurish cannoneers were mowed down by the first volley from the Swiss who, with the armed noblemen, despite a shortage of ammunition, fired steadily into the rabble until the courtyard was piled high with dead and dying *sansculottes*. They had captured their cannon and all but driven them off, when a message arrived from Louis ordering the Swiss to cease fire. It was their death-warrant. Disciplined to the last, they obeyed dourly and were at once hacked and clubbed to death, their severed heads being tossed into the air to be caught on pike points – 615 officers and men were slaughtered, and over a hundred more were later murdered in prison.

Triumphantly the mob swept into the Tuileries. Some of the noblemen escaped through secret passages, Malesherbes among them. Others preferred to stay and die, like the octogenarian M. de Mailly, who remembered Louis XIV and who had taken command of the defence; leaning on a cane the old man tried to fight to the death with his court sword but was disarmed and led away – to perish beneath the guillotine. Mme Campan saw two courtiers, hats pulled down over their eyes and gripping their swords, who told her, 'We die at our posts – it is our duty.' She herself survived only because she was a woman. All male palace servants were butchered, from master chefs to lowly grooms and scullions – many were Jacobins themselves and had not anticipated any danger. Years afterwards Napoleon, not unaccustomed to bloodshed, said he had never seen such carnage as that which he watched at the Tuileries (from the window of a nearby furniture shop). That night he wrote to his brother Joseph, 'If Louis XVI had put in an appearance on horseback, he would have won.'

Marie Antoinette's gamble had failed. We know now that the Duke of Brunswick never had a chance of reaching Paris in time. Yet she had not risked everything without reason. Most contemporary observers thought the French army in its then condition would be brushed aside easily by disciplined Austrian and Prussian troops. Moreover the Tuileries could

have been held. The dream of Bourbon monarchy restored
by an armed congress was not as unrealistic as it sounds.
Twenty-five years later such a congress did in fact take place –
the Congress of Vienna.

At the Manège the royal family were greeted respectfully
by the President of the Assembly, Vergniaud. 'You can count
on the Legislative Assembly's loyalty,' he declaimed pompously. 'We are all sworn to give our lives if necessary to
defend the rights of the people and the lawfully constituted
authority.' Then, for their own safety, they were placed in the
recording clerks' gallery behind the President's chair.

11

The Temple

I do suppose, that such a Termination of the misery
and captivity of three years, attended with humiliations
and mortifications of every sort, could hardly be
exceeded by any Effort of imagination; and this but
preparatory to the dreadful Death that awaits them

Edmund Burke, 17 August 1792

I think she is doomed

The Princesse de Lamballe

THE PRESIDENT of the Assembly's loyal welcome was
meaningless. The attack on the Tuileries had been part of a
coup d'état – the new Revolution, which Marie Antoinette had
long foreseen. Organized by Danton, the extreme Left had
also seized the Hôtel de Ville where it installed a Commune
with which to frighten the Assembly into doing what it
wanted. So terrified were the deputies that two-thirds of
them stayed away from the Manège, while those who did
attend dared not oppose the Commune's wishes.

Louis, his family and Mmes de Lamballe and de Tourzel
had to stay in the gallery until ten p.m. that night. It was little
more than a cupboard, only ten foot square, and grew
unbearably hot. For twelve hours they were given nothing to
eat or drink, but at last a compassionate doorkeeper went out
and bought them some biscuits and a bottle of wine with his
own money. All the Queen could take was a single glass of
water.

An English spectator, Dr John Moore, who was watching from the Manège's public gallery, says a person near him thought Marie Antoinette's face 'indicated rage and the most provoking arrogance. I perceived nothing of that nature [but rather] dignified composure'. However Gérard's theatrical sketch of the scene is as prejudiced as Moore's neighbour. Outraged figures symbolizing the betrayed French people are pointing scornfully at the recorders' box, in which one can see the royal family. The King looks despondent enough, but the Queen glares out like some she wolf at bay. The Revolution never denied her courage. She certainly needed it.

Throughout that long and dreadful day blood-stained, powder-blackened *sansculottes* kept on bursting in to the Manège to deposit plunder from the Tuileries – including Marie Antoinette's jewels – or to drag in half-dead Swiss prisoners to exhibit before cutting their throats at the Abbaye prison. Danton, Marat and Robespierre, the men behind the Commune, forced the abject Vergniaud – who had welcomed Louis so pompously – to announce the suspension of the monarchy and the replacement of the Assembly by a new 'Convention'. The former royal family would be confined in the Luxembourg, Monsieur's old palace. Then, after nearly fourteen hours of stifling, cramped confinement and exposure to the public gaze, they were taken to the cells of the adjoining convent of the Feuillants. (There was a certain irony in the name.) All through the night there was a mob outside, trying to break in and howling for their blood – in particular for that of the Queen. 'I think she is doomed,' said the terrified Mme de Lamballe to Mme de Tourzel.

Next morning, Saturday 11 August, they were all put back into the squalid gallery at seven-thirty a.m., and again on Sunday, returning to the convent each night. Reliable informants told Edmund Burke just what this meant, and within a week he was writing 'this miserable King and his family . . . staid as a miserable prisoner at the Bar to hear all the barbarous Eloquence of their bloody declamations against him, preparatory to the Sentence of formal deprivation. . . This late Master of seven Magnificent Palaces, lying in a little Chamber of retreat, without Table, Chair or bed, for three days with his whole family of Children all huddled together under the disgusting Necessities of Nature.' However they at least had proper meals, while listening to speech upon speech demanding the establishment of a republic. On the Sunday there were objections to the Luxembourg as their place of confinement – it had too many secret passages and 'hidden exits'. The Commune's representatives also objected to an hotel in the Place Vendôme and instead proposed the Temple. The fearful deputies agreed hastily. At six p.m. on Monday the royal party, accompanied by their old mentor Pétion, climbed into two carriages and were driven to the Temple, which was in the Marais.

The Temple did not then have the sinister name it was soon to acquire. The seat of the Grand Priory of France of the Knights of Malta, it was their most important house in France, a complex of many buildings enclosed by a long circular wall. Apart from the church, its most important edifice was an elegant seventeenth-century palace, the official residence of the Grand Prior. As recently as 1789 the Bailiff de la Brillane had celebrated his appointment as the Order's ambassador to the court of Versailles with a splendid banquet to which everyone known to be in favour with Marie Antoinette had been invited. Technically the Temple still belonged to the Knights, but they had deserted it. The Grand Prior (Artois's son, Berry) and his administrator the Bailiff de Crussol were *émigrés*, together with most of their brethren, while the ambassador Brillane had died of apoplexy and the chargé d'affaires, the Chevalier d'Estourmel – who had subsidized the flight to Varennes – had had a nervous breakdown.

The royal family arrived at the palace, which they knew very well, and sat down to an excellent meal in the Salle des Quatres Glaces – where the young Mozart and his sister had once given a concert. The great room was lit by a multitude of candles, though the Dauphin, only seven, was so tired that he fell asleep. To their astonishment they were then told that their quarters would not be in the palace but in the grim twelfth-century tower at the other end of the compound. (Strangely enough, Marie Antoinette had long ago taken a dislike to the building and had often asked for it to be demolished.) While the desolate old barrack – each floor of which formed a single room – was being refurbished, they were to be housed in the 'Little Tower' next to it, in the small but comfortable apartment of the Knights' archivist, who was summarily ejected despite his frenzied protests. It had blue-and-white striped velvet chairs, some mildly erotic prints on its sky-blue walls and was comparatively cosy. There was not room for the unfortunate King, who had to sleep in an alcove downstairs on a bug-ridden mattress for the first night. Mmes de Lamballe and de Tourzel were taken off to the prison of La Force. Louis, Marie Antoinette and the family were to spend well over a month in the Little Tower.

Brunswick's army quickly recaptured Verdun, the last strongpoint before Paris. After the storming of the Tuileries hundreds of aristocrats – mainly liberals – non-juring priests and other royalist supporters had been rounded up and put in gaol. On 2 September, infuriated by the invasion and by rumours of royalist plots, the Commune set in motion several days of massacre. Summary courts were held in nine prisons, the 'condemned' being forced to pass between two rows of 'executioners' – butchers recruited from the abattoirs and violent criminals specially let out of gaol, equipped with swords, pikes, axes and cleavers, and paid six francs a day plus free wine. More than 1,400 people were murdered with the most appalling cruelty, including some little girls of ten. Among the victims was Mme de Lamballe who, despite fainting during her interrogation, refused to swear 'an oath of hatred against King, Queen and Crown'. She was then thrust between the waiting butchers, crying, 'Oh! how horrible!' when she saw the bodies of those who had preceded her, but was dispatched with merciful speed. Her corpse was raped, then her head, heart and sexual organs were ripped out and stuck on spikes. The murderers then set off for the Temple with these prizes, dragging her naked, mutilated trunk with them as well. On the way they had her hair dressed and powdered by a *coiffeur* – they were going to ask the Queen to kiss her.

When this horrible rabble reached the Temple, one of the more decent guards hastily drew the curtains of Marie Antoinette's apartment. Another told her brutally, 'He's trying to stop you seeing la Lamballe's head, which they've brought to show you how the people take their revenge on tyrants. If I were you, I'd appear at the window.' The Queen moaned and then fainted. Years later her daughter commented, 'It was the only moment in her life when she ever lost her self-control.' At last the mob went away with its ghastly trophies. Fortunately Marie Antoinette never learnt the details of her friend's death. Such was the city's blood-lust that the 'people' slaughtered the ordinary female criminals of the Salpêtrière and the vagrants, paupers and lunatics of the Bicêtre. By some miracle Mme de Tourzel escaped and eventually got away to the country.

On 20 September 1792 the newly elected Convention, the Revolution's third assembly since 1789, met for the first time, in the Tuileries. All its deputies, whether Jacobins or Girondins – by now thoroughly frightened – agreed on the abolition of the monarchy on 21 September, and the French Republic was proclaimed the following day. Astonishingly, Brunswick's dysentery-ridden army was halted by the French artillery at Valmy the very same week, to general amazement. It began to retreat and within a few weeks had recrossed the French frontier. One excellent reason for its departure was that both the Austrians and the Prussians were concerned about eastern Europe – Russia was about to invade Poland.

Although the King and Queen were not allowed news-papers, they were kept informed of events outside by a twenty-nine-year-old kitchen hand called François Turgy, who was a devoted royalist and a typically tough and resourceful Parisian. He had been in service at Versailles and at the Tuileries – where he had escaped the massacre – and had cunningly contrived to get work at the Temple. Here he communicated with the royal family by whispers, by notes concealed in bottles or jugs and by pre-arranged hand signals – for example, if the Convention was discussing the monarchy, he was to touch his hair with the fingers of his left hand. A whole repertory of gestures told the story of Brunswick's advance and retreat. Louis and Marie Antoinette must have been horribly disappointed when they heard that the Duke had turned back, but Turgy was then given more signals to make should the English land on the French coast. The Queen was incapable of despair.

The Temple was not ready for several weeks. Partitions had to be erected to make more rooms, and blinds put over the windows to stop the prisoners from looking out. Adjoining buildings were demolished. The Commune was determined to isolate the 150-foot high keep, with its ten-foot thick walls and winding stair guarded by no less than twelve wicket gates, from the rest of Paris. On the second floor was a small, dark garret for Cléry (Louis's faithful valet, who had managed to rejoin his master at the end of August) and a bedroom for the King and the Dauphin. On the third floor were the bedrooms of Marie Antoinette, Madame Elisabeth and Madame Royale, and also a bathroom. To judge from the pieces which survive in the Musée Carnavalet, the furniture was that of a cheap boarding-house of the period, though the Queen had a clavichord, a green damask bedspread and a green-and-white damask armchair. Louis's rooms were ready first and he moved in at the end of September. The rest of the family did not join him until the end of the following month.

At this time the royal family were treated reasonably well, despite their close confinement. Marie Antoinette, her sister-in-law and her daughter were allowed to order any number of dresses, hats and shoes since they had brought nothing from the Tuileries. They were also supplied with books. They ate extremely well. Dinner included a choice from three soups, four entrées and six roasts – champagne, claret and madeira were served, though the Queen drank only water. However, apart from Cléry and Turgy, the servants left much to be desired, notably the disagreeable Tison couple. Both were elderly; the man, a former customs official, was sullen and bad-tempered, the woman obsequious and sly; he laid the table, she waited on the ladies, together they did the general cleaning. A further irritation were the guards and municipal officials, who lounged about wearing their hats in the royal presence.

It is only too plain from the Journal of Jean-Baptiste Cléry that these guards and officials deliberately behaved with as much insolence as possible, whether in the Temple or when the royal family were taking their short daily airing. They danced, sang obscene songs, puffed pipe-smoke at them, insisted on sitting in their rooms, interrupted the Dauphin's lessons, referred to the King as 'Capet' and scribbled menacing graffiti on the walls – '*Madame Veto*'s going to swing'. On one occasion a man actually followed her into her bedroom when she wanted to change her clothes. Marie Antoinette ignored all insults with icy dignity, and once rebuked her son for forgetting to say good-morning to a guard. She even partly tamed Antoine Simon, one of the six Commissioners appointed to inspect the expenses of the Temple and who was always there. This failed cobbler of nearly sixty from the Paris back-streets, who was living off the savings of his charwoman wife, was semi-literate, dirty, foul-mouthed and evil-tempered. Nevertheless he grew surprisingly obliging and went on shopping errands for the Queen.

The humble backgrounds of so many of the Commune's officials – lemonade-sellers, gardeners, wigmakers as well as a cobbler – and the use of such words as 'democrat' and 'equality' may give an impression of socialism, an impression that the poor were benefiting from the Revolution. Admittedly there were many new jobs to be filled and *sansculottes* were often ostentatiously employed. But it was only window-dressing by the bourgeoisie in their war on the nobility. All too many of these proletarian officials died in want and misery, while the urban poor were swollen by hordes of unemployed footmen, chefs, grooms, valets and ladies' maids, together with a swarm of lesser ecclesiastical employees – parish clerks, beadles, sacristans, church cleaners –

who literally starved to death in circumstances of the utmost degradation. Neither the more determined peasants who had seized their seigneurs' estates nor the bourgeoisie who were making fortunes out of the Revolution were interested in the problems of such people. Even when the Jacobin extremists made their greatest parade of 'democracy' in 1793, the upper bourgeois remained more or less in the ascendant, however discreetly, determined to prevent social as well as counter revolution. Men like Simon were their dupes.

Despite all vexations, the royal family began a routine in the Little Tower, which they carried on in the Temple for as long as possible. Louis rose at six a.m. and after saying his prayers went to read in the Order of Malta's library. (Huë, another valet, tells us that on one occasion the King pointed to the works of Rousseau and Voltaire and whispered to him, 'Those two men are responsible for ruining France.') At nine a.m. he joined his wife and family for breakfast in the little dining-room, and then spent the rest of the morning with them. He and Marie Antoinette gave the children lessons until one p.m. when they all took some exercise, a promenade along the Temple compound's avenue of horse-chestnuts – the Dauphin and his father sometimes flew a kite or played quoits. They dined at two, waited on by Cléry, after which Louis and the Queen often had a game of backgammon. At four o'clock they took a siesta. Then the King read and his wife embroidered – sometimes she read to herself, among her books being an old favourite, Fanny Burney's *Evelina*. In the evenings she or Madame Elisabeth would read aloud to the rest of the family. The children were put to bed after supper at nine p.m., Marie Antoinette retiring shortly afterwards.

This gentle, domestic existence was far from what or-dinary Parisians were being taught to think of 'the menagerie in the Temple'. Hébert, in his popular paper the *Père Duchesne*, asked his readers to imagine 'the rhinoceros [the King] foaming with rage at finding himself chained up, panting from his consuming thirst for blood. That, feature for feature, is the true likeness of Louis, the traitor, snorting through the night like a hog on its dunghill, doing nothing but growl in the day-time, happy only when he sees his grub arrive, devouring a capon at one gulp and muttering to himself, "How I would like to do the same to a Jacobin or a *sansculotte*."' Hébert goes on: 'As for the Austrian, she is no longer the tigress swimming in pools of blood that she was on St Lawrence's Day [10 August]. She has assumed the deceitful face of a she-cat; she has an air of miaouing gently; she shows smooth velvet paws, biding her time until she can scratch again.'

The royal family's position suddenly became much more dangerous. On 19 November a locksmith called Gamein informed Citizen Roland – still Minister of the Interior – that during the previous May he had constructed a secret iron safe at the Tuileries on the King's instructions. Roland immediately had it broken open and discovered Louis's correspondence with Mirabeau and other politicians which revealed all too plainly his hostility to the Revolution from the very beginning. Paris was in uproar when it learnt of the royal 'perfidy'. The bones of Mirabeau, 'Tribune of the People', were disinterred from the Panthéon and flung into a ditch. Two days later the Anglo-American deputy for the Pas de Calais, Tom Paine, demanded in the Convention that the former King should be tried – 'A weak and narrow-minded man, badly reared like all his kind, given as it is said, to frequent excesses of drunkenness,' declaimed this inveterate boozer, while urging that 'some compassion' should be shown. But Robespierre and his terrible disciple Saint-Just were soon arguing that there was no need for a trial since the people had already found Louis guilty of kingship, which in itself was a crime. Terrified of the mob, which they knew was controlled by the Jacobins, the Girondins were far too frightened to oppose such ruthless sophistry. On 8 December the Convention ordered the preparation of an indictment.

Three days later 'Louis Capet' was summoned to appear before the deputies. He was brought to the bar, and 'he in whose presence no one has the right to sit' was kept standing for some considerable time. He answered his interrogators with such dignity and sagacity that even Marat was impressed. He was granted counsel, his lawyers being the venerable Malesherbes – his former household minister – Tronchet, another old man, and a young advocate Raymond de Sèze; all three were perfectly aware that by appearing for the King they might well have signed their own death-warrants. They had a fortnight in which to prepare their brief.

In the meantime the defendant was not allowed to see his wife and children or his sister. He was deprived of his razors and penknives, even of the knives and forks with which he ate, the guards going to ludicrous lengths to see that he did not try to poison himself. He also had to put up with interminable deputations from the Convention. However Cléry and Turgy managed to pass reassuring messages from him to Madame Elisabeth, who presumably handed them on to the Queen. On Christmas Day he sat down and wrote his will, a most moving document. It is too long to quote in full, apart from the paragraph addressed to Marie Antoinette: 'I entreat my wife to forgive me for all the misfortunes she has had to suffer because of me, and for any vexations I may have caused her during our marriage, and she may be assured that I harbour nothing whatsoever against her, should indeed she suppose that there was anything with which she might reproach herself.'

On 26 December Louis again appeared before the Convention. Maître de Sèze answered all the charges, but since he based his defence on the principle embodied in the constitution of 1791, that so long as the King acted constitutionally his person was inviolable, he had little effect. Louis himself said a few words, rejecting in particular the accusation that he had 'shed the people's blood' on 10 August. He was then returned to his solitary confinement in the Temple, while the Convention debated his fate for the next three weeks.

The Jacobins, the men of the Mountain – so called because they filled the higher rows at the back of the chamber – were determined to kill the King. Led by Robespierre and Marat they clamoured for his death, not without reason: so long as he remained alive he was a threat to the Revolution, whether in prison or in exile. At home he would be a focus for intrigue, abroad the potential leader of an army of revenge. Fearful for their own lives, the Girondins tried cravenly to save Louis without actually defending him – they suggested a referendum or at any rate a respite. Only a few deputies were brave enough to dare to speak up for him, among them gallant, crack-brained Tom Paine, who proposed banishment – 'Ah, citizens, give not the tyrant of England the triumph of seeing the man perish on the scaffold who aided my so much loved America to break his chains.' Paine, 'the enemy of Kings', tried again and again till the very last moment to save him – to Marat's fury. It was useless. After Louis had been found guilty, almost unanimously, and after a referendum had been rejected, there was a vote on how he should be punished. Deputy after deputy mounted the tribune to vote – a few for banishment, many for death but a postponement, and a narrow majority of fifty-three for death. Among those who voted unequivocally for death was Philippe Egalité, deputy for a Paris constituency, whose mistresses were watching from the public gallery. (He horrified even the Jacobin leaders. Danton muttered to Robespierre, 'Miserable wretch – he of all people could have refused to vote!') A final attempt on 20 January to procure a respite was defeated by seventy votes. According to law the sentence had to be carried out within the next twenty-four hours.

Malesherbes immediately brought the news to his master, falling at his feet in tears. Louis embraced the faithful old man emotionally, though he had expected the sentence and faced the prospect of the knife with phlegmatic equanimity. His only complaint to his venerable counsel was that the French had never learnt to appreciate his wife's sterling qualities. 'Poor woman,' he groaned, 'promised a throne and then ending like this!' Significantly he blamed her misfortunes not on the people but on a vicious court, and on the fact that none of his older female relations had taken her under their wing.

Marie Antoinette had been so distraught that her health suffered. From 1 January she was given 'medical soup' on a doctor's order, but nevertheless began to lose weight – a dressmaker had to be summoned to take in her clothes. She simply could not believe that the Convention wanted to kill the amiable, kindly, infinitely well-intentioned human being who was her husband. However she learnt the verdict at once, by means of a stentorian news vendor whom sympathizers had paid to stand within earshot of the Temple.

At half-past eight on the evening of 20 January she and her children, together with Madame Elisabeth, were at last allowed to see the King again, going down to his room on the floor below them – 'a scene of sorrow which continued for an hour and a quarter,' says Cléry. Little Madame Royale fainted. The Queen wanted to spend the night with her husband, but was not allowed. When Louis forced them to leave, he promised that he would come and say good-bye the next morning. 'You promise?' they all insisted. 'Yes, I promise. Farewell. Farewell!' Although the doors of their rooms were shut, for a long time Cléry on the stairs could hear Marie Antoinette and her sister-in-law sobbing.

Meanwhile Louis XVI made his confession to a non-juring priest recommended by Madame Elisabeth. This was the Abbé Edgeworth de Firmont, a Franco-Irishman and unshakeably resolute Papist, who was himself already in some danger. The King then ate an excellent meal and slept soundly till five the next morning. From that time on drums and bugles sounded continuously throughout Paris. Louis's first words to Cléry were, 'I slept very well – I needed it, as yesterday was very tiring.' He dressed and packed what possessions he still had into small parcels, including his wedding ring which he told the valet to give to his wife. The Queen was woken at six – if she had ever slept, since she had spent the night fully dressed on her bed, weeping – by someone asking for Mme Tison's missal which was needed for the Mass below. She was given no other news of what was happening.

Edgeworth celebrated Mass, served by the King and Cléry, the former receiving Communion. Louis did not, as he had promised, say good-bye to his family. 'Tell the Queen, my dear children, and my sister that although I promised to see them this morning, I decided to spare them the pain of such a cruel parting. Tell them what it cost me not to see them once again.' In fact the Abbé had warned him that Marie Antoinette would find 'this additional agony' almost unendurable. The King replied, 'You're right – she'd find it unbearable. It's much better to forgo the happiness of seeing her once more and to let her live in hope a little longer.'

Santerre, the brewer from the faubourg Saint-Antoine, who was now a General and Commandant of the Temple, came to escort Louis to his execution. At eight-thirty a.m. the King, accompanied by Edgeworth, was driven in the Mayor of Paris's carriage to the Place de la Révolution (formerly Place Louis Quinze, now Place de la Concorde). On the way they recited together psalms from the Abbé's breviary. When Louis arrived and climbed up the scaffold, drums began to roll, but the drummers ceased when he bellowed at them to keep quiet. Only with reluctance did he submit to having his hands bound. He shouted, 'Frenchmen, I die innocent.' The drums started to roll again. His last words were interrupted by the guillotine itself – 'May my blood strengthen the happiness of the Fr . . .' As the knife crashed down Edgeworth cried, 'Son of St Louis, ascend to Heaven.' The head was held up to the crowd by a young guard. There was a long, uneasy silence, then a wild and almost defiant shout of '*Vive la Nation!*'

Even at the time many Frenchmen would have agreed with Taine that the King's execution was 'the suicide of France'. Like Charles I, nothing had so become his life as the way in which he left it. Uneasy republicans hastily circulated a lie, that Louis's neck was so fat that he began to scream as the blade cut through it. Gouverneur Morris wrote a true account, however, to Thomas Jefferson. 'The late King of this country has been publicly executed. He died in a manner becoming his dignity . . . the great mass of Parisian citizens mourn'd the fate of their unhappy Prince. I have seen grief such as for the untimely death of a beloved parent. Everything wears the appearance of solemnity which is

awfully distressing.' In London an English cartoonist published a vicious picture of a drunken, terrified Louis taking
leave of a screaming, raddled Marie Antoinette. Nevertheless
most English people were horrified. The Prime Minister,
William Pitt, referred to Louis's killing as 'the foulest and
most atrocious deed which the history of the world has yet
had occasion to attest' – ignoring the fact that his own
countrymen had committed exactly the same crime in the
previous century.

The royal family realized it was all over when they heard
the cannon booming out at ten-thirty a.m. Although her
children cried loudly, Marie Antoinette was so choked with
grief that for a long time she remained speechless. When they
had recovered from their first shock, she, her daughter and
her sister-in-law knelt before her seven-year-old son according to ancient custom, in acknowledgement of his new status
as King Louis XVII – *'le roi est mort, vive le roi!'* Henceforward the royal ladies treated him as their sovereign, though
almost the only courtesy they could pay him was to see that
he was served first at meals.

The Commune allowed the Queen to go into what they
thought was mourning, sending a dressmaker to 'the widow
Capet' as they now called her. She was given a black cap,
black dresses, black petticoats, black stockings and black
shoes, even a black fan. (In fact, white was the mourning
colour for a Queen of France.) She rarely spoke, never again
went down into the garden – she did not wish to pass her
husband's door – and sat in an old armchair, sometimes
knitting but usually just musing. A person who saw her in
these miserable days informs us 'she was painfully thin', and a
last portrait painted in the Temple at this time shows a
frozen-faced wreck of a woman, with burnt-out eyes.
However, she continued to give her son daily lessons and saw
that he was polite to the guards – she would not give up hope
that one day he would ascend his throne and be anointed at
Rheims.

Among the guards was a certain François-Adrien Toulan,
a thirty-two-year-old bookseller from Toulouse, who had

The Dauphin, Louis-Charles, briefly to be Louis XVII, by Kucharski

taken a prominent part in the storming of the Tuileries on 10 August. He had all the hot enthusiasm of the Midi, and when he first arrived at the Temple his manner was so aggressive and threatening that the royal family loathed the sight of him. Yet this bloodthirsty fanatic soon succumbed to pity at the spectacle of their misery – some of his comrades thought that he actually fell in love with the Queen. Another potential ally was Citizen Lepitre, formerly a teacher of Latin and proprietor of a small boarding-school. The latter, twenty-nine but with a bad limp, was a timid, venal pedant who had only adopted revolutionary principles for reasons of expedience. He discreetly made it clear to the prisoners that he was a Royalist sympathizer.

Toulan became accustomed to doing Marie Antoinette numerous small services. He decided to do more. One day in February he suddenly told her that he would help her to escape, with all her family. He then contacted the Chevalier de Jarjayes, who had secretly remained in Paris and who at once visited the Queen, dressed as the Temple lamplighter. Jarjayes's plan required the co-operation of two others besides Toulan, so Turgy and Lepitre were recruited. The schoolmaster insisted on being paid lavishly but was worth it, since he was head of the Commune's passport committee. It was a very simple scheme – the Queen and Madame Elisabeth would literally walk out of the Temple at night dressed in cocked hats, tail coats and voluminous trousers like municipal guards, together with Madame Royale in the rags of one of the lamplighters' little boys, and carrying the King in a dirty linen basket. Three fast little carriages would then drive them at breakneck speed to Dieppe and a boat for England. (A berlin was declined by Marie Antoinette, who had plainly learnt a lesson from Varennes.) The Tisons were to be drugged with doctored snuff.

Alas, the Jarjayes plan – which might just conceivably have worked – was ruined, through no fault of the plotters. In mid-April Dumouriez suddenly made his dramatic desertion to the Austrians and in the ensuing panic the Commune ordered that no more passports must be issued for the time being. Lepitre lost his nerve, refusing to make out the vital documents. Even Jarjayes was badly shaken, though he thought he could still manage to bring the Queen out. But she refused to go without her son. 'We dreamed a beautiful dream, that's all,' she wrote to the Chevalier. 'Nothing could ever make me happy again if I abandoned my children.' Considerate as always, she told Jarjayes that he must leave Paris as quickly as possible, for his own safety – 'I think the sooner you go the better. I am so worried for your poor wife.' By means of Toulan – who skilfully extracted them from a sealed room – she gave the Chevalier her husband's watch seal and wedding ring to take to her brothers-in-law at Coblenz. She also entrusted him with a wax impression of her own seal to bring to Fersen – it was Axel's crest of a pigeon with the motto '*Tutto a te mi guida*' (Everything leads me to you). In this last letter she asked Jarjayes to tell Fersen that 'the inscription has never been more true'.

Unfortunately the Tisons had clearly had their eye on Toulan and Lepitre for a long time. They were in a bad mood after their daughter was stopped from visiting them and in April, in a fit of pique, complained about the two guards to the Mayor of Paris when he chanced to visit the Temple. Tison said that he had seen Marie Antoinette and Madame Elisabeth with pens and sealing wax, and his wife confirmed his story by producing a candlestick from Madame Elisabeth's room spotted with the wax. Even so, for the time being, the Commune thought its security measures perfectly adequate.

One may perhaps wonder why Fersen did not try to visit his adored friend in her prison. After all Jarjayes had managed it. But Axel never went near Paris, wandering through the Lowlands and Germany with Mrs O'Sullivan. For the whole of the first half of 1793 he was still optimistic that Austrian troops would speedily enter Paris and restore the monarchy. Admittedly, since Dumouriez's defection the French army had virtually collapsed. But the Emperor was distracted by other matters, notably Poland – he was determined to share in any further dismemberment of that tragic land beset by both Prussians and Russians. Fersen, for once approaching reality, proposed ransoming Marie Antoinette to the government in Vienna. Before anything could come of this, the political scene changed totally in France.

Yet while Axel dreamt, French Royalists all but succeeded in rescuing the Queen a second time. A rich and rather shady banker, the Baron de Batz, had stayed in the capital despite its dangers. He was a fanatical counter-revolutionary, spending his fortune on plot after plot; he had even hoped to rescue the King on his way to the scaffold by simply drawing his sword and shouting to bystanders to follow him – no one did, so he melted away into the crowd before he could be caught. There were many warrants out for this arch-conspirator, the authorities searching everywhere, but he was a master of disguise, concealed by countless aliases, a real-life Scarlet Pimpernel. (Fittingly, he belonged to the same family as the model for Dumas's d'Artagnan.) In June he collected a band of like-minded enthusiasts who dedicated themselves to saving Marie Antoinette. An adept at bribery, Batz swiftly had a senior official at the Temple in his pay – Michonis, a former lemonade-seller – together with the Temple district's military superintendent, Captain Cortey. Within a very short time the Baron and his friends had themselves enrolled as guards and were on sentry duty at the Temple. 'Citizen Forguet' – Batz's latest alias – intended to march the entire royal family out in military uniform on the night of 21 June. At eleven p.m. the Queen was waiting. Michonis was about to knock on her door as everything was ready – there were thirty Royalists in the guardroom.

Suddenly, without any warning, the Commissioner Simon arrived. He had received an anonymous message that Michonis would 'betray' him that night. When the old cobbler reported it to the Commune he was told not to take it seriously. Nevertheless Simon decided to make certain that the prisoners were still in the Temple. There were too many guards present who were not in the conspiracy for the wretched man to be knocked on the head, so Batz and his conspirators marched off – without the royal family. This was the end of the Baron's plot, though it was never discovered by the authorities.

By now the political atmosphere had changed radically. In April 1793 a Committee of Public Safety had been nominated by the Convention. At the end of May the Committee and the Commune overthrew the Girondins, and the Jacobins swiftly proscribed them. Most fled but were nearly all caught and executed, including Mme Roland; her husband killed himself with a swordstick, while Pétion died in a field from exposure and starvation. The fall and destruction of the Girondins inaugurated the Terror, when the Committee of Public Safety swept aside all legality. The new Jacobin regime adopted extreme measures to save the Republic, which was threatened not only by foreign invasion but by the revolt of the ferocious Vendéens, dourly Catholic and Royalist peasants in the west whose poverty had become intolerable. Paris was in a bloodthirsty and merciless mood. Even so Marie Antoinette hoped that the Vendéens would save her and her children.

In the last weeks of June the Committee of Public Safety decided to take Louis XVII away from his mother. In the meantime Mme Tison had been going off her head, as Madame Royale later wrote, 'talking ceaselessly about her sins, about the ruin of her family, and about prison and the scaffold'. She thought Toulan and Lepitre had been put to death as a result of her accusations. (Later Toulan was in fact guillotined, though Lepitre survived.) She also 'had terrible dreams which made her worse'. When on 29 June she was informed secretly of the Committee's decision to separate the little King from his mother, Madame Tison went completely insane, throwing herself at the Queen's feet and begging for forgiveness – 'I am the cause of your death and of Madame Elisabeth's' – and finally collapsing in convulsions. It took eight men to remove the raving woman to the public madhouse.

Marie Antoinette herself did not hear of the decision until 3 July. She had gone to bed when at ten p.m. a group of municipal officers entered her room and announced that she and her son were to be confined separately. The man who read the order did so in a shaking voice. The officials' report states that 'the parting was effected with all the kindness necessary in such circumstances, the people's officers having shown extreme consideration'. Madame Royale remembered a rather different scene, the terrified child clinging to the Queen. After an hour of fruitless argument 'my mother agreed to surrender her son and, raining tears on him, as if she realized very well that she would never see him again, gave him up to the officers. The poor boy kissed us all frantically and left crying.'

The King was taken downstairs to his father's former bedroom where his 'tutor', Simon, was waiting for him. He had been chosen as the man best qualified 'to turn an aristocrat into a democrat'. Here one may remark that the 'democratic' bourgeois of the Convention who had appointed him would never have allowed their own sons to be brought up by someone of Simon's social background.

Louis XVII was at first so miserable that he had to be locked in his room. From the floor above Marie Antoinette heard him sobbing for two days, and a week later he asked some visiting members of the Committee of Public Safety if there really was 'a law to separate him from his mama'. But gradually he was changed and corrupted by Citizen Simon. Listening, the Queen was to hear him swearing horribly 'about God, his family and aristocrats' and also singing the Marseillaise – a noble tune in our own day but an inexpressibly evil one for her. She watched ceaselessly from a chink through her shutters and occasionally, though very rarely, managed to catch a glimpse of him playing in the garden.

Marie Antoinette was crushed by the blow, and told her sister-in-law that she was afraid God had forsaken her – 'I no longer dare to pray.' This was soon cured. For so instinctively devout a woman as the Queen, a serene mystic like Madame Elisabeth, with her total and infectious belief, must have been a tower of strength.

Despite all the efforts of the Committee of Public Safety,

the French Republic's position continued to deteriorate. The Austrians took Valenciennes at the end of July, and then the wild Vendéens captured Saumur and it looked as though all Brittany would join them. There were five enemy armies on French soil and Royalist outbreaks all over the country – the port of Toulon proclaimed Louis XVII King and admitted English and Spanish warships. A young Norman Royalist, Charlotte Corday, stabbed the great Marat to death in his bath. A new Committee of Public Safety came into being, whose chief personality was Maximilien de Robespierre. With him began a life and death struggle to save the Revolution. Anyone who was not wholeheartedly for it was regarded as against it.

At two o'clock in the morning of 2 August there was a loud banging on Marie Antoinette's door. Four police officers entered her room, led by Michonis – who had once tried to help her escape. One of them read out a decree of the Convention. She was to be transferred immediately to the prison of the Conciergerie, to await her trial before the Extraordinary Tribunal. She had to dress in the men's presence. All she was allowed to take with her were a small bundle of clothes, her watch, a vial of smelling-salts, and a handkerchief.

[12]

The Conciergerie

d'une prison à un cachot, la différence est si peu de chose

Beaumarchais

Elle est morte, cette grande reine, et par sa morte elle a laissé un regret éternel

Bossuet

BEAUMARCHAIS'S quip that there is small difference between a cell and a prison applied only to the polite world he knew before the Revolution. The Conciergerie was very different from the Temple. On the Île de la Cité, the prison was among the vast complex of law courts which until recently had been called the Palais Royal (not to be confused with Orléans's residence) but was now renamed the Palace de Justice. In August 1793 it already contained nearly 300 political prisoners, who were beginning to know it as 'the waiting-room for the guillotine'. The cell in which Marie Antoinette was placed was less than twelve foot square. Since it was half below ground and not far from the Seine its stone walls dripped with moisture, though partly covered by torn paper hangings on wooden frames. The floor, also of stone, was bare. Its furniture comprised a bed—made with decent linen specially supplied by the prison governor's wife—a small table, a cane armchair, two small cane chairs, a washbowl and a screen. The sole ornament was a rusty nail high up the wall, on which the prisoner at once hung her gold watch. She was allowed neither writing nor sewing materials. Yet she had one trusted companion with her in the cell, a pug dog she must have brought from the Temple – perhaps with Michonis's connivance – and which she somehow managed to keep throughout. (It survived her, and was still at the Conciergerie in 1796.)

She intended to live, and her children were the reason. She was frightened of only two things. She feared indignity (affronts to her dignity as a woman rather than as a Queen) and she dreaded what might happen to the little King and his sister. She could overcome the first fear, but never the second. It gave her the strength to fight for her life.

Marie Antoinette had brought with her only what she wore – her black mourning dress and her black widow's cap. Mme Richard, the prison governor's wife, was too frightened to lend the Queen any of her own clothes or to buy some for her, but she and her maid Rosalie had the black dress patched discreetly and the cap made into two small ones. However, after ten days Michonis (the same official who had been in Batz's plot) brought her a parcel from Madame Elisabeth. It contained two cambric chemises trimmed with lace, handkerchiefs, coloured ribbons, a white wrapper 'for the mornings', some fine linen *fichus*, two pairs of black silk stockings and a pair of smart shoes. This was a godsend, since by now her black dress was ragged and patched with muslin, and her shoes were covered in mould from the cell damp. In delight she told Mme Richard and Rosalie, 'I can see my poor sister-in-law's hand, from the neat way they're packed.' Mme Richard dared not give her a chest for the clothes. Instead she had a cardboard box placed in the cell. According to Rosalie, it was considered a treasure by the former patron of such cabinet-makers as Jacob and Molitor.

We know the routine of Marie Antoinette's day at the Conciergerie from eye-witness accounts collected after the Bourbon Restoration. The most helpful is that dictated by Mme Richard's young and illiterate servant girl, Rosalie Lamorlière – 'native of Breteuil in Picardy'. Others are less reliable. But it is likely we do not possess the whole story.

The majority of prison officials and guards were better disposed towards the Queen than was suspected, but they were not going to risk their lives by confessing to each other that they had done her a kindness. Undoubtedly they connived at mitigating her imprisonment – some actually planned to help her escape.

Her worst afflictions were the heat and closeness of the cell in a torrid August, and sheer boredom. She also had to endure the permanent company of two guards, Sergeant Dufresne and the gendarme Gilbert, who drank, smoked and played cards or backgammon at the little table, or else simply stared at her. As she was never allowed out of her cell, she had to relieve herself behind the screen (though this was less of a humiliation than might be supposed, if one is to believe the memoirs of those who knew Versailles). They were an amiable pair and Gilbert regularly brought her flowers. Sometimes she watched them playing backgammon, a game she understood very well.

Marie Antoinette rose at seven in the morning, when Rosalie came to help dress her hair. It was first scented with powder, then parted in front, the ends being tied on top with white ribbon in a sort of chignon. Overall she wore one of her black caps. The day's principal events were her two meals, though she had never been interested in food. They were simple but excellent. At dinner she had soup, a ragout of beef, chicken or duck – which she liked best – a plate of vegetables and a dessert. Supper was just as good, though less copious. Everything was served on pewter plates and dishes. Mme Richard was embarrassed at not being able to provide silver, but Rosalie polished the pewter to make it as bright as possible. The maid was struck by the way in which the prisoner ate – 'stripping the bones with unbelievable skill and thoroughness. She seldom left any vegetables'. The food was brought personally by Mme Richard, market women taking extra care to give her the best available when she told them for whom it was intended.

Rosalie also remembered that Marie Antoinette said grace before and after each meal. She was as lonely as a Carthusian hermit and one may surmise that she prayed a good deal. No doubt she still considered Madame Elisabeth's favourite advice of 'resignation to God's will' not particularly helpful. She was able to receive more tangible spiritual consolation. The Conciergerie's unofficial chaplain was a non-juring priest, the Abbé Emery, superior to the seminary of Saint-Sulpice, a man whose holiness was matched only by his indestructibility and whose advice was later sought even by Napoleon. Some time before 14 September he had a note smuggled in to the Queen. It read, 'Prepare yourself to receive absolution. To-night, at midnight, I shall stand outside your door and say the words of forgiveness over you.' Emery went at the specified hour and, hearing her sigh, managed to talk to her for a few moments before pronouncing the absolution.

Mme Richard mustered up enough courage to lend her a few books. These included *Captain Cook's Travels* and *A History of Famous Shipwrecks* – she told Mme Richard that she 'enjoyed reading really frightening adventures'. She spent more time simply musing – staring into space and ceaselessly turning her two diamond rings round and round, taking them off and putting them on again, 'as if they were toys' Rosalie tells us. Luckily the authorities had not thought of confiscating them – she cried when they took away her watch during the first week.

In her musing Marie Antoinette must often have wondered why she was suffering such a fate. Certainly no contemporary Frenchman – or Frenchwoman – could understand what was happening. Between 1789 and 1799 France endured a decade of horror worse than any since the Hundred Years War. The proudest nobility in Europe was proscribed and plundered, hunted to death or else driven out to starve abroad. The richest Church in Christendom came crashing down, amid savage martyrdoms. There was bloody civil war, both sides cutting each other's throats mercilessly. There was foreign invasion and brigandage, and a collapse of law and order over wide areas. There was unparalleled inflation and unemployment, famine and starvation. The monarchy was not alone in its ruin. Louis XVI had blamed it all on Voltaire and Rousseau, the Queen on cowardly noblemen who had deserted their King after opening the floodgates. She could not realize, nor could she be expected to realize, that the mighty and prosperous realm whose sovereign she had married had long been doomed to such a cataclysm. The social, administrative and economic structure of late eighteenth-century France made it inevitable that the government would become bankrupt sooner or later, while French society could never reform itself, or be reformed, without a total breakdown. Marie Antoinette was very like some casualty in a modern war, incapable of understanding why or even how hostilities had begun, knowing only that a frightful death approached.

No doubt she thought of the men she had loved. She may even have agreed, however reluctantly, with Roederer – the betrayer of the Tuileries – that Louis XVI had destroyed her by his weakness, and that the King's 'calm in moments of danger was only stolidity, his bravery in disaster only resignation', though even so, in the last letter she would ever write she says she hopes to rejoin her husband in the next world. Of Fersen, who had bungled Varennes and abandoned her for months after, who had written those ridiculous letters to the Tuileries – 'hide in a cellar' – who had not come to her in the Temple like Jarjayes (he had not even tried). Of her dead imperial brothers, who had refused to take her danger seriously. Also of her nephew in beloved Schönbrunn, much too busy to bother about an unknown aunt. Above all of her son, Louis XVII: she had a tiny locket with a portrait of him concealed in her bodice, together with one of his little yellow gloves containing a lock of his hair.

The occasionally excellent Mme Richard, wanting to cheer the Queen, brought her own youngest small boy to visit her. 'Fanfan' was a good-looking, fair-haired child, about the same age as Louis-Charles. On seeing him Marie Antoinette at once burst into tears and began kissing him passionately. Rosalie, who was there, tells us that the Queen said she thought about her son every hour of the day and night. The maid also remembers her kissing the locket and the glove, adding that she would discuss her own desperate situation or any other misfortune without a trace of emotion or despondency but the very mention of her children invariably sent her into floods of tears.

In any case Marie Antoinette was already wretched enough. The uncertainty of her position must have been much more frightening than any positive menace – she was kept in total ignorance of the charges to be brought against her, knowing only that she would be tried in due course. She did not expect a death sentence, and lived in dread of an even crueller imprisonment in some deep and solitary dungeon.

However France – or, rather, the Revolution – was now in terrible danger. Josias, Prince of Coburg (a member of the same family as the present Queen of England), was a much more formidable general than Brunswick and his Austrian troops had taken Valenciennes at the end of July. On 12 September he took Le Quesnoy and on 28 September he invested Maubeuge, and he continued to threaten Paris until mid-October. The capital was therefore menaced by an enemy army throughout Marie Antoinette's confinement in the Conciergerie. Danton, and perhaps even Robespierre too, had at first hoped to use her as a bargaining counter with her fellow countrymen, but had come to realize that the Emperor was not going to change his policy simply to save his aunt. Understandably, extremists began to clamour for a show trial. Billaud-Varenne, an influential member of the Committee of Public Safety, started to put pressure on Robespierre, while every influential body in Paris was deluged with letters from all over France demanding that she be tried – 'The widow Capet must be judged'; 'Do Marie Antoinette's crimes, the crimes of a blasphemous woman driven by a demon, have to become even blacker before she can be condemned?'; 'The modern Messalina . . . must be handed over to the vengeance of the law'; 'She must pay with her filthy blood'. Not only were the Jacobins determined that the Queen should be tried but – in the interests of what they believed to be good for France – they were equally insistent that she must be found guilty, even in the unlikely event of her being innocent. (A hundred years later the French Right would demand the condemnation of Captain Dreyfus in a similar spirit of perverted patriotism – both Marie Antoinette and Dreyfus symbolized opposition to a particular concept of France, and were thus enemies of the French, and friends of Germany.)

Three people were planning the Queen's judicial murder. All were inadequate, not to say unbalanced, personalities who would never have achieved prominence in any normal society. Historians differ widely about Maximilien de Robespierre. For some he is the Revolution's murderous evil genius, for others the last custodian of its idealism and a scapegoat on whom all its excesses have been unjustly blamed. This bloodless little lawyer from Arras, with his neatly formal clothes, powdered hair and green spectacles, his cat-like face and thin, harsh voice, still only thirty-four, was by now the most powerful man in France. If hardly a Prime Minister, let alone a dictator, he nevertheless dominated the Committee of Public Safety. As a former criminal judge and provincial public prosecutor, he knew all about the machinery of trials and tribunals. While he may have been more merciful than is generally acknowledged, even his warmest admirers admit that he was completely ruthless in forwarding the progress of the Revolution. Once he decided that Marie Antoinette's death would be of use, she was doomed. He seems to have reached this conclusion by the beginning of October at latest.

Like so many revolutionaries, Robespierre belonged to the lesser nobility, if only to the very lowest ranks of the *noblesse de la robe*. So too did Fouquier-Tinville, whose proper name was Antoine-Quentin Fouquier de Tinville d'Hérouël, and who was likewise a lawyer. He differed from the Revolution's leaders in being middle aged, in his late forties. He had been a failure in his professional life, a bankrupt forced to sell his legal office and become a clerk at a police station. Nevertheless, because of his fashionably violent opinions he was now Public Prosecutor of the Revolutionary Tribunal – a body to

whom Danton had said at its creation the previous March,
'Let us be terrible, to spare the people from being terrible.'
Fouquier-Tinville obeyed Danton's instructions to the full.
He had already sent dozens to the scaffold, dozens which
would become thousands, including some 900 women – in
his own words, he made 'heads tumble like slates off roofs'.
He was even terrible in appearance, having a pale, sinister
face with a low, scowling forehead, bushy black eyebrows
and bloodless white lips. In court he invariably adopted a
brutal manner, brusque and bullying. To cap everything he
was also a hypocrite – it seems that he was a secret Catholic.

Jacques-René Hébert was another gifted failure to whom
the Revolution had given a career in public life. Although
from a comfortable bourgeois background – his father was a
goldsmith at Alençon – he had nearly starved before 1789. He
had lost one poorly paid job as a doctor's secretary for
stealing and another as a theatre box-office clerk for
embezzlement, and was so wretched that he actually thought
of emigrating to China. But he could write and was in some
ways the Dr Goebbels of the Jacobins. His gutter paper, the
Père Duchesne, was written in a prose scattered with oaths and
obscenities and was often disgusting – even bestial – but it
was also brilliant and exactly what the wilder population of
the poorest Paris faubourgs wanted. They trusted the big,
coarse-spoken Duchesne with his moustache and pipe, the
personification of a working-class sage, who voiced his
opinions in language which could be understood in the back
streets, at best full of earthy common sense and rough
humour, at worst full of the most savage mob violence. (The
modern French Left claims Hébert as the founder of popular
journalism.)

Those who met the real Duchesne must have been sadly
disappointed. Hébert was a foppish little man drenched in
scent – he stank of musk – with a thin, reedy voice and an
embarrassing tendency to shriek when frightened, which was
only too often. His short hair was combed fashionably
forward *à la Brutus* over a beaming face like that of a well-
behaved errand-boy. When not ranting on the rostrum, he

had excellent, even self-effacing manners and lived a quiet bourgeois life with an ex-nun whom he had married. After Christianity, he now hated Marie Antoinette more than anything in the world. Ambitious and with a crazy cunning, he hoped to exploit his audience's sympathy with his phobias to advance his career. At a meeting of the Committee of Public Safety at the end of September he declared, 'I've promised my readers to give them Antoinette's head. If there's any delay in letting me have it, I'll go and cut it off myself.' Beyond question Hébert was a psychopath, yet his influence must never be underestimated. It was he who orchestrated the outcry for the Queen's trial and condemnation, and during the trial he was to work closely with Fouquier-Tinville (who later sent him to the guillotine as well).

Hébert has horrified nearly all Marie Antoinette's biographers. Certainly he was abusive and foul mouthed to the point of lunacy every time he mentioned 'the arch-tigress', 'the slut', or 'the whore', whose neck he so much wanted to 'shave with the national razor'. Yet he was only continuing in the footsteps of such pamphleteers as Choderlos de Laclos and Champcenetz de Riquebourg and all the others once financed by Monsieur and Orléans. It was they, not *Père Duchesne*, who first called the Queen a nymphomaniac and a Lesbian. If the half-unhinged Hébert believed them, as appears to have been the case, it was not entirely his fault.

His outburst to the Committee was prompted by the knowledge that enemies of the Revolution were actively plotting to rescue Marie Antoinette from the Conciergerie. Her escape would have been a disastrous moral blow to the Jacobins. An attempt had already been discovered in early September, the so-called 'Carnation Plot'.

Towards the end of August Michonis had entered the Queen's cell on one of his routine visits of inspection, accompanied by a fat-faced young man in a dingy brown suit with two carnations in his button-hole. She recognized him at once: it was the Chevalier de Rougeville who had saved her from the mob at the Tuileries the previous June. He took the flowers from his coat and 'with a look full of meaning' threw them behind her screen. He then left with Michonis, without saying a word.

The Chevalier was a strange mixture, far more colourful than Alexandre Dumas makes him in the *Chevalier de la Maison-Rouge*. His real name was Alexandre Gousse, the 'Rougeville' being a little estate of his father, who was a tax collector, though he was certainly a Chevalier of the Order of St Louis. He claimed quite untruthfully to have been an equerry to Monsieur, to have served in the King's Bodyguard, and to have been an aide-de-camp to General Washington during his time in America. He was in fact a boastful and rather seedy adventurer, a sponging philanderer, but he was also a very brave man. Oddly enough he came from Arras, the same town as Robespierre.

The carnations had little notes wrapped round them. One offered her money – 'three or four hundred *louis*' – and the other said the writer had 'a safe and well prepared plan of escape' if she wished to try. Rougeville returned after only a few minutes whereupon Marie Antoinette immediately accepted his proposal. It had been made possible by Michonis, who may well have been the scheme's originator. The Queen at once attempted to enlist the help of the gendarme Gilbert who, to begin with, agreed. She also confirmed her acceptance of Rougeville's offer with an answer pricked out by a pin on a scrap of paper, which still survives – the words have been deciphered as, 'I am under constant guard. I talk to nobody. I trust you. I will come.'

Just before eleven p.m. on the night of Friday 2 September Michonis and Rougeville again entered the Queen's cell. The two guards including Gilbert had each been bribed by the Chevalier with fifty *louis* apiece. Michonis flourished a handful of official papers at M. Richard, the governor, and told him that by order of the Convention he was taking the prisoner back to the Temple. A carriage was waiting outside, but its real destination was Mme de Jarjayes' château in the country near Paris, preparatory to crossing the German frontier. Michonis, Rougeville and Marie Antoinette had passed through all the wicket gates and had reached the street door, when Gilbert stepped forward and refused to let the Queen leave. He had lost his nerve, and denounced the plot the following day. The Chevalier wisely fled, going to ground in a gypsum quarry at Montmartre before escaping to Belgium. (He lived until 1814, when he was shot for Royalist activities by Napoleon's government.) Michonis tried to brazen it out but was arrested. He survived, thanks to Marie Antoinette's skilful concealment of the part he had played during the ensuing interrogations.

Her cell was searched from top to bottom, her rings were confiscated, as was temporarily even her underwear, apart from what she was wearing. Ten days later she was moved to a new and smaller cell, the former prison dispensary, blocked by a massive door with two locks and two bolts and by iron grilles over the windows. Instead of the secretly sympathetic M. and Mme Richard, who had been suspended, there was a new gaoler, M. Bault from the La Force prison, responsible with his life for the safe keeping of his charge. He was so terrified that at their first meeting he told her rudely that it was his job to do her hair. Later he explained to Rosalie, still mercifully with the Queen, 'I really am sorry to have upset that poor woman, but my position here is so difficult that I'm frightened of the slightest thing. I can't forget that my friend Richard and his wife are in prison. For God's sake, Rosalie, don't do anything silly or it's the end of me.'

The new cell was a place of misery, at first stiflingly hot but then miserably cold and chillingly damp. Later Bault was threatened with the guillotine by Fouquier-Tinville for daring to ask for another blanket for her. She was not allowed a lamp or candles – at night the sole illumination came from the dim lantern in the female prisoners' exercising yard outside. The worst thing was the lack of privacy, every one of her actions being watched through a grille by a gendarme. Rosalie did her best. She remembered, 'At bedtime I made the various little tasks last as long as possible in order that my revered mistress would not be left alone in the dark until the very last moment.' She also tried to ward off the cold and damp, warming the Queen's nightdress by the fire in her own room each evening.

Not surprisingly Marie Antoinette fell ill. Rougeville had already noticed her 'extreme weakness', which made him worry about her fitness for a long journey. She now suffered from fainting fits, from agonizing menstrual pains which sent her to bed, and from severe haemorrhages. In addition, her sight was failing. Even the authorities were concerned, and for a fortnight she was given medicine and nourishing soup.

Most of what we know about the Queen's life during the second part of her imprisonment at the Conciergerie comes from Rosalie's naive account. The memoirs of other witnesses, such as Mme Bault, are much less trustworthy, while not even Rosalie saw everything. Astonishingly, it seems that the new gendarmes, although threatened with every menace, connived at some most unrevolutionary visitors to the cell.

The Abbé Magnin, who had access to the Conciergerie to visit the Abbé Emery, sent a message to her saying that if she wished he would celebrate Mass in her cell. 'In those awful days,' Magnin tells us, 'we had very small chalices which unscrewed, together with miniature missals and portable altar stones barely broader than a chalice base. All these items fitted into a small bag easily hidden in our pockets.' Since he was a non-juring priest, Marie Antoinette accepted gratefully. The Abbé had noticed that two gendarmes guarding the cell showed some respect for the Queen and he discovered that they were devout Catholics. One night at the beginning of October he was conducted to the cell by none other than Bault. After hearing the Queen's confession, 'without losing a moment we prepared everything necessary on a little table' and he said Mass. He gave Communion to Marie Antoinette and also to the two gendarmes. Magnin firmly believed that the sacraments filled her with 'the courage to suffer, without complaining, all the torments awaiting her'. Shortly afterwards he fell ill and never saw her again. However he adds that she was given Communion on the night of 12–13 of the same month by M. Cholet, a priest from the Vendée. These visits have been questioned because she says in her last letter that she does not know if any non-juring priests still exist. In fact she was protecting them, just as she protected Michonis.

Many other people waited longer in the Conciergerie for the trial which was going to send them to the guillotine, but nearly all did so in less wretched discomfort. Small luxuries could be procured, as well as clothes, blankets and warmth, light and good company. They were allowed to walk about the corridors and courtyards chatting to each other. Ladies wore negligées in the morning, full toilette at noon, smart gowns in the evening. Few prisoners approached the Queen's importance in the eyes of the Convention, and they were spared such savagely close confinement and surveillance. By contrast the Conciergerie, as she experienced it, broke her health and ruined a once magnificent constitution. Damp, cold, darkness, loneliness, and obsessive fear for her children transformed the once strapping mistress of Versailles into a thin, blinking, red-eyed, white-haired creature who, racked with pain, shook constantly, an old woman of thirty-seven who had all but lost the sight of one eye. It was in this state that she had to come forth from the shadows and face the most daunting ordeal of her not uneventful life.

On 3 October the Convention decided to try the widow Capet as soon as possible. But Fouquier-Tinville postponed the trial since he was worried by the lack of evidence, especially documents. Hébert tried to help. His unhinged mind suggested a solution. He went to the Temple and coaxed and bullied the little King into signing a statement that his mother had committed incest with him and had also taught him to masturbate. Fouquier-Tinville was misguided enough to believe that such 'evidence' would help the case against the Queen – in charity one must question his sanity too.

By now Royalist prisoners in the courtyard adjoining Marie Antoinette's cell had warned her that her trial was imminent, by talking at the top of their voices. At last Hébert's rantings in the *Père Duchesne* about 'the shame of womankind' were to bear fruit – he had declaimed, 'We must give the *sansculottes* their fill. If they are to kill all our enemies, their enthusiasm must be fuelled with Antoinette's death.' Shortly before midnight on 12 October an usher and some gendarmes burst into her cell and told her to dress. She was feeling particularly weak, having had another haemorrhage that day besides suffering noticeably from the cold, though she had been heartened by M. Cholet's visit earlier in the evening. After dressing as quickly as she could behind her screen, she was led through damp corridors, up and down stairs, across courtyards, to the great Gothic hall of the Palais de Justice. Once the home of the Parlement of Paris and where the Kings had held their *lits de justice*, it was the French equivalent of Westminster Hall. The tapestries with the royal arms had gone and it had been renamed the 'Hall of Liberty' – somewhat ironically the new decorations included a cheaply painted allegory of the Declaration of Rights. That night the vast room was lit by only two candles.

This was the preliminary hearing. The public prosecutor, Fouquier-Tinville, and the examining magistrate, Nicolas Hermann, both wore black, their ceremonial bonnets crowned by tall ostrich plumes. A few specially invited spectators peered down through the darkness from the public galleries, though they could see little. It was noticed that the Queen seemed alarmed when, hearing noises from the gallery, she turned and saw nothing. She sat on a bench, opposite a table behind which were Fouquier-Tinville, Hermann and a recording clerk. Hermann asked the questions.

She gave her name. 'I am Marie Antoinette of Lorraine-Austria, widow of Louis Capet, once King of France.' Fouquier-Tinville intervened with insulting pedantry, 'Where were you living at the time of your arrest?' She replied simply that she had not been arrested, merely removed from the care of the National Assembly. But Hermann's questions were serious. Martial-Joseph-Armand Hermann, President of the Revolutionary Tribunal, was a former advocate and provincial judge from Arras like

Robespierre, to whom he was devoted. An experienced and skilful cross-examiner, he hoped to trap the Queen into admitting that she was the enemy of the Revolution, that she had intrigued with foreign powers, and that she had influenced Louis and was responsible for his decision to escape from Paris. There were no less than thirty-five questions to be answered.

Marie Antoinette showed considerable shrewdness and subtlety in her replies. Although she knew very well that such charges as intriguing with the Emperor could be substantiated if her enemies could find the right papers, she calmly denied the accusations where she was most vulnerable. (The documents were certainly in the Convention's hands, but in so muddled a state that they did not know how to use them.) When told she was responsible for the war with the Austrians, she pointed out that it was France which had declared war and that in doing so her husband had had to read out a declaration specially drafted for him by his ministers. Referring to the flight to Varennes she was told, 'You opened the doors and made sure everyone left,' to which she answered, 'I don't think an open door shows that one is constantly governing another person's actions.' She swept aside other accusations, some of which were in fact justified, with equal skill. 'You never stopped trying to destroy liberty for an instant,' said Hermann. 'You meant to reign whatever the price and to re-ascend the throne by climbing over the bodies of slaughtered patriots.' She replied simply, 'We didn't need to re-ascend the throne – we were already there.' Hermann did no better when he attempted to show that she was guilty of inciting the Guards to attack the people at the notorious Versailles banquet in 1789, of forcing Louis to sign the vetoes, or of being directly involved in the defence of the Tuileries.

Unable to do much with specific charges, Hermann tried to make her discredit herself on broad issues. 'Do you think kings are necessary for the people's happiness?' 'An individual cannot decide on such matters.' 'Surely you regret that your son has lost the throne he might have ascended had not the people, aware of their rights at last, destroyed it?' 'I never regret anything on my son's behalf when his country is happy.'

Finally they asked her if she wanted counsel, and she agreed to the court's appointing Maîtres Tronson du Coudray and Chauveau-Lagarde. Surprisingly, she could not have been given better men. Both were able, energetic and courageous, particularly Chauveau-Lagarde, a year younger than the Queen but who lived on until 1841 – he had already defended Charlotte Corday and would later defend Madame Elisabeth. Then the prisoner was taken down to her cell.

In his capacity as Public Prosecutor, Fouquier-Tinville now proceeded to draft the indictment, working through the night in a tower of the Palais de Justice. He concocted an extraordinary farrago of abuse, containing absurd insults as well as the wildest accusations. Marie Antoinette was compared to Messalina, Fredegonde, Brunhilda, Catherine de Medici and Marie de Medici – the first two being actually described as Queens of France – and was called 'a scourge and a bloodsucker of the French ever since her arrival'. She had intrigued with the Emperor and sent him vast sums of money, she had stirred up the Flanders Regiment at Versailles, she was responsible for the civil wars and for the slaughter of 'patriots' during the storming of the Tuileries – where, it was also alleged, she had abused the King as a coward and made him bite lead bullets to keep up his courage – and she had betrayed the French plans for invading Belgium. Fouquier-Tinville was only guessing in the last charge – he had no evidence. He was even stupid enough to include Hébert's filthy inventions. 'Finally,' said the Public Prosecutor in ending his so called indictment, 'the widow Capet, although immoral in every possible way, is so thoroughly perverted and so accustomed to every enormity that, regardless of her duty as a mother and of the laws of nature, she did not shrink from indulging with her own son Louis-Charles Capet, as the latter attests, in indecencies of which the mere mention arouses a shudder of horror.'

The very morning after the preliminary hearing the

indictment was delivered to Chauveau-Lagarde. He at once took it to the Queen at the Conciergerie, together with the news that her trial would begin on the following day. The lawyer was horrified by the indictment, but his client was quite unmoved. Nevertheless Chauveau-Lagarde was prepared to fight and told her that she must apply to the Convention for an adjournment so that he could study the evidence. When she refused to do so, he told her, 'Pride has nothing to do with the business in hand, and you mustn't let it stop you making use of what might be an advantage. Surely it is your duty to save your life, not just for your own sake, but for your children's sake?' Marie Antoinette allowed herself to be persuaded and, as instructed, applied to the Convention. Her letter included the words, 'I owe it to my children to do everything in my power to justify their mother's conduct.' She received no reply and did not obtain an adjournment. A year later, after his fall, the letter was found underneath Robespierre's mattress. It has been plausibly surmised that one reason for refusing the adjournment was Fouquier-Tinville's calculation that without it she would stand trial during her period, when she would be at her weakest, based perhaps on information supplied by her doctor – significantly the medicine and nourishing soup was stopped the day after the preliminary hearing.

Fouquier-Tinville was busily making sure of the court. Hermann would be assisted by four other 'patriot' judges, while the twelve jurors were no less reliable. The latter included a wigmaker, a cobbler, a café proprietor, a hatter, a printer, a musician, a lemonade-seller, two carpenters, a surgeon, an ex-priest and a former marquis. The humbler were clearly avid readers of the *Père Duchesne* – one simple soul refers to the Queen in an illiterate scrawl to his brother as 'the ferocious beast who had devoured a large part of the Republic' – while the more privileged were sound 'patriots', two being personal friends of Robespierre. There were as many as forty-one witnesses, though nearly half of these proved not worth calling, since they were found to be 'ignorant of the matters in question', and the remainder were scarcely better. The public gallery was to be packed with carefully selected *sansculottes* and fishwives. Among them were *tricoteuses* famed for bringing their knitting to every trial and execution, and for their bloodthirsty screams. Even so, the trial was to be essentially a confrontation of one woman by many men.

At eight a.m. on the morning of Monday 14 October, Queen Marie Antoinette was brought into the 'Hall of Liberty' and led to a small wooden chair on a little platform, where everyone could see her, though at first she was kept standing. There was a gasp of general astonishment at the appearance of the once beautiful woman, whose legs could scarcely support her emaciated frame and who was obviously half blind. A newspaper reporter told his readers, 'She is amazingly changed.' The accused was allowed to sit, and sat drumming the arms of her chair with her fingers as though playing a harpsichord. The first two hours were spent listening to a witness who recounted the extravagance of the 'feasts and orgies at Versailles' between 1779 and 1789, ending with the banquet for the Flanders Regiment. Another witness followed, but scarcely carried conviction when he described seeing bottles which the accused kept under her bed to make the Swiss Guards drunk. The prosecution droned on, going through the indictment without much method. It could not produce a single document in the Queen's handwriting, save for a notebook containing the names of her doctor and her laundress. However she undoubtedly failed to carry conviction when she denied that she had been aware of her husband's intention to use troops in 1789 or that she had enriched the Polignac family. From the gallery the *tricoteuses* shrieked that the accused ought to give her answers standing. On the whole, however, she made an excellent defence, sweeping aside any serious charges or replying with studied ambiguity.

The prosecution then played its trump card. Hébert was called and repeated his disgusting allegations. He added that the real object of her 'criminal intercourse' had been to ensure that she would be able to dominate her son if he came to the throne. Shaking, she answered that she had no knowledge of such incidents. After questioning on other matters, a juror insisted that 'Antoinette' reply to Hébert's charges. She rose to her feet and replied, 'If I did not reply, it was simply because human nature cannot answer such a charge against a mother.' Turning round, she cried, 'I appeal to all mothers in this room.' Eye-witnesses report that an electric shock ran through the court. There were feminine cries of support and even the *tricoteuses* applauded. Uproar broke out in the gallery and several women fainted.

Marie Antoinette whispered to Chauveau-Lagarde, 'Was my answer too dignified?' He replied, 'Madame, simply be yourself and you will always be perfect. Why do you ask?' 'I heard a common-looking person say to her neighbour, "Look, isn't she proud."' Chauveau-Lagarde comments in his memoirs that the Queen had complete control of herself and still had hope.

Plainly alarmed, Hermann rang his bell and restored order. He managed to redress the balance a very little by extracting the admission that Fersen had supplied the berlin for the flight to Varennes. Then he adjourned. It was noticed that the judges looked extremely worried as they left the court.

Late that evening, at a little dinner party for his friends at Vénua's famous restaurant, Robespierre met one of the jurors. He asked him how the trial was going. Hearing of Hébert's charges and the Queen's triumphant defence, the 'Incorruptible' burst into a fury. 'The fool!' he shouted. 'Can't he be satisfied with the Capet woman being a Messalina, instead of having to turn her into an Agrippina as well – and giving her a public triumph at the last moment?' Clearly he was deeply alarmed and feared that Hébert's antics might have saved the Queen. It is also plain that the incident had shaken even so prejudiced a jury.

During the adjournment Marie Antoinette discussed the witnesses' testimony with Chauveau-Lagarde. He was impressed by her summary and agreed with her that it was nothing but lies. He even considered that the prosecution was in danger of defeating itself 'by its sheer grossness, vileness and spite'. The Queen still thought she might save herself.

The court reassembled. It listened to such ridiculous charges as sending the Emperor Josef 200 million gold francs and of carrying a brace of pistols with which to murder Citizen Egalité. The hearing did not end until eleven o'clock at night.

Next morning Marie Antoinette was back in court at nine a.m. This day was to last for eighteen hours, during which the prosecution concentrated on her extravagances and her gifts to favourites, on her political intrigues with the Emperor, on her influence over Louis and on her part in the defence of the Tuileries. Night fell and the hearing went on and on in the dim candlelight. In his summing up for the defence, Chauveau-Lagarde argued for two hours. When he had finished the Queen thanked him. 'How tired you must be, M. Chauveau-Lagarde! I deeply appreciate all the trouble you are taking.' Fouquier-Tinville was so angry that he had him arrested in court. Hermann's summing-up for the prosecution was as outrageous as the indictment, but subtler. He claimed that 'Antoinette' stood accused by the entire French people for her political conduct during the last five years and told the jurors that they must find her guilty if they considered that she had helped foreign powers to invade France and had plotted a civil war. In effect he was telling them to ignore the evidence and to trust to their own prejudices – of which he was only too well aware.

The jury went out to consider its verdict at three a.m. on 16 October. Many observers thought she would at least escape the death penalty and merely be deported, since she had answered so skilfully. (Across the Channel the Duchess of Devonshire was so impressed by her performance that she wrote 'her answers, her cleverness, composure, greatness of mind blaze forth in double splendour'.) The Queen herself still hoped. At four a.m. the jury returned, and she was brought back into court to hear the verdict. It was 'Guilty'. Fouquier-Tinville demanded the death penalty, which was read out by Hermann. The court dispersed, the jurors, weary but proud, to a banquet specially ordered for them by the Public Prosecutor – like some harvest-home.

On the way back to her cell Marie Antoinette became so exhausted that she almost fell down the stairs. She was helped along by the court usher, Lieutenant de Busne, who – to some spectators' fury – did so bareheaded with his hat under his arm, as though he had been at Versailles. He was already under suspicion for having brought her a glass of water during the trial. He ordered some candles and also writing materials for her, and sat in her cell for the remainder of the night. Just before dawn he was taken out and arrested on account of excessive courtesy to the condemned.

The Queen's final night lasted barely three hours. Yet she somehow mustered enough strength to write, in a firm hand, a letter to Madame Elisabeth. It is very well known, but since it tells us more than anything else about Marie Antoinette's character and personality it cannot be omitted:

It is to you, sister, that I am writing for the last time. I have just been sentenced to death, though hardly a shameful death since it is only shameful for criminals, and I can go to be reunited with your brother. No less innocent than he was, I hope I will be able to show the same courage that he had at the end. I am quite calm, as one always is when one's conscience is clear, though I am deeply upset at having to abandon my children. You know that I lived only for them, and for you, kind, loving sister. In the goodness of your heart you sacrificed everything to stay with us, and now I am leaving you in an awful situation. I only learnt during the trial that my daughter had been separated from you. Alas, the poor child! I don't dare write to her since it wouldn't reach her. I don't even know if you will receive this letter. Nevertheless I send you my blessing to give to them, and hope that one day when they are older they will be able to rejoin you and enjoy your affectionate care. If only they would remember what I have always tried to teach them – that firm principles and dedication to duty are the only proper foundation for a life – then their mutual love and confidence in each other will make them happy. Will my daughter please remember that because she is older it is her duty to help her brother with any advice derived from her being an elder sister, and may both of them always remember that in whatever situation they may find themselves in, they can never be really happy unless they agree. They should learn from our example, how much consolation we had from our affection for each other despite all misfortunes, and how sharing happiness with a friend redoubles it – and where can one find a truer, more loving friend than among one's family? I hope my son never forgets his father's last words, which I repeat – 'He must never try to avenge our deaths.' I should say something about him which pains me, because I know the boy must have hurt you a good deal. Please forgive him, dear sister, remembering his age and how easy it is to make a child say what you want, especially when he doesn't understand. I hope that one day he will be all the more aware how much beyond price your kindness has been to both of them.

All that remains is to tell you my last thoughts. I wanted to write them down at the beginning of the trial but, besides being forbidden to write, everything has happened so quickly that I didn't have time. I die in the Catholic, Apostolic and Roman religion, in the faith of my father in which I was brought up and which I have always professed. I do not expect any spiritual consolation and I don't even know if any priests of that faith are still here – I think that even if they are it would be much too dangerous for them to visit me. I sincerely beseech God to pardon me for all the sins I have committed since I was born and I trust that in His goodness He will hear my last petitions, and especially those I have made for many years that, of His mercy and goodness, he will receive my soul. I ask pardon of everyone of my acquaintance, and especially of you sister, for any distress I may unwittingly have caused you. I forgive all my enemies any harm they may have done me. I take my leave of my aunts, my brothers and my sisters. Once I had friends too. One of my deepest regrets is the thought of being cut off from them and their worries. Do please let them know that I thought of them until the very last moment of my life.

Good-bye, my good and loving sister. I only hope this letter reaches you. Always remember me. I send you my fondest love, and send it as well to my poor dear children. My God, it is agony to leave them. Good-bye. Good-bye. Now I must busy myself with spiritual matters. Perhaps they will bring a [State] priest since I am a prisoner, but I solemnly swear that I will have nothing to say to him and will treat him as a total stranger.

This letter was never delivered. Later, it too was found under the Incorruptible's mattress. Marie Antoinette signed it but did not date it. At 'half-past four in the morning' – probably much later since she had no means of telling the time – she also wrote a little note for her children. It read simply, 'Oh, my God, have pity on me! My eyes have no tears left to weep for you, my poor children. Good-bye! Good-bye!' It was not delivered.

When Rosalie came to rouse her at seven a.m. she found the Queen wide awake on her bed, still fully dressed, her head resting on her hand, and crying. No one could face the prospect of being beheaded with equanimity – apart from Louis XVI – but it is not too much to suppose her tears stemmed as much from sheer weariness and nervous tension as fear. The far more frightened maid told her, 'Madame you ate nothing at supper yesterday and scarcely anything all day.' Marie Antoinette murmured, 'I need nothing to eat, child – my life is over.' However, to please the girl she swallowed a few spoonfuls of soup which Rosalie had kept warm on her stove throughout the night. Then she told her to go away and to come back at eight to help her dress. When she did so, the Queen asked for her assistance in changing her chemise, since she had had a severe haemorrhage – the doctor had given Fouquier-Tinville excellent advice – and it was ruined. A gendarme came to the end of the bed and, despite her protests, insisted on watching her dress – 'My orders are I must see all your movements.' With what Rosalie calls 'as much modesty as possible' she continued to do so. Despite her pitifully inadequate wardrobe she was determined to go to her death wearing white, the correct colour for the mourning of a Queen of France. She put on her white wrapper over a clean black chemise, a white muslin fichu round her neck and a small white bonnet overall. She also found a hole behind the hangings, in which she hid the bloodstained chemise.

Rosalie left the doomed woman. She remembered many years later 'I went away without being bold enough to say good-bye or curtsey for the last time, as I was afraid of bothering her or upsetting her, I shut myself up in my room where I cried, and I prayed for her.'

The Abbé Girard, a 'constitutional' priest now arrived. Despite his official status he was not even wearing clerical clothes. She refused his nervously proffered offices, saying scornfully, 'You may tell anyone who asks you that God's mercy is available to all.' She enquired of the gendarme calmly, 'Do you think the people will allow me to reach the scaffold without tearing me to pieces?' She greeted the turnkey, confiding in an embarrassed voice, 'Larivière, do you know that they're going to put me to death? Please tell your kind mother that I am grateful for her care of me and would like her to pray for me.' She then knelt down to pray herself.

At 10 a.m. her prayers were interrupted when Hermann entered the cell with the clerk of the court and two other officials. She was still kneeling by her bed. Despite her protesting that she had heard it before, Hermann insisted on reading out the sentence again, though he bared his head while doing so – a courtesy normally omitted – as did his companions. Before he finished, a huge man came into the room. It was the executioner, Henri Sansom, whose father had beheaded Louis XVI only nine months ago. He told her to hold out her hands. 'Must they be bound?' asked Marie Antoinette. 'Louis XVI's were not.' Hermann ordered the

Marie Antoinette leaves the Conciergerie –
a contemporary English impression by William Hamilton, RA

man to do his duty and, anxious to please his masters, he tied them much too tightly behind her back, with some brutality. He then snatched off her bonnet and cropped her hair with a pair of scissors, putting the shorn locks into his pocket to burn later, after which he replaced the bonnet.

At eleven a.m., led like a tethered animal by a cord tied to her hands, she was taken to the gate of the Conciergerie. Here, instead of a carriage of the sort in which her husband had ridden to his death, a rubbish cart drawn by two dray horses awaited her. Seeing an unprotected vehicle from which the mob might drag her with ease, she suffered yet another humiliation. She was seized by a looseness of the bowels and had to ask Sansom to untie her hands so that she could relieve herself, which she did in a corner of the prison wall. Then her hands were retied and the executioner pushed her up a small step-ladder into the cart, where she was made to sit on a plank with her back to the horses. Beside her sat the Abbé Girard, already badly shaken. Sansom stood leaning against the side, holding the cord. Both men held their hats under their arms.

Astonishingly, even now she might have been rescued. Two barbers, a fourteen-year-old shoeblack, and a blind hunchback woman who made lace had enlisted nearly 500 men who hoped to do so. They included more barbers, together with grocers, butchers, wine-sellers, house painters and even a dealer in junk, besides troops from the barracks at Vanves. They expected to recruit still more support and had found the money to purchase 1,500 pistols. Originally they intended to storm the Conciergerie – after lighting the surrounding street-lamps in the daytime so that, without oil, they would go out during the night and provide cover. Police agents somehow dissuaded them, whereupon the lacemaker decided that the Queen must be saved on her way to the scaffold, in the rue Saint-Honoré. Alas, the police infiltrators panicked the plotters. No more than eighty came and even these had lost their nerve and dared not act. The conspiracy is well documented. It seems that not all the Parisian working classes believed what they read in the *Père Duchesne* or what 'democrats' shouted at them.

It was a fine, fresh day with a slight mist. The cart set off along the muddy streets towards the Place de la Révolution, surrounded by soldiers on foot and on horseback. When it came to the rue Saint-Honoré, mocking hand claps and yells of hatred began – 'There goes the Austrian! Death to the Austrian!' The Jacobin artist David drew the Queen as she jolted past. His sketch is of a battered, shabby woman without any beauty or majesty, but it is also of a seemingly emotionless woman who is sitting rigidly erect with her head held high – the jutting Habsburg lip gives the impression not of a pout, as in days gone by, but of strength and determination. Not even the hostile David was able to impute any hint of fear. The revolutionary papers admitted her courage – the *Père Duchesne* reports 'the whore was bold and insolent right up to the very end'. Once she nearly fell off the plank, but recovered. She sat with so little movement that some spectators thought she was already dead.

One of the mounted escort was an actor named Grammont, avid for cheap publicity. Suddenly he stood up in his stirrups, flourished his sabre and shouted, 'Here's the wicked Antoinette! She's finally finished, my friends.' She ignored his clowning, though she stared contemptuously at a woman screaming insults – she recognized her as a former servant at Versailles.

After nearly an hour the cart finally reached the Place de la Révolution. It was filled with a multitude who had been waiting all morning, and there was a roaring trade in cakes and lemonade and in the usual pornographic pamphlets about Marie Antoinette's private life. Since she had last seen the great square, the statue of Louis XV had been toppled from its pedestal and replaced by a towering figure of the goddess of liberty.

The Queen got down quickly from the cart, refusing any help although her hands were still tied. An eye-witness tells us that she climbed up the steep ladder to the scaffold 'with an air of bravado' and appeared even calmer and more un-troubled than when she had ridden out from the Con-ciergerie. She walked across the platform so fast that she trod on Sansom's foot. He cursed, whereupon she spoke her last words. 'I beg your pardon Monsieur – I didn't do it on purpose.' She shook off her bonnet and was manhandled to the upright plank of the guillotine to which she was strapped. She closed her eyes. The plank was pushed over and down and she was thrust forward under the wooden collar, which was locked on her neck. Only four minutes had passed since she climbed up the scaffold. Sansom released the heavy knife, there was a crash – her head dropped into the basket. He held it up amid repeated yells of triumph and then the satisfied crowd dispersed amiably. After a while the body was removed in a wheelbarrow, the head between the legs, for burial in an unmarked grave.

Bishop Bossuet had preached a sermon at the funeral of Henrietta Maria, Charles I's widow. It contains a passage which could serve as an epitaph for Marie Antoinette. 'She is dead, this great Queen, and her death must for ever be regretted by . . . those who had the honour of serving or even knowing her. There is no need to weep any more over her humiliations, because they have become her glory. Had she been more fortunate throughout her life, she would undoubtedly have received the respect due to her, but her story could never have been such a fine one.'

Postscript

ROBESPIERRE, Fouquier-Tinville and Hébert – the last moaning with fear in the tumbril – all followed Marie Antoinette to the guillotine. So also did Hermann, three judges, five members of the jury and fourteen witnesses. The gendarme Gilbert shot himself. Mme Richard was stabbed to death by a mad prisoner.

Philippe Egalité, who was certainly no less guilty than Hébert of the Queen's destruction, was guillotined only three weeks after her. Characteristically, his last address was restricted to 'one short, obscene word'. In 1830 his son usurped the throne but the French soon rejected an Orléanist monarchy. He is the ancestor of today's Orléanist Pretender, whose regicide descent can never be forgotten even now in certain traditionalist circles in France.

As for those whom Marie Antoinette left behind at the Temple, Madame Elisabeth was executed on 10 May 1794, an experience borne with her habitual serenity. So close had been her imprisonment that only on the way to the scaffold did she learn that her beloved 'sister' had gone before her. Her corpse was thrown naked into a common grave. Louis XVII died in the Temple in June 1795, his body weirdly deformed by the King's Evil like his elder brother – his mother's suspicions only too justified. Worse still, he had been deliberately broken in spirit and degraded by ill-treatment as vile as any ever inflicted on a child. 'The saddest thing for France,' commented the Comte d'Hézecques, 'is that every member of the Convention was responsible for his long martyrdom.' Madame Royale – once *Mousseline la Sérieuse* – was handed over to the Austrians in exchange for French prisoners of war. Later she married her uncle Artois's son, the Duc d'Angoulême, destined to be the last Dauphin. She never recovered from her experience in the Temple, living on, frozen and embittered, until 1851 – the year before Napoleon III became Emperor of the French. She was only seventy-two, yet already she seemed like a ghost from remote antiquity.

Count von Fersen returned to Sweden. There he grew stranger and more introspective than ever, while becoming *Riksmarskalk* (Earl Marshal) and a power in the land. In 1810 popular rumour unjustly accused him of murdering the Crown Prince. Despite warnings that his life was in danger, Fersen insisted on attending the funeral, and was beaten and kicked to death by a Stockholm mob. It was the anniversary of the flight to Varennes.

Mme Campan was only saved from the guillotine by the fall of Robespierre. With an invalid husband heavily in debt, an aged mother and a small son to support, her sole assets were an almost worthless *assignat* for 500 francs. Undaunted she set up a boarding-school at Saint Germain which prospered wonderfully, and during the Empire Napoleon appointed her headmistress of the institution at Ecouen for the education of the daughters of recipients of the Legion of Honour. However the Imperial favour caused her to be frowned on by the restored Bourbons, who dissolved the establishment at Ecouen. She spent her last years in quiet but comfortable retirement at Mantes, where she died in 1822. Her *Mémoires sur la Vie privée de la Reine Marie Antoinette* were published the following year and, even if a little discredited, are a testimony to her very genuine affection for her mistress.

After the Restoration, Monsieur, by then Louis XVIII, had the bones of his brother and his sister-in-law disinterred and reburied in the royal sepulchre at Saint-Denis. Louis, who had done a good deal in his time to discredit Marie Antoinette, also built a 'Chapelle Expiatoire' in their memory, next to the Madeleine. Here Masses of atonement are still offered annually. Among the congregation of modern French Royalists one may sometimes see descendants of those courtiers whose slanderous tongues contributed so much to the destruction of Marie Antoinette.

Bibliography

Contemporary works

BESENVAL, BARON DE, *Mémoires*, Paris, 1805.

BOIGNE, COMTESSE DE, *Mémoires*, Paris, 1907–8.

BOUILLÉ, MARQUIS DE, *Mémoires sur la Révolution*, London, 1797.

BURKE, EDMUND, *Reflections on the Revolution in France*, London, 1790.

— *A Letter from Mr. Burke to a Member of the National Assembly*, London, 1791.

— *Correspondence* (ed. T. W. Copeland), Cambridge, 1967–78.

CAMPAN, MME DE, *Mémoires sur la Vie Privée de la Reine Marie Antoinette*, Paris, 1823.

CHÂTEAUBRIAND, VICOMTE A. R. DE, *Mémoires d'outre tombe*, Paris, 1849–50.

CLÉRY, J.B., *Journal de ce qui s'est passé à la tour du Temple pendant le captivité de Louis XVI*, London, 1798.

CROY, DUC DE, *Journal inédit du Duc de Croy*, Paris, 1906.

DAMAS, DUC DE, *Mémoires relatifs à la Révolution*, Paris, 1823.

EDGEWORTH DE FIRMONT, ABBÉ, *Mémoires*, Paris, 1816.

FERSEN, COUNT VON, *Le comte de Fersen et la cour de France* (ed. R. M. de Klinckowström), Paris, 1877–78.

— *Fersen et Marie Antoinette; correspondance et journal intime inédits du comte Axel de Fersen* (ed. A. Söderhjelm), Paris, 1934.

— *Lettres d'Axel Fersen à son père* (ed. F. U. Wrangel), Paris, 1929.

GENLIS, MME DE, *Mémoires*, Paris, 1825.

GOGUELAT, BARON DE, *Mémoire de M. le baron de Goguelat*, Paris, 1823.

GRIMM, BARON DE, *Correspondance littéraire*, Paris, 1829–31.

HÉZECQUES, COMTE D', *Souvenirs d'un page*, Paris, 1895.

JEFFERSON, THOMAS, *Writings* (ed. P. L. Ford), New York, 1893–9.

LA TOUR DU PIN, MARQUISE DE, *Journal d'une femme de cinquante ans*, Paris, 1913.

LAUZUN, L. A. DE GONTAUT-BIRON, DUC DE, *Mémoires*, Paris, 1822.

LIGNE, PRINCE DE, *Mémoires du Prince de Ligne*, Brussels, 1861.

LOUIS XVI, *Correspondance secrète sur Louis XVI, Marie Antoinette, la Cour et la Ville* (ed. M. F. A. de Lescure), Paris, 1866.

— *Negotiations secrètes de Louis XVI et du Baron de Breteuil avec la cour de Berlin, décembre 1791 à juillet 1792* (ed. J. Flammermont), Paris.

LUYNES, DUC DE, *Mémoires sur la cour de Louis XV*, Paris, 1860–65.

MAGNIN, ABBÉ, *Déclaration* (in *Le Monde* of 31 May), Paris, 1863.

MALLET DU PAN, J., *Mémoires et Correspondances de Mallet du Pan*, Paris, 1851.

MARIE ANTOINETTE, *Lettres de Marie Antoinette* (ed. M. de La Rocheterie & le Marquis de Beaufort), Paris, 1895–96.

— *Marie Antoinette, Fersen et Barnave; Leur Correspondance* (ed. O. G. de Heidenstamm), Paris, 1913.

— *Correspondance secrète de Marie Antoinette et de Barnave* (ed. A. Söderhjelm), Paris, 1934.

MARIA THERESA, *Correspondance secrète entre Marie Thérèse et le Comte de Mercy-Argenteau avec les lettres de Marie Thérèse et de Marie Antoinette* (ed. A. Arneth & M. A. Geffroy), Paris, 1874.

— *Correspondance entre Marie Thérèse et Marie Antoinette* (ed. G. Girard), Paris, 1933.

MORRIS, GOUVERNEUR, *A Diary of the French Revolution*, New York, 1939.

NAPOLEON, *Correspondance de Napoléon I*, Paris, 1858–69.

— *Mémorial de Ste-Hélène*, Paris, 1828.

OBERKIRCH, BARONNE D', *Mémoires*, Paris, 1835.

PAINE, THOMAS, *The Rights of Man*, London, 1791–92.

ROEDERER, BARON, *Chronique de cinquante jours*, Paris, 1832.

SAINT-PRIEST, COMTE DE, *Correspondance*, Paris, 1845.

STAEL-HOLSTEIN, BARONNE DE, *Oeuvres complètes*, London, 1820.

TALLEYRAND, PRINCE DE, *Memoirs*, London, 1805.

THRALE, MRS, *The French Journals of Mrs Thrale and Dr. Johnson* (ed. M. Tyson & H. Guppy), Manchester, 1832.

TOURZEL, DUCHESSE DE, *Mémoires de Tourzel*, Paris, 1883.

TURGY, L. F., *Fragments historiques sur la captivité de la famille royale*, Paris, 1818.

VÉRI, ABBÉ DE, *Journal* (ed. A. M. P. G. de Nolhac), Paris, 1928.

VIGÉE-LEBRUN, MME, *Souvenirs*, Paris, 1835.

WALPOLE, HORACE, *The Letters of Horace Walpole* (ed. H. P. Toynbee), O. U. P., 1905.

YOUNG, ARTHUR, *Travels in France in 1787, 1788 and 1789*, Bury St. Edmunds, 1791.

Modern studies

ALMERAS, HENRI DE, *Marie Antoinette et les pamphlets royalistes et révolutionnaires*, Paris, 1907.

ARMAILLE, COMTESSE DE LA FOREST D', *Marie Thérèse et Marie Antoinette*, Paris, 1870.

BELLOC, H., *Marie Antoinette*, London, 1911.

— *The French Revolution*, London, 1911.

BOUTELOUP, J. A., *La Rôle Politique de Marie Antoinette*, Paris, 1924.

BOUTRY, M. DE, *Autour de Marie Antoinette*, Paris, 1906.

CARLYLE, T., *The French Revolution*, London, 1837.

CASTELOT, ANDRÉ, *Marie Antoinette*, Paris, 1953.

CASTRIES, DUC DE, *L'Agonie de la Royauté*, Paris, 1959.

COBBAN, A., *A History of Modern France*, London, 1962–5.

CRONIN, VINCENT, *Louis and Antoinette*, London, 1974.

CURZON, E. H. P. DE, *La Maison du Temple de Paris*, Paris, 1888.

DUMAS, ALEXANDRE, *La Route de Varennes*, Paris, 1889.

FAŸ, B., *Louis XVI, ou la Fin d'un Monde*, Paris, 1961.

FUNCK-BRENTANO, F., *L'affaire du Collier*, Paris, 1901.

— *Les Derniers jours de Marie Antoinette*, Paris, 1933.

GONZALEZ PALACIOS, G., *Il Luigi XVI*, Milan, 1966.

LACOUR GAYET, R., *Calonne*, Paris, 1963.

LEFEBVRE, GEORGES, *La Révolution française*, Paris, 1957.

LENÔTRE, G., *La captivité et la mort de Marie Antoinette*, Paris, 1902.

— *Le drame de Varennes*, Paris, 1905.

MIGNET, *Histoire de la Révolution française*, Paris, 1824.

MOSSIKER, F., *The Queen's Necklace*, London, 1961.

NOLHAC, A. M. P. G. DE, *La Reine Marie Antoinette*, Paris, 1936.

— *Marie Antoinette, dauphine*, Paris, 1898.

— *Autour de la Reine*, Paris, 1926.

PERNOUD, R., and FLAISSIER, S., *La Révolution*, Paris, 1959.

SOBOUL, ALBERT, *Précis de la Révolution française*, Paris, 1962.

SOREL, ALBERT, *L'Europe et la Révolution française*, Paris, 1885–1904.

STRYIENSKI, CASIMIR, *Mesdames de France, Filles de Louis XV*, Paris, 1911.

THOMPSON, E. P., *English Witnesses of the French Revolution*, Oxford, 1938.

— *Leaders of the French Revolution*, Oxford, 1929.

TOCQUEVILLE, A. DE, *L'Ancien Régime et la Révolution*, Paris, 1877.

ZWEIG, STEFAN, *Marie Antoinette*, London, 1952.

Index